P9-CMM-327

DESIRING
GOD

WITHDRAWN

JOHN PIPER

DESIRING GOD

Meditations *of a* Christian Hedonist

MULTNOMAH
BOOKS

DESIRING GOD, REVISED EDITION
PUBLISHED BY MULTNOMAH BOOKS
12265 Oracle Boulevard, Suite 200
Colorado Springs, Colorado 80921

Scripture quotations, unless otherwise indicated, are taken from the The Holy Bible, English Standard Version, © 2001 by Crossway Bibles, a division of Good News Publishers. Used by permission. All rights reserved. Scripture quotations marked (NASB) are taken from the New American Standard Bible © 1960, 1977, 1995 by the Lockman Foundation. Used by permission. Scripture quotations marked (RSV) are taken from the Revised Standard Version Bible © 1946, 1952 by the Division of Christian Education of the National Council of the Churches of Christ in the United States of America. Scripture quotations marked (KJV) are taken from the King James Version.

Italics added in Scripture are the author's emphasis.

ISBN: 978-1-60142-310-8
ISBN: 978-1-60142-391-7 (electronic)

Copyright © 1986, 1996, 2003, 2011 by Desiring God Foundation

Cover design by Kristopher K. Orr
Cover image by George Kavanagh

All rights reserved. No part of this book may be reproduced or transmitted in any form or by any means, electronic or mechanical, including photocopying and recording, or by any information storage and retrieval system, without permission in writing from the publisher.

Published in the United States by WaterBrook Multnomah, an imprint of the Crown Publishing Group, a division of Random House Inc., New York.

MULTNOMAH and its mountain colophon are registered trademarks of Random House Inc.

Library of Congress Cataloging-in-Publication Data:
    Piper, John, 1946–
        Desiring God / revised and expanded by John Piper.
                p. cm.
    Includes bibliographical references and indexes.
    1. God—Worship and love. 2. Desire for God. 3. Happiness—Religious aspects—Christianity.
    4. Praise of God. I. Title.
        BV4817 .P56 2003
        248.4—dc19   2002154750

Printed in the United States of America
2011—First Revised Edition

10 9 8 7 6 5 4 3 2 1

SPECIAL SALES
Most WaterBrook Multnomah books are available at special quantity discounts when purchased in bulk by corporations, organizations, and special-interest groups. Custom imprinting or excerpting can also be done to fit special needs. For information, please e-mail SpecialMarkets@WaterBrook Multnomah.com or call 1-800-603-7051.

Twenty-five years ago
I dedicated this book
to my father,

WILLIAM SOLOMON HOTTLE PIPER.

The sweet indebtedness I still feel to him
is now only intensified
by the joy of knowing that today
his happiness is sinless
in the presence of Christ.

CONTENTS

PREFACE

There is a kind of happiness and wonder that makes you serious.

C. S. LEWIS

The Last Battle

This is a serious book about being happy in God. It's about happiness because that is what our Creator commands: "Delight yourself in the LORD" (Psalm 37:4). And it is serious because, as Jeremy Taylor said, "God threatens terrible things if we will not be happy."

The heroes of this book are *Jesus,* who "endured the cross for the joy that was set before him;" and *the apostle Paul,* who was "sorrowful, yet always rejoicing;" and *Jonathan Edwards,* who deeply savored the sweet sovereignty of God; and *C. S. Lewis,* who knew that the Lord "finds our desires not too strong but too weak;" and all the *missionaries* who have left everything for Jesus and in the end said, "I never made a sacrifice."

Twenty-five years have passed since *Desiring God* first appeared in 1986. The significance of a truth is judged in part by whether over time it has transforming power in very different circumstances. What about the message of this book? Its context today is dramatically different from when it was first published.

Things have changed personally and culturally. Since its first edition, my body and mind have passed from being forty years old to being sixty-five years old. My marriage advanced from a seventeen-year-old marriage to a forty-two-year-old marriage. My pastorate at Bethlehem Baptist Church has extended from six years to thirty-one years. My sons have grown through their single teen years into married adulthood, and they have made me a grandfather twelve times over. In 1986 there were no daughters. Now there is Talitha Ruth, whose motto at fifteen is "a girl should get so lost in God, that a guy has to seek *Him* to find *her*."

Culturally the world is a different place. Consider some of the events: Tiananmen Square, the collapse of the Berlin Wall, the disintegration of the Soviet Union, Rwandan genocide, Columbine High School, the global AIDS pandemic, Y2K, 9/11, the rise of jihadist terrorism, the ceaseless Middle East wars, tsunamis, the historic Obama presidency. Or consider the transformation of popular culture by developments that were not prominent before 1986: laptops, smart phones, debit cards, DVDs, iPods, pay-at-the-pump gasoline, digital cameras, PowerPoint, Purell, Viagra, flat-screen TVs, public use of the Internet, blogging, Web commerce, YouTube, Twitter, Facebook, and a ceaseless rush of computer-related innovations.

In other words, things have changed. This is the world I live in with profound appreciation and serious concern. But, as personally astute and as culturally awake as I try to be, what seems plain to me is that the really important, deep, and lasting things in life have not changed. And therefore my commitment to the message of this book has not changed. The truth that I unfold here is my life. That *God is most glorified in us when we are most satisfied in Him* continues to be a spectacular and precious truth in my mind and heart. It has sustained me into my seventh decade of life, and I do not doubt that, because of Jesus, it will carry me Home.

Along the way, I added a chapter called "Suffering: The Sacrifice of Christian Hedonism." The reason was partly biblical, partly global, and partly autobiographical. Biblically, it is plain that God has appointed suffering for all His children. "Through many tribulations we must enter the kingdom of God" (Acts 14:22). "Indeed, all who desire to live a godly life in Christ Jesus will be persecuted" (2 Timothy 3:12).

Globally, it is increasingly plain that a bold stand for the uniqueness of Christ crucified, not to mention the finishing of the Great Commission among hostile peoples, will cost the church suffering and martyrs. The post-9/11 world has been troubled with terrorism and war. If the message of this book is to have any credibility, it must give an account of itself in this world of fear and suffering. Increasingly I am drawn to the apostle's experience described in the words "sorrowful, yet always rejoicing" (2 Corinthians 6:10).

Autobiographically, the years since the first edition of *Desiring God* have been the hardest. One of the older women of our church quipped to us at our twenty-fifth wedding anniversary, "The first twenty-five are the hardest." We have not found it to be so. We are nearing the end of the second twenty-five, and undoubtedly they have been the hardest.

The body ages and things go wrong. Marriage, we found, passes through deep water as husband and wife pass through midlife and beyond. We made it. But we will not diminish the disquietude of those years. We were not ashamed to seek help. God has been good to us—much more kind than we deserve. As we ended our fourth decade of marriage, I thought I might be far enough along to write a seasoned book on marriage. It is called *This Momentary Marriage: A Parable of Permanence*.[1] The paradox of that title is at the root of what we have learned. Now, moving through our seventh decade of life and our fifth decade of marriage, the roots are deep, the covenant is solid, the love is sweet. Life is hard, and God is good.

The other "marriage" in my life (with Bethlehem Baptist Church) has been a mingling of sweetness and sorrow. As I sit here pondering the years, the sweetness so outweighs the sorrow that I have no desire to dwell on the pain. It was all in God's good plan—for us and for the people. The apostle Paul spoke a deep pastoral reality when he said, "If we are afflicted, it is for your comfort and salvation" (2 Corinthians 1:6). But there is a joy without which pastors cannot profit their people (Hebrews 13:17). Mercifully, God has preserved it for thirty-one years. And the truth of this book has been His means.

During these twenty-five years since *Desiring God* first appeared, I have been testing it and applying its vision in connection with more of life and ministry and

---

1. John Piper, *This Momentary Marriage: A Parable of Permanence* (Wheaton, Ill.: Crossway Books, 2009).

God. The more I do so, the more persuaded I become that it will bear all the weight I can put on it.[2] The more I reflect and the more I minister and the more I live, the more all-encompassing the vision of God and life in this book becomes.

The older I get, the more I am persuaded that Nehemiah 8:10 is crucial for living and dying well: "The joy of the LORD is your strength." As we grow older and our bodies weaken, we must learn from the Puritan pastor Richard Baxter (who died in 1691) to redouble our efforts to find strength from spiritual joy, not natural supplies. He prayed, "May the Living God, who is the portion and rest of the saints, make these our carnal minds so spiritual, and our earthly hearts so heavenly, that loving Him, and *delighting in Him, may be the work of our lives.*"[3] When delighting in God is the work of our lives (which I call Christian Hedonism), there will be an inner strength for ministries of love to the very end.

J. I. Packer described this dynamic in Baxter's life: "The hope of heaven brought him joy, and joy brought him strength, and so, like John Calvin before him and George Whitefield after him (two verifiable examples) and, it would seem, like the apostle Paul himself…he was astoundingly enabled to labor on, accomplishing more than would ever have seemed possible in a single lifetime."[4]

But not only does the pursuit of joy in God give strength to endure; it is the key to breaking the power of sin on our way to heaven. Matthew Henry, another Puritan pastor, put it like this: "The joy of the Lord will arm us against

2. If you wish, you can test this for yourself by consulting the books in which I have tried to apply the vision of this book to the nature of God (*The Pleasures of God*, Multnomah, 2000); the gravity and gladness of preaching (*The Supremacy of God in Preaching*, Baker, 2004); the power and the price of world evangelization (*Let the Nations Be Glad*, Baker, 2010); the daily battle against unbelief and sin (*The Purifying Power of Living by Faith in Future Grace*, Multnomah, 1995); the spiritual disciplines of fasting and prayer (*A Hunger for God*, Crossway, 1997); a hundred practical issues in life and culture (*A Godward Life*, Multnomah, 1997, and *Taste and See*, Multnomah, 2005); the radical call to pastoral ministry (*Brothers, We Are Not Professionals*, Broadman & Holman, 2002); the goal of everyday life (*Don't Waste Your Life*, Crossway, 2003); the ultimate good of the gospel (*God Is the Gospel*, Crossway, 2005), the reality of the new birth (*Finally Alive*, Christian Focus, 2009), and the life of the mind (*Think*, Crossway, 2010).
3. Richard Baxter, *The Saints' Everlasting Rest* (Grand Rapids, Mich.: Baker, 1978), 17, emphasis added. I have been asked so many times what this "work" looks like, that I wrote another book to answer that question with as many specifics as I could. It is called *When I Don't Desire God: How to Fight for Joy* (Crossway, 2004) and is meant to be a fuller application of what I have written here.
4. J. I. Packer, "Richard Baxter on Heaven, Hope, and Holiness," in *Alive to God: Studies in Spirituality*, ed. J. I. Packer and Loren Wilkinson (Downers Grove, Ill.: InterVarsity, 1992), 165.

the assaults of our spiritual enemies and put our mouths out of taste for those pleasures with which the tempter baits his hooks."[5]

This is the great business of life—to "put our mouths out of taste for those pleasures with which the tempter baits his hooks." I know of no other way to triumph over sin long-term than by faith to die with Christ to our old seductions, that is, to gain a distaste for them because of a superior satisfaction in God. One of the reasons this book is still "working" after twenty-five years is that this truth simply does not and will not change. God remains gloriously all-satisfying. The human heart remains a ceaseless factory of desires. Sin remains powerfully and suicidally appealing. The battle remains: Where will we drink? Where will we feast? Therefore *Desiring God* is still a compelling and urgent message. Feast on God.

I never tire of saying and savoring the truth that God's passion to be glorified and our passion to be satisfied are *one* experience in the Christ-exalting act of worship—singing in the sanctuary and suffering in the streets. Baxter said it like this:

> [God's] glorifying himself and the saving of his people are not
> two decrees with God, but one decree, to glorify his mercy in
> their salvation, though we may say that one is the end of the
> other: so I think they should be with us together indeed.[6]

We get the mercy; He gets the glory. We get the happiness in Him; He gets the honor from us.

If God would be pleased to use this book to raise up one man or woman in this line of serious and happy saints who inspired it, then those of us who have rejoiced in the making of this book would delight all the more in the display of God's grace. It has indeed been a happy work. And my heart overflows to many:

---

5. Matthew Henry, *Commentary on the Whole Bible*, vol. 2 (Old Tappan, N.J.: Fleming H. Revell, n.d., orig. 1708), 1096.
6. Richard Baxter, *The Saints' Everlasting Rest*, abr. John T. Wilkinson (1650; reprint, London: Epworth, 1962), 31.

Steve Halliday believed in the book from the beginning. If he hadn't asked to see the sermons in 1983, there may be no *Desiring God.*

I remain ever in debt to Daniel Fuller in all I do. It was his class in 1968 where the seminal discoveries were made. It was from him that I learned how to dig for gold rather than rake for leaves when I take up the Scriptures. He remains a treasured friend and teacher.

The church that I love and serve has made my writing life possible. The partnership that I enjoy with the elders and staff is priceless. There is a chapter yet to be completed. It is called "The Camaraderie of Christian Hedonism." May the Spirit Himself continue to write it on the tablets of our hearts!

The successive editions of this work over the years have been made possible by the skills and insights and labors of Justin Taylor followed by David Mathis. New and better editions would not have been possible without their help.

Finally, a word about my father. He has gone to heaven since I dedicated the book to him. But the dedicatory words I wrote in 1986 are still true twenty-five years later. When the first edition of *Desiring God* was published, I gave my father a copy with these words written on the dedicatory page:

When grace abounds, the yoke of the law is easy and the commandment is light. You have been to me grace upon grace these 41 years, and therefore I find nothing easier or lighter than to obey the holy statute: Honor thy father.

Respectfully with all my heart,
Johnny

I look back to my childhood and see mother laughing so hard at the dinner table that the tears ran down her face. She was a very happy woman. But especially when my father came home on Monday. He had been gone two weeks in the work of evangelism. Or sometimes three of four. She would glow on Monday mornings when he was coming home.

At the dinner table that night (these were the happiest of times in my memory) we would hear about the victories of the gospel. Surely it is more exciting to be the son of an evangelist than to sit with knights and warriors. As I grew older I saw more of the wounds. But he spared me most of that until I was mature enough to "count it all joy." Holy and happy were those Monday meals. Oh, how good it was to have Daddy home!

John Piper
2011
Minneapolis, Minnesota

"It was good of you to look for Quentin."
"Good!" she exclaimed. "Good! O Anthony!"
"Well, so it was," he answered. "Or good in you.
How accurate one has to be with one's prepositions!
Perhaps it was a preposition wrong that set the whole world awry."

Charles Williams
The Place of the Lion

HOW I BECAME A CHRISTIAN HEDONIST

You might turn the world on its head by changing one word in your creed. The old tradition says:

The chief end of man is to glorify God
and
enjoy Him forever.

And? Like ham *and* eggs? Sometimes you glorify God *and* sometimes you enjoy Him? Sometimes He gets glory, sometimes you get joy? *And* is a very ambiguous word! Just how do these two things relate to each other?

Evidently, the old theologians didn't think they were talking about two things. They said "chief end," not "chief ends." Glorifying God and enjoying Him were one end in their minds, not two. How can that be?

That's what this book is about.

Not that I care too much about the intention of seventeenth-century theologians. But I care tremendously about the intention of God in Scripture. What does God have to say about the chief end of man? How does God teach us to give Him glory? Does He command us to enjoy Him? If so, how does this quest for joy in God relate to everything else? Yes, everything! "Whether you eat or drink, or whatever you do, do all to the glory of God" (1 Corinthians 10:31).

The overriding concern of this book is that in all of life God be glorified the way He Himself has appointed. To that end this book aims to persuade you that

The chief end of man is to glorify God
by
enjoying Him forever.

How I Became a Christian Hedonist

When I was in college, I had a vague, pervasive notion that if I did something good because it would make me happy, I would ruin its goodness.

I figured that the goodness of my moral action was lessened to the degree that I was motivated by a desire for my own pleasure. At the time, buying ice cream in the student center just for pleasure didn't bother me, because the moral consequences of that action seemed so insignificant. But to be motivated by a desire for happiness or pleasure when I volunteered for Christian service or went to church—that seemed selfish, utilitarian, mercenary.

This was a problem for me because I couldn't formulate an alternative motive that worked. I found in myself an overwhelming longing to be happy, a tremendously powerful impulse to seek pleasure, yet at every point of moral decision I said to myself that this impulse should have no influence.

One of the most frustrating areas was that of worship and praise. My vague notion that the higher the activity, the less there must be of self-interest in it caused me to think of worship almost solely in terms of duty. And that cuts the heart out of it.

Then I was converted to Christian Hedonism. In a matter of weeks I came to see that it is unbiblical and arrogant to try to worship God for any other reason than the pleasure to be had in Him. (Don't miss those last two words: *in Him*. Not His gifts, but Him. Not ourselves, but Him.) Let me describe the series of insights that made me a Christian Hedonist. Along the way, I hope it will become clear what I mean by this strange phrase.

1. During my first quarter in seminary, I was introduced to the argument for Christian Hedonism and one of its great exponents, Blaise Pascal. He wrote:

> All men seek happiness. This is without exception. Whatever different means they employ, they all tend to this end. The cause of some going to war, and of others avoiding it, is the same desire in both, attended with different views. The will never takes the least step but to this object. This is the motive of every action of every man, even of those who hang themselves.[1]

This statement so fit with my own deep longings, and all that I had ever seen in others, that I accepted it and have never found any reason to doubt it. What struck me especially was that Pascal was not making any moral judgment about this fact. As far as he was concerned, seeking one's own happiness is not a sin; it is a simple given in human nature. It is a law of the human heart, as gravity is a law of nature.

This thought made great sense to me and opened the way for the second discovery.

2. I had grown to love the works of C. S. Lewis in college. But not until later did I buy the sermon called "The Weight of Glory." The first page of that sermon is one of the most influential pages of literature I have ever read. It goes like this:

> If you asked twenty good men today what they thought the highest of the virtues, nineteen of them would reply, Unselfishness. But if you asked almost any of the great Christians of old he would have replied, Love. You see what has happened? A negative term has been substituted for a positive, and this is of more than philological importance. The negative ideal of Unselfishness carries with it the suggestion not primarily of securing good things for others, but of going without them

---

1. Blaise Pascal, *Pascal's Pensees,* trans. W. F. Trotter (New York: E. P. Dutton, 1958), 113, thought #425.

ourselves, as if our abstinence and not their happiness was the important point. I do not think this is the Christian virtue of Love. The New Testament has lots to say about self-denial, but not about self-denial as an end in itself. We are told to deny ourselves and to take up our crosses in order that we may follow Christ; and nearly every description of what we shall ultimately find if we do so contains an appeal to desire.

If there lurks in most modern minds the notion that to desire our own good and earnestly to hope for the enjoyment of it is a bad thing, I submit that this notion has crept in from Kant and the Stoics and is no part of the Christian faith. Indeed, if we consider the unblushing promises of reward and the staggering nature of the rewards promised in the Gospels, it would seem that Our Lord finds our desires not too strong, but too weak. We are half-hearted creatures, fooling about with drink and sex and ambition when infinite joy is offered us, like an ignorant child who wants to go on making mud pies in a slum because he cannot imagine what is meant by the offer of a holiday at the sea. We are far too easily pleased.[2]

There it was in black and white, and to my mind it was totally compelling: It is not a bad thing to desire our own good. In fact, the great problem of human beings is that they are far too easily pleased. They don't seek pleasure with nearly the resolve and passion that they should. And so they settle for mud pies of appetite instead of infinite delight.

I had never in my whole life heard any Christian, let alone a Christian of Lewis's stature, say that all of us not only seek (as Pascal said), but also *ought to seek,* our own happiness. Our mistake lies not in the intensity of our desire for happiness, but in the weakness of it.

3. The third insight was there in Lewis's sermon, but Pascal made it more explicit. He goes on to say:

---

2. C. S. Lewis, *The Weight of Glory and Other Addresses* (Grand Rapids, Mich.: Eerdmans, 1965), 1–2.

There once was in man a true happiness of which now remain to him only the mark and empty trace, which he in vain tries to fill from all his surroundings, seeking from things absent the help he does not obtain in things present. But these are all inadequate, because the infinite abyss can only be filled by an infinite and immutable object, that is to say, only by God Himself.[3]

As I look back on it now, it seems so patently obvious that I don't know how I could have missed it. All those years I had been trying to suppress my tremendous longing for happiness so I could honestly praise God out of some "higher," less selfish motive. But now it started to dawn on me that this persistent and undeniable yearning for happiness was not to be suppressed, but to be glutted—on God! The growing conviction that praise should be motivated solely by the happiness we find in God seemed less and less strange.

4. The next insight came again from C. S. Lewis, but this time from his *Reflections on the Psalms*. Chapter 9 of Lewis's book bears the modest title "A Word about Praise." In my experience it has been *the* word about praise—the best word on the nature of praise I have ever read.

Lewis says that as he was beginning to believe in God, a great stumbling block was the presence of demands scattered through the Psalms that he should praise God. He did not see the point in all this; besides, it seemed to picture God as craving "for our worship like a vain woman who wants compliments." He goes on to show why he was wrong:

But the most obvious fact about praise—whether of God or any-thing—strangely escaped me. I thought of it in terms of compliment, approval, or the giving of honor. I had never noticed that all enjoyment spontaneously overflows into praise.... The world rings with praise—lovers praising their mistresses, readers their favorite poet, walkers praising the countryside, players praising their favorite game....

---

3. Pascal, *Pensees,* 113.

My whole, more general difficulty about the praise of God depended on my absurdly denying to us, as regards the supremely Valuable, what we delight to do, what indeed we can't help doing, about everything else we value.

I think we delight to praise what we enjoy because the praise not merely expresses but completes the enjoyment; it is its appointed consummation.[4]

This was the capstone of my emerging Hedonism. Praising God, the highest calling of humanity and our eternal vocation, did not involve the renunciation, but rather the consummation of the joy I so desired. My old effort to achieve worship with no self-interest in it proved to be a contradiction in terms. God is not worshiped where He is not treasured and enjoyed. Praise is not an alternative to joy, but the expression of joy. Not to enjoy God is to dishonor Him. To say to Him that something else satisfies you more is the opposite of worship. It is sacrilege.

I saw this not only in C. S. Lewis, but also in the eighteenth-century pastor Jonathan Edwards. No one had ever taught me that God is glorified by our joy in Him. That joy in God is the very thing that makes praise an honor to God, and not hypocrisy. But Edwards said it so clearly and powerfully:

God glorifies Himself toward the creatures also in two ways: 1. By appearing to…their understanding. 2. In communicating Himself to their hearts, and in their rejoicing and delighting in, and enjoying, the manifestations which He makes of Himself.… *God is glorified not only by His glory's being seen, but by its being rejoiced in.* When those that see it delight in it, God is more glorified than if they only see it.… He that testifies his idea of God's glory [doesn't] glorify God so much as he that testifies also his approbation of it and his delight in it.[5]

---

4. C. S. Lewis, *Reflections on the Psalms* (New York: Harcourt, Brace & World, 1958), 94–5.
5. Jonathan Edwards, "Miscellanies," in *The Works of Jonathan Edwards,* vol. 13, ed. Thomas Schafer (New Haven: Yale University Press, 1994), 495, miscellany #448, emphasis added. See also #87 (pp. 251–2); #332 (p. 410); #679 (not in the New Haven volume).

This was a stunning discovery for me. I *must* pursue joy in God if I am to glorify Him as the surpassingly valuable Reality in the universe. Joy is not a mere option alongside worship. It is an essential component of worship.[6]

We have a name for those who try to praise when they have no pleasure in the object. We call them hypocrites. This fact—that praise means consummate pleasure and that the highest end of man is to drink deeply of this pleasure—was perhaps the most liberating discovery I ever made.

5. Then I turned to the Psalms for myself and found the language of Hedonism everywhere. The quest for pleasure was not even optional, but commanded: "Delight yourself in the LORD, and he will give you the desires of your heart" (Psalm 37:4).

The psalmists sought to do just this: "As a deer pants for flowing streams, so pants my soul for you, O God. My soul thirsts for God, for the living God" (Psalm 42:1–2). "My soul thirsts for you; my flesh faints for you, as in a dry and weary land where there is no water" (Psalm 63:1). The motif of thirsting has its satisfying counterpart when the psalmist says that men "drink their fill of the abundance of Your house; and You give them to drink of the river of Your delights" (Psalm 36:8, NASB).

I found that the goodness of God, the very foundation of worship, is not a thing you pay your respects to out of some kind of disinterested reverence. No, it is something to be enjoyed: "Oh, taste and see that the LORD is good!" (Psalm 34:8). "How sweet are your words to my taste, sweeter than honey to my mouth!" (Psalm 119:103).

As C. S. Lewis says, God in the Psalms is the "all-satisfying Object." His people adore Him unashamedly for the "exceeding joy" they find in Him (Psalm 43:4). He is the source of complete and unending pleasure: "In your presence there is fullness of joy; at your right hand are pleasures forevermore" (Psalm 16:11).

That is the short story of how I became a Christian Hedonist. I have now been brooding over these things for some forty years, and there has emerged a

---

6. I will deal in chapter 10 with the place of sadness in the Christian life and how it can be a part of worship, which is never perfect in this age. True evangelical brokenness for sin is a sadness experienced only by those who taste the pleasures of God's goodness and feel the regret that they do not savor it as fully as they ought.

philosophy that touches virtually every area of my life. I believe that it is biblical, that it fulfills the deepest longings of my heart, and that it honors the God and Father of our Lord Jesus Christ. I have written this book to commend these things to all who will listen.

Many objections rise in people's minds when they hear me talk this way. I hope the book will answer the most serious problems. But perhaps I can defuse some of the resistance in advance by making a few brief, clarifying comments.

First, Christian Hedonism as I use the term does not mean God becomes a means to help us get worldly pleasures. The pleasure Christian Hedonism seeks is the pleasure that is in God Himself. He is the end of our search, not the means to some further end. Our exceeding joy is He, the Lord—not the streets of gold or the reunion with relatives or any blessing of heaven. Christian Hedonism does not reduce God to a key that unlocks a treasure chest of gold and silver. Rather, it seeks to transform the heart so that "the Almighty will be your gold and your precious silver" (Job 22:25).

Second, Christian Hedonism does not make a god out of pleasure. It says that one has already made a god out of whatever he finds most pleasure in. The goal of Christian Hedonism is to find most pleasure in the one and only God and thus avoid the sin of covetousness, that is, idolatry (Colossians 3:5).

Third, Christian Hedonism does not put us above God when we seek Him out of self-interest. A patient is not greater than his physician. I will say more about this in chapter 3.

Fourth, Christian Hedonism is not a "general theory of *moral justification*."[7] In other words, nowhere do I say: An act is right because it brings pleasure. My aim is not to decide what is right by using joy as a moral criterion. My aim is to own up to the amazing, and largely neglected, fact that some dimension of joy is a moral duty in all true worship and all virtuous acts. I do not say that loving God is good because it brings joy. I say that God commands that we find joy in

---

7. One of the most extended and serious critiques of Christian Hedonism to appear since *Desiring God* was first published is in Richard Mouw, *The God Who Commands* (Notre Dame: Notre Dame Press, 1990). The quotation is taken from p. 33 (emphasis added).

loving God: "Delight yourself in the LORD" (Psalm 37:4). I do not say that loving people is good because it brings joy. I say that God commands that we find joy in loving people: "[Let] the one who does acts of mercy [do so] with cheerfulness" (Romans 12:8).[8]

I do not come to the Bible with a hedonistic theory of moral justification. On the contrary, I find in the Bible a divine command to be a pleasure-seeker—that is, to forsake the two-bit, low-yield, short-term, never-satisfying, person-destroying, God-belittling pleasures of the world and to sell everything "with joy" (Matthew 13:44) in order to have the kingdom of heaven and thus "enter into the joy of your master" (Matthew 25:21, 23). In short, I am a Christian Hedonist not for any philosophical or theoretical reason, but because God commands it (though He doesn't command that you use these labels!).

Fifth, I do not say that the relationship between love and happiness is this: "True happiness requires love." This is an oversimplification that misses the crucial and defining point. The distinguishing feature of Christian Hedonism is not that pleasure seeking demands virtue, but that virtue consists essentially, though not only, in pleasure seeking.

The reason I come to this conclusion is that I am operating here not as a philosophical hedonist, but as a biblical theologian and pastor who must come to terms with divine commands:

- to *"love* mercy," not just *do* it (Micah 6:8, KJV),
- to do "acts of mercy, *with cheerfulness"* (Romans 12:8),
- to *"joyfully"* suffer loss in the service of prisoners (Hebrews 10:34),
- to be a *cheerful* giver (2 Corinthians 9:7),
- to make *our joy* the joy of others (2 Corinthians 2:3),
- to tend the flock of God willingly and *"eagerly"* (1 Peter 5:2), and
- to keep watch over souls *"with joy"* (Hebrews 13:17).

---

8. Additional texts revealing the God-given duty of joy in God include Deuteronomy 28:47; 1 Chronicles 16:31, 33; Nehemiah 8:10; Psalm 32:11; 33:1; 35:9; 40:8, 16; 42:1–2; 63:1, 11; 64:10; 95:1; 97:1, 12; 98:4; 104:34; 105:3; Isaiah 41:16; Joel 2:23; Zechariah 2:10; 10:7, Philippians 3:1; 4:4. Additional texts mentioning the divine command of joy in loving others include 2 Corinthians 9:7 (cf. Acts 20:35); Hebrews 10:34; 13:17; 1 Peter 5:2.

When you reflect long and hard on such amazing commands, the moral implications are stunning. Christian Hedonism attempts to take these divine commands with blood-earnestness. The upshot is piercing and radically life changing: The pursuit of true virtue includes the pursuit of the joy because joy is an essential component of true virtue. This is vastly different from saying, "Let's all be good because it will make us happy."

Sixth, Christian Hedonism is not a distortion of historic Reformed catechisms of faith. This was one of the criticisms of Richard Mouw in his book, *The God Who Commands:*

> Piper might be able to alter the first answer in the Westminster Shorter Catechism—so that glorifying *and* enjoying God becomes glorifying *by* enjoying the deity—to suit his hedonistic purposes, but it is a little more difficult to alter the opening lines of the Heidelberg Catechism: That I, with body and soul, both in life and death, am not my own but belong unto my faithful Savior Jesus Christ.[9]

The remarkable thing about the beginning of the Heidelberg Catechism is not that I can't change it for hedonistic purposes, but that I don't have to. It already places the entire catechism under the human longing for "comfort." Question one: "What is your only *comfort* in life and death?" The pressing question for critics of Christian Hedonism is: Why did the original framers of the four-hundred-year-old catechism structure all 129 questions so that they are an exposition of the question "What is my only comfort?"

Even more remarkable is to see the concern with "happiness" emerge explicitly in the second question of the catechism, which provides the outlines for the rest of the catechism. The second question is: "How many things are necessary for thee to know, that thou in this *comfort (Troste)* mayest live and die *happily (seliglich)?*" Thus, the entire catechism is an answer to the concern for how to live and die *happily.*

---

9. Mouw, *The God Who Commands,* 36.

The answer to the second question of the catechism is: "Three things: first, the greatness of my sin and misery; second, how I am redeemed from all my sins and misery; third, how I am to be thankful to God for such redemption." Then the rest of the catechism is divided into three sections to deal with these three things: "The First Part: Of Man's Misery" (questions 3–11); "The Second Part: Of Man's Redemption" (questions 12–85); and "The Third Part: Of Thankfulness" (questions 86–129). What this means is that *the entire Heidelberg Catechism is written to answer the question "What must I know to live happily?"*

I am puzzled that anyone would think that Christian Hedonism needs to "alter the opening lines to the Heidelberg Catechism." The fact is, the entire catechism is structured the way Christian Hedonism would structure it. Therefore, Christian Hedonism does not distort the historic Reformed catechisms. Both the Westminster Catechism and the Heidelberg Catechism begin with a concern for man's enjoyment of God, or his quest to "live and die happily." I have no desire to be doctrinally novel. I am glad that the Heidelberg Catechism was written four hundred years ago.

TOWARD A DEFINITION OF CHRISTIAN HEDONISM

Fresh ways of looking at the world (even when they are centuries old) do not lend themselves to simple definitions. A whole book is needed so people can begin to catch on. Quick and superficial judgments will almost certainly be wrong. Beware of conjecture about what lies in the pages of this book! The surmise that here we have another spin-off from modern man's enslavement to the centrality of himself will be very wide of the mark. Ah, what surprises lie ahead!

For many, the term *Christian Hedonism* will be new. Therefore, I have included the appendix: "Why Call It Christian Hedonism?" If this is a strange or troubling term, you may want to read those pages before plunging into the main chapters.

I would prefer to reserve a definition of Christian Hedonism until the end of the book, when misunderstandings would have been swept away. A writer often wishes his first sentence could be read in light of his last—and vice versa! But, alas, one must begin somewhere. So I offer the following advance definition in hope that it will be interpreted sympathetically in light of the rest of the book.

Christian Hedonism is a philosophy of life built on the following five convictions:

1. The longing to be happy is a universal human experience, and it is good, not sinful.
2. We should never try to deny or resist our longing to be happy, as though it were a bad impulse. Instead, we should seek to intensify this longing and nourish it with whatever will provide the deepest and most enduring satisfaction.
3. The deepest and most enduring happiness is found only in God. Not from God, but in God.
4. The happiness we find in God reaches its consummation when it is shared with others in the manifold ways of love.
5. To the extent that we try to abandon the pursuit of our own pleasure, we fail to honor God and love people. Or, to put it positively: The pursuit of pleasure is a necessary part of all worship and virtue. That is:

The chief end of man is to glorify God
by
enjoying Him forever.

THE ROOT OF THE MATTER

This book will be predominantly a meditation on Scripture. It will be expository rather than speculative. If I cannot show that Christian Hedonism comes from the Bible, I do not expect anyone to be interested, let alone persuaded. There are a thousand man-made philosophies of life. If this is another, let it pass. There is only one rock: the Word of God. Only one thing ultimately matters: glorifying God the way He has appointed. That is why I am a Christian Hedonist. That is why I wrote this book.

Our God is in the heavens;
he does all that he pleases.

PSALM 115:3

There has been a wonderful alteration in my mind,
in respect to the doctrine of God's sovereignty.... The doctrine
has very often appeared exceeding pleasant, bright and sweet.
Absolute sovereignty is what I love to ascribe to God.

JONATHAN EDWARDS

The climax of God's happiness
is the delight He takes
in the echoes of His excellence
in the praises of His people.

JOHN PIPER

CHAPTER 1

THE HAPPINESS OF GOD

Foundation for Christian Hedonism

The ultimate ground of Christian Hedonism is the fact that God is uppermost in His own affections:

> *The chief end of* God *is to glorify God*
> *and enjoy Himself forever.*

The reason this may sound strange is that we are more accustomed to think about our duty than God's design. And when we do ask about God's design, we are too prone to describe it with ourselves at the center of God's affections. We may say, for example, that His design is to redeem the world. Or to save sinners. Or to restore creation. Or the like.

But God's saving designs are penultimate, not ultimate. Redemption, salvation, and restoration are not God's ultimate goal. These He performs for the sake of something greater: namely, the enjoyment He has in glorifying Himself. The bedrock foundation of Christian Hedonism is not God's allegiance to us, but to Himself.

If God were not infinitely devoted to the preservation, display, and enjoyment of His own glory, we could have no hope of finding happiness in Him.

But if He does in fact employ all His sovereign power and infinite wisdom to maximize the enjoyment of His own glory, then we have a foundation on which to stand and rejoice.

I know this is perplexing at first glance. So I will try to take it apart a piece at a time, and then put it back together at the end of the chapter.

GOD'S SOVEREIGNTY:
THE FOUNDATION OF HIS HAPPINESS AND OURS

"Our God is in the heavens; he does all that he pleases" (Psalm 115:3). The implication of this text is that God has the right and power to do whatever makes Him happy. That is what it means to say that God is sovereign.

Think about it for a moment: If God is sovereign and can do anything He pleases, then none of His purposes can be frustrated.

The LORD brings the counsel of the nations to nothing; he frustrates the plans of the peoples. The counsel of the LORD stands forever, the plans of his heart to all generations. (Psalm 33:10–11)

And if none of His purposes can be frustrated, then He must be the happiest of all beings. This infinite, divine happiness is the fountain from which the Christian Hedonist drinks and longs to drink more deeply.

Can you imagine what it would be like if the God who ruled the world were not happy? What if God were given to grumbling and pouting and depression, like some Jack-and-the-beanstalk giant in the sky? What if God were frustrated and despondent and gloomy and dismal and discontented and dejected? Could we join David and say, "O God, you are my God; earnestly I seek you; my soul thirsts for you; my flesh faints for you, as in a dry and weary land where there is no water" (Psalm 63:1)?

I don't think so. We would all relate to God like little children who have a frustrated, gloomy, dismal, discontented father. They can't enjoy him. They can only try not to bother him, or maybe try to work for him to earn some little favor.

Therefore if God is not a happy God, Christian Hedonism has no foundation. For the aim of the Christian Hedonist is to be happy in God, to delight in God, to cherish and enjoy His fellowship and favor. But children cannot enjoy the fellowship of their Father if He is unhappy. Therefore the foundation of Christian Hedonism is the happiness of God.

But the foundation of the happiness of God is the sovereignty of God: "Our God is in the heavens; he does all that he pleases" (Psalm 115:3). If God were not sovereign, if the world He made were out of control, frustrating His design again and again, God would not be happy.

Just as our joy is based on the promise that God is strong enough and wise enough to make all things work together for our good, so God's joy is based on that same sovereign control: He makes all things work together for His glory.

If so much hangs on God's sovereignty, we should make sure the biblical basis for it is secure.

THE BIBLICAL BASIS FOR GOD'S SOVEREIGN HAPPINESS[1]

The sheer fact that God is God implies that His purposes cannot be thwarted—so says the prophet Isaiah:

"I am God, and there is no other; I am God, and there is none like me, declaring the end from the beginning and from ancient times things not yet done, saying, 'My counsel shall stand, and I will accomplish all my purpose.'" (Isaiah 46:9–10)

The purposes of God cannot be frustrated; there is none like God. If a purpose of God came to naught, it would imply that there is a power greater than God's. It would imply that someone could stay His hand when He designs to do a thing. But "none can stay his hand," as the newly awakened Nebuchadnezzar says:

1. For a much fuller defense of God's sovereignty in all that He does, see John Piper, *The Pleasures of God: Meditations on God's Delight in Being God* (Sisters, Ore.: Multnomah, 2000), 47–75, 121–55 and *The Justification of God: An Exegetical and Theological Study of Romans 9:1–23* (Grand Rapids, Mich.: Baker, 1993). See also Wayne Grudem, *Systematic Theology: An Introduction to Biblical Doctrine* (Grand Rapids, Mich.: Zondervan), 315–54; John M. Frame, *The Doctrine of God*, Theology of Lordship Series (Phillipsburg, N.J.: Presbyterian & Reformed, 2002), 47–79, 274–88, 313–39, and the relevant chapters in *Still Sovereign: Contemporary Perspectives on Election, Foreknowledge, and Grace*, ed. Thomas R. Schreiner and Bruce A. Ware (Grand Rapids, Mich.: Baker, 2000).

His dominion is an everlasting dominion, and his kingdom endures from generation to generation; all the inhabitants of the earth are accounted as nothing, and he does according to his will among the host of heaven and among the inhabitants of the earth; and none can stay his hand or say to him, "What have you done?" (Daniel 4:34–35)

HIS SOVEREIGNTY COVERS CALAMITIES

This was also Job's final confession after God had spoken to him out of the whirlwind: "I know that you can do all things, and that no purpose of yours can be thwarted" (Job 42:2). "Our God is in the heavens; he does all that he pleases" (Psalm 115:3).

This raises the question whether the evil and calamitous events in the world are also part of God's sovereign design. Jeremiah looks over the carnage of Jerusalem after its destruction and cries:

My eyes are spent with weeping; my stomach churns; my bile is poured out to the ground because of the destruction of the daughter of my people, because infants and babies faint in the streets of the city. (Lamentations 2:11)

But when he looked to God, he could not deny the truth:

Who has spoken and it came to pass, unless the Lord has commanded it? Is it not from the mouth of the Most High that good and bad come? (3:37–38)

"SHALL WE RECEIVE GOOD
FROM GOD AND NOT EVIL?"

If God reigns as sovereign over the world, then the evil of the world is not outside His design: "Does disaster come to a city, unless the LORD has done it?" (Amos 3:6).

This was the reverent saying of God's servant Job when he was afflicted with boils: "Shall we receive good from God, and shall we not receive evil?" (Job 2:10). He said this even though the text says plainly that "Satan went out from the presence of the LORD and struck Job with loathsome sores" (Job 2:7). Was Job wrong to attribute to God what came from Satan? No, because the inspired writer tells us immediately after Job's words: "In all this Job did not sin with his lips" (Job 2:10).

The evil Satan causes is only by the permission of God. Therefore, Job is not wrong to see it as ultimately from the hand of God. It would be unbiblical and irreverent to attribute to Satan (or to sinful man) the power to frustrate the designs of God.

WHO PLANNED THE MURDER OF CHRIST?

The clearest example that even moral evil fits into the designs of God is the crucifixion of Christ. Who would deny that the betrayal of Jesus by Judas was a morally evil act?

Yet in Acts 2:23, Peter says, "This Jesus, delivered up according to the definite plan and foreknowledge of God, you crucified and killed by the hands of lawless men." The betrayal was sin, but it was part of God's ordained plan. Sin did not thwart His plan or stay His hand.

Or who would say that Herod's contempt (Luke 23:11) or Pilate's spineless expediency (Luke 23:24) or the Jews' "Crucify, crucify him!" (Luke 23:21) or the Gentile soldiers' mockery (Luke 23:36)—who would say that these were not sin? Yet Luke, in Acts 4:27–28, records the prayer of the saints:

> Truly in this city there were gathered together against your holy servant
> Jesus, whom you anointed, both Herod and Pontius Pilate, along with
> the Gentiles and the peoples of Israel, to do whatever your hand and
> your plan had predestined to take place.

People lift their hand to rebel against the Most High only to find that their rebellion is unwitting service in the wonderful designs of God. Even sin cannot frustrate the purposes of the Almighty. He Himself does not commit sin, but

He has decreed that there be acts that are sin,[2] for the acts of Pilate and Herod were predestined by God's plan.

GOD TURNS IT WHEREVER HE WILL

Similarly, when we come to the end of the New Testament and to the end of history in the Revelation of John, we find God in complete control of all the evil kings who wage war. In Revelation 17, John speaks of a harlot sitting on a beast with ten horns. The harlot is Rome, drunk with the blood of the saints; the beast is the Antichrist; and the ten horns are ten kings who "hand over their power and authority to the beast…[and] make war on the Lamb" (vv. 13–14).

But are these evil kings outside God's control? Are they frustrating God's designs? Far from it. They are unwittingly doing His bidding: "For God has put it into their hearts to carry out his purpose by being of one mind and handing over their royal power to the beast, until the words of God are fulfilled" (Revelation 17:17). No one on earth can escape the sovereign control of God: "The king's heart is a stream of water in the hand of the LORD; he turns it wherever he will" (Proverbs 21:1; cf. Ezra 6:22).

The evil intentions of men cannot frustrate the decrees of God. This is the point of the story of Joseph's fall and rise in Egypt. His brothers sold him into slavery. Potiphar's wife slandered him into the dungeon. Pharaoh's butler forgot him in prison for two years. Where was God in all this sin and misery? Joseph answers in Genesis 50:20. He says to his guilty brothers, "As for you, you meant evil against me, but God meant it for good, to bring it about that many people should be kept alive, as they are today."

The hardened disobedience of men's hearts leads not to the frustration of God's plans, but to their fruition.

Consider the hardness of heart in Romans 11:25–26: "Lest you be wise in your own conceits, I want you to understand this mystery, brothers: a partial

---

2. For an explanation and defense of this statement, see "Is God Less Glorious Because He Ordained that Evil Be?", the transcript of a presentation given in 1998 at The Jonathan Edwards Institute. Available online at: http://www.desiringgod.org/resource-library/conference-messages/is-god-less-glorious-because-he-ordained-that-evil-be: "Is God Less Glorious Because He Ordained That Evil Be? Jonathan Edwards on the Divine Decrees."

hardening has come upon Israel, until the full number of the Gentiles has come in. And in this way all Israel will be saved." Who is governing the coming and going of this hardness of heart so that it has a particular limit, and then gives way at the appointed time to the certain salvation of "all Israel"?

Or consider the disobedience in Romans 11:31. Paul speaks to his Gentile readers about Israel's disobedience in rejecting their Messiah: "So they [Israel] too have now been disobedient in order that by the mercy shown to you [Gentiles] they also may now receive mercy." When Paul says that Israel was disobedient in order that Gentiles might get the benefits of the gospel, whose purpose does He have in mind?

It could only be God's. For Israel certainly did not conceive of their disobedience as a way of blessing the Gentiles—or winning mercy for themselves in such a roundabout fashion! Is not then the point of Romans 11:31 that God rules over the disobedience of Israel and turns it precisely to the purposes He has planned?

THERE IS NO SUCH THING AS MERE COINCIDENCE

God's sovereignty over men's affairs is not compromised even by the reality of sin and evil in the world. It is not limited to the good acts of men or the pleasant events of nature. The wind belongs to God whether it comforts or whether it kills.

> For I know that the LORD is great, and that our Lord is above all gods. Whatever the LORD pleases, he does, in heaven and on earth, in the seas and all deeps. He it is who makes the clouds rise at the end of the earth, who makes lightnings for the rain and brings forth the wind from his storehouses. (Psalm 135:5–7)

In the end, one must finally come to see that if there is a God in heaven, there is no such thing as mere coincidence, not even in the smallest affairs of life: "The lot is cast into the lap, but its every decision is from the LORD" (Proverbs 16:33). Not one sparrow "will fall to the ground without your Father's will" (Matthew 10:29, RSV).

THE STRUGGLE AND SOLUTION OF JONATHAN EDWARDS

Many of us have gone through a period of deep struggle with the doctrine of God's sovereignty. If we take our doctrines into our hearts where they belong, they can cause upheavals of emotion and sleepless nights. This is far better than toying with academic ideas that never touch real life. The possibility at least exists that out of the upheavals will come a new era of calm and confidence.

It has happened for many of us the way it did for Jonathan Edwards. Edwards was a pastor and a profound theologian in New England in the early 1700s. He was a leader in the First Great Awakening. His major works still challenge great minds of our day. His extraordinary combination of logic and love make him a deeply moving writer. Again and again when I am dry and weak, I pull down my collection of Edwards's works and stir myself up with one of his sermons.[3]

He recounts the struggle he had with the doctrine of God's sovereignty:

From my childhood up, my mind had been full of objections against the doctrine of God's sovereignty.... It used to appear like a horrible doctrine to me. But I remember the time very well, when I seemed to be convinced, and fully satisfied, as to this sovereignty of God....

But never could I give an account, how, or by what means, I was thus convinced, not in the least imagining at the time, nor a long time after, that there was any extraordinary influence of God's Spirit in it; but only that now I saw further, and my reason apprehended the justice and reasonableness of it. However, my mind rested in it; and it put an end to all those cavils and objections.

And there has been a wonderful alteration in my mind, in respect to the doctrine of God's sovereignty, from that day to this; so that I scarce ever have found so much as the rising of an objection against it, in the most absolute sense.... I have often since had not only a con-

---

3. The most accessible version of Edwards's works is *The Works of Jonathan Edwards*, 2 vols., published both by Banner of Truth and Hendrickson. The complete works also have been published in individual volumes by Yale University Press.

viction but a delightful conviction. The doctrine has very often appeared exceeding pleasant, bright, and sweet. Absolute sovereignty is what I love to ascribe to God. But my first conviction was not so.[4]

It is not surprising, then, that Jonathan Edwards struggled earnestly and deeply with the problem that stands before us now. How can we affirm the happiness of God on the basis of His sovereignty when much of what God permits in the world is contrary to His own commands in Scripture? How can we say God is happy when there is so much sin and misery in the world?

Edwards did not claim to exhaust the mystery here. But he does help us find a possible way of avoiding outright contradiction while being faithful to the Scriptures. To put it in my own words, he said that the infinite complexity of the divine mind is such that God has the capacity to look at the world through two lenses. He can look through a narrow lens or through a wide-angle lens.

When God looks at a painful or wicked event through His narrow lens, He sees the tragedy of the sin for what it is in itself, and He is angered and grieved: "I have no pleasure in the death of anyone, declares the Lord GOD" (Ezekiel 18:32).

But when God looks at a painful or wicked event through His wide-angle lens, He sees the tragedy of the sin in relation to everything leading up to it and everything flowing out from it. He sees it in relation to all the connections and effects that form a pattern, or mosaic, stretching into eternity. This mosaic in all its parts—good and evil—brings Him delight.[5]

---

4. Jonathan Edwards, "Personal Narrative," in *Jonathan Edwards: Representative Selections*, ed. C. H. Faust and T. H. Johnson (New York: Hill & Wang, 1962), 58–9.
5. Edwards treats this problem by distinguishing two kinds of willing in God (which is implied in what I have said). God's "will of command" (or revealed will) is what He commands in Scripture (Thou shalt not kill, etc.). His "will of decree" (or secret will, or sovereign will) is what He infallibly brings to pass in the world. Edwards's words are complex, but they are worth the effort if you love the deep things of God:

   When a distinction is made between God's revealed will and his secret will, or his will of command and decree, "will" is certainly in that distinction taken in two senses. His will of decree, is not his will in the same sense as his will of command is. Therefore, it is no difficulty at all to suppose, that the one may be otherwise than the other: his will in both senses is his inclination. But when we say he wills virtue, or loves virtue, or the happiness of his creature; thereby is intended, that virtue, or the creature's happiness, absolutely and simply considered, is agreeable to the inclination of his nature.

"IT WAS THE WILL OF THE LORD TO CRUSH HIM"

For example, the death of Christ was the will and work of God the Father. Isaiah writes, "We esteemed him stricken, smitten by God.… It was the will of the LORD to crush him; he has put him to grief" (53:4, 10). Yet surely, as God the Father saw the agony of His beloved Son and the wickedness that brought Him to the cross, He did not delight in those things in themselves (viewed through the narrow lens). Sin in itself, and the suffering of the innocent, is abhorrent to God.

Nevertheless, according to Hebrews 2:10, God the Father thought it was fitting to perfect the Pioneer of our salvation through suffering. God willed what He abhorred. He abhorred it in the narrow-lens view, but not in the wide-angle view of eternity. When the universality of things was considered, the death of the Son of God was seen by the Father as a magnificent way to demonstrate His righteousness (Romans 3:25–26) and bring His people to glory (Hebrews 2:10) and keep the angels praising Him forever and ever (Revelation 5:9–13).

Therefore, when I say that the sovereignty of God is the foundation of His happiness, I do not ignore or minimize the anger and grief God can express against evil. But neither do I infer from this wrath and sorrow that God is a frustrated God who cannot keep His creation under control. He has designed from all eternity, and is infallibly forming with every event, a magnificent mosaic of redemptive history.[6] The contemplation of this mosaic (with both its dark and bright tiles) fills His heart with joy.

His will of decree is his inclination to a thing, not as to that thing absolutely and simply, but with respect to the universality of things, that have been, are, or shall be. So God, though he hates a thing as it is simply, may incline to it with reference to the universality of things. Though he hates sin in itself, yet he may will to permit it, for the greater promotion of holiness in this universality, including all things, and at all times. So, though he has no inclination to a creature's misery, considered absolutely, yet he may will it, for the greater promotion of happiness in this universality.

Jonathan Edwards, "Concerning the Divine Decrees," in *The Works of Jonathan Edwards*, vol. 2 (Edinburgh: Banner of Truth, 1974), 527–8.

6. The term *redemptive history* simply refers to the history of God's acts recorded in the Bible. It is called redemptive history not because it isn't real history, but because it is history viewed from the perspective of God's redeeming purpose revealed along the Bible's storyline.

And if our Father's heart is full of deep and unshakable happiness, we may be sure that when we seek our happiness in Him, we will not find Him "out of sorts" when we come. We will not find a frustrated, gloomy, irritable Father who wants to be left alone, but a Father whose heart is so full of joy that it spills over onto all those (Christian Hedonists) who are thirsty.

GOD'S HAPPINESS IS IN HIMSELF

I began this chapter by saying that the ultimate ground of Christian Hedonism is the fact that God is uppermost in His own affections:

> *The chief end of God is to glorify God*
> *and enjoy Himself forever.*

What we have seen so far is that God is absolutely sovereign over the world, that He can therefore do anything He pleases, and that He is therefore not a frustrated God, but a deeply happy God, rejoicing in all His works (Psalm 104:31) when He considers them in relation to all of redemptive history.

What we have not yet seen is how this unshakable happiness of God is indeed a happiness in *Himself.* We have seen that God has the sovereign power to do whatever He pleases, but we have not yet seen specifically what it is that pleases Him. Why is it that contemplating the mosaic of redemptive history delights the heart of God? Is this not idolatry—for God to delight in something other than Himself?

So now we must ask: What does make God happy? What is it about redemptive history that delights the heart of God? The way to answer this question is to survey what God pursues in all His works. If we could discover what one thing God pursues in everything He does, we would know what He delights in most. We would know what is uppermost in His affections.

GOD DELIGHTS IN HIS GLORY

The high points of redemptive history, which include Creation, the call of Abraham, the Exodus, the giving of the Law, the temple, the life, ministry, and death of Jesus, and the Christian life, reveal God's ultimate goal in all He does. Jonathan Edwards has written the best book on the subject, *The End for Which God Created the World*.[7] If what follows seems out of sync with Scripture, I urge you to examine the supporting evidence in Edwards's book.

My conclusion is that God's own glory is uppermost in His own affections. In everything He does, His purpose is to preserve and display that glory. To say that His own glory is uppermost in His own affections means that He puts a greater value on it than on anything else. He delights in His glory above all things.

Glory is not easy to define. It is like beauty. How would you define beauty? Some things we have to point at rather than define. But let me try. God's glory is the beauty of His manifold perfections. It can refer to the bright and awesome radiance that breaks forth in visible manifestations. Or it can refer to the infinite moral excellence of His character. In either case it signifies a reality of infinite greatness and worth. C. S. Lewis helps us with his own effort to point at it:

> Nature never taught me that there exists a God of glory and of infinite majesty. I had to learn that in other ways. But nature gave the word glory a meaning for me. I still do not know where else I could have found one. I do not see how the "fear" of God could have ever meant to me anything but the lowest prudential efforts to be safe, if I had never seen certain ominous ravines and unapproachable crags.[8]

God's ultimate goal is to preserve and display His infinite and awesome greatness and worth, that is, His glory.

God has many other goals in what He does. But none of them is more ultimate than this. They are all subordinate. God's overwhelming passion is to exalt

---

7. Reprinted in its entirety in John Piper, *God's Passion for His Glory: Living the Vision of Jonathan Edwards* (Wheaton, Ill.: Crossway, 1998).
8. Quoted from *The Four Loves*, in *A Mind Awake: An Anthology of C. S. Lewis,* ed. Clyde Kilby (New York: Harcourt, Brace & World, 1968), 202.

the value of His glory. To that end, He seeks to display it, to oppose those who belittle it, and to vindicate it from all contempt. It is clearly the uppermost reality in His affections. He loves His glory infinitely.

This is the same as saying: He loves himself infinitely. Or: He Himself is uppermost in His own affections. A moment's reflection reveals the inexorable justice of this fact. God would be unrighteous (just as we would) if He valued anything more than what is supremely valuable. But He Himself is supremely valuable. If He did not take infinite delight in the worth of His own glory, He would be unrighteous. For it is right to take delight in a person in proportion to the excellence of that person's glory.

GOD DELIGHTS IN THE GLORY OF HIS SON

Another moment's reflection reminds us that this is exactly what we affirm when we affirm the eternal divinity of God's Son. We stand at the foothills of mystery in all these things. But the Scriptures have given us some glimpses of the heights. They teach us that the Son of God is Himself God: "In the beginning was the Word, and the Word was with God, and the Word was God" (John 1:1). "In him the whole fullness of deity dwells bodily" (Colossians 2:9).

Therefore, when the Father beheld the Son from all eternity, He was beholding the exact representation of Himself. As Hebrews 1:3 (RSV) says, the Son "reflects the glory of God and bears the very stamp of his nature." And 2 Corinthians 4:4 (RSV) speaks of "the glory of Christ, who is the likeness of God."

From these texts we learn that through all eternity God the Father has beheld the image of His own glory perfectly represented in the person of His Son. Therefore, one of the best ways to think about God's infinite enjoyment of His own glory is to think of it as the delight He has in His Son, who is the perfect reflection of that glory (John 17:24–26).

When Christ entered the world and proceeded to fulfill all righteousness, God the Father said, "This is my beloved Son, with whom I am well pleased" (Matthew 3:17). As God the Father contemplates the image of His own glory in the person of His Son, He is infinitely happy. "Behold my servant, whom I uphold, my chosen, in whom my soul delights" (Isaiah 42:1).

Within the triune Godhead (Father, Son, and Holy Spirit), God has been uppermost in His own affections for all eternity. This belongs to His very nature, for He has begotten and loved the Son from all eternity. Therefore, God has been supremely and eternally happy in the fellowship of the Trinity.[9]

GOD DELIGHTS IN THE GLORY OF HIS WORK

In creation, God "went public"[10] with the glory that reverberates joyfully between the Father and the Son. There is something about the fullness of God's joy that inclines it to overflow. There is an expansive quality to His joy. It wants to share itself. The impulse to create the world was not from weakness, as though God were lacking in some perfection that creation could supply. "It is no argument of the emptiness or deficiency of a fountain, that it is inclined to overflow."[11]

God loves to behold His glory reflected in His works. So the eternal happiness of the triune God spilled over in the work of creation and redemption. And since this original happiness was God's delight in His own glory, therefore the happiness that He has in all His works of creation and redemption is nothing

---

9. If one should ask what place the Holy Spirit has in this understanding of the Trinity, I would direct attention to two works of Jonathan Edwards: "Treatise on Grace" and "An Essay on the Trinity." He sums up his understanding of the Trinity in these words:

   And this I suppose to be that blessed Trinity that we read of in the Holy Scriptures. The Father is the deity subsisting in the prime, unoriginated and most absolute manner, or the deity in its direct existence. The Son is the deity generated by God's understanding, or having an idea of Himself and subsisting in that idea. The Holy Ghost is the deity subsisting in act, or the divine essence flowing out and breathed forth in God's infinite love to and delight in Himself. And I believe the whole Divine essence does truly and distinctly subsist both in the Divine idea and Divine love, and that each of them are properly distinct persons.

   Jonathan Edwards, "An Essay on the Trinity," in *Treatise on Grace and Other Posthumously Published Writings*, ed. Paul Helm (Cambridge: James Clarke, 1971), 118.

   In other words, the Holy Spirit is the delight that the Father and the Son have in each other, and He carries in Himself so fully all the essence of the Father and the Son that He Himself stands forth as a third Person in His own right.

   Jonathan Edwards, "Treatise on Grace," in *Treatise on Grace,* 63.
10. I borrow this phrase from Daniel Fuller's book *The Unity of the Bible: Unfolding God's Plan for Humanity* (Grand Rapids, Mich.: Zondervan, 1992). See especially chapters 8 and 9.
11. Edwards, "Dissertation Concerning the End for Which God Created the World," in *The Works of Jonathan Edwards,* 102. This "Dissertation" is of immense value in handling the whole question of God's goal in history. For the complete text, as well as footnotes to aid your study, see Piper, *God's Passion for His Glory.*

other than a delight in His own glory. This is why God has done all things, from creation to consummation, for the preservation and display of His glory. All His works are simply the spillover of His infinite exuberance for His own excellence.

IS GOD FOR US OR FOR HIMSELF?

But now the question arises: If God is so utterly enamored of His own glory, how can He be a God of love? If He unwaveringly does all things for His own sake, how then can we have any hope that He will do anything for our sake? Does not the apostle say, "[Love] does not seek its own" (1 Corinthians 13:5, NASB)?

Now we begin to see how the issue of God's happiness can make or break the philosophy of Christian Hedonism. If God were self-centered in such a way that He had no inclination to love His creatures, then Christian Hedonism would be dead. Christian Hedonism depends on the open arms of God. It depends on the readiness of God to accept and save and satisfy the heart of all who seek their joy in Him. But if God is on an ego trip and out of reach, then it is in vain that we pursue our happiness in Him.

Is God for us or for Himself? It is precisely in answering this question that we will discover the great foundation for Christian Hedonism.

IS HE VAIN OR LOVING TO COMMAND OUR PRAISE?

The Bible is replete with commands to praise God. God commands it because this is the ultimate goal of all He does—"to be glorified in his saints, and to be marveled at among all who have believed" (2 Thessalonians 1:10). Three times in Ephesians 1 this great aim is proclaimed: "In love He predestined us to adoption as sons...to the praise of the glory of His grace" (vv. 4–6, NASB); we have been predestined and appointed to "be to the praise of His glory" (v. 12, NASB); the Holy Spirit "is the guarantee of our inheritance until we acquire possession of it, to the praise of his glory" (v. 14).

All the different ways God has chosen to display His glory in creation and redemption reach their culmination in the praises of His redeemed people. God governs the world with glory precisely that He might be admired, marveled at, exalted, and praised. The climax of His happiness is the delight He takes in the echoes of His excellence in the praises of the saints.

But again and again I have found that people stumble over this truth. People do not like to hear that God is uppermost in His own affections, or that He does all things for His own glory, or that He exalts Himself and seeks the praise of men.

Why? There are at least two reasons. One is that we just don't like people who are like that. The other is that the Bible teaches us not to be like that. Let's examine these objections and see if they can apply to God.

IS GOD A SECOND-HANDER?

First, we just don't like people who seem to be enamored with their own intelligence or strength or skill or good looks or wealth. We don't like scholars who try to show off their specialized knowledge or recite for us all their recent publications. We don't like businessmen who talk about how shrewdly they have invested their money and how they stayed right on top of the market to get in low and out high. We don't like children to play one-upmanship (Mine's bigger! Mine's faster! Mine's prettier!). And unless we are one of them, we disapprove of men and women who dress not functionally and simply, but to attract attention with the latest style.

Why don't we like all that? I think at root it's because such people are inauthentic. They are what Ayn Rand calls "second-handers." They don't live from the joy that comes through achieving what they value for its own sake. Instead, they live secondhand from the compliments of others. They have one eye on their action and one on their audience. We simply do not admire second-handers. We admire people who are secure and composed enough that they don't need to shore up their weaknesses and compensate for their deficiencies by trying to get compliments.

It stands to reason, then, that any teaching that puts God in the category of a second-hander will be unacceptable to Christians. And for many, the teaching that God seeks to show off His glory and get the praise of men does in fact put Him in the category of a second-hander. But should it?

One thing is certain: God is not weak and has no deficiencies: "From him and through him and to him are all things" (Romans 11:36). He is not "served by human hands, as though he needed anything, since he himself gives to all men life and breath and everything" (Acts 17:25). Everything that exists owes its existence to Him, and no one can add anything to Him that is not already flowing from Him. Therefore, God's zeal to seek His own glory and to be praised by men cannot be owing to His need to shore up some weakness or compensate for some deficiency. He may look, at first glance, like one of the second-handers, but He is not like them, and the superficial similarity must be explained another way.

"LOVE SEEKS NOT ITS OWN"—EXCEPT IN THE JOY OF OTHERS

The second reason people stumble over the teaching that God exalts His own glory and seeks to be praised by His people is that the Bible teaches us not to be like that. For example, the Bible says that love "does not seek its own" (1 Corinthians 13:5, NASB). How can God be loving and yet be utterly devoted to "seeking His own" glory and praise and joy? How can God be for us if He is so utterly for Himself?

The answer I propose is this: Because God is unique as an all-glorious, totally self-sufficient Being, He must be for Himself if He is to be for us. The rules of humility that belong to a creature cannot apply in the same way to its Creator. If God should turn away from Himself as the Source of infinite joy, He would cease to be God. He would deny the infinite worth of His own glory. He would imply that there is something more valuable outside Himself. He would commit idolatry.

This would be no gain for us. For where can we go when our God has become unrighteous? Where will we find a Rock of integrity in the universe when the heart of God has ceased to value supremely the supremely valuable? Where shall we turn with our adoration when God Himself has forsaken the claims of infinite worth and beauty?

No, we do not turn God's self-exaltation into love by demanding that God cease to be God. Instead, we must come to see that God is love precisely because He relentlessly pursues the praises of His name in the hearts of His people.

DELIGHT IS INCOMPLETE UNTIL IT IS EXPRESSED

Consider this question: In view of God's infinite power and wisdom and beauty, what would His love for a human being involve? Or to put it another way: What could God give us to enjoy that would prove Him most loving? There is only one possible answer: *Himself!* If He withholds Himself from our contemplation and companionship, no matter what else He gives us, He is not loving.

Now we are on the brink of what for me was a life-changing discovery. What do we all do when we are given or shown something beautiful or excellent? We *praise* it! We praise new little babies: "Oh, look at that nice round head! And all that hair! And her hands! Aren't they perfect?" We praise a lover after a long absence: "Your eyes are like a cloudless sky! Your hair like forest silk!" We praise a grand slam in the bottom of the ninth when we are down by three. We praise the October trees along the banks of the St. Croix.

But the great discovery for me, as I said, came while I was reading "A Word about Praise" in C. S. Lewis's *Reflections on the Psalms*. His recorded thoughts— born from wrestling with the idea that God not only wants our praise, but commands it—bear looking at again, in fuller form:

> But the most obvious fact about praise—whether of God or any thing—strangely escaped me. I thought of it in terms of compliment, approval, or the giving of honor. I had never noticed that all enjoyment spontaneously overflows into praise unless (sometimes even if) shyness or the fear of boring others is deliberately brought in to check it. The world rings with praise—lovers praising their mistresses, readers their favorite poet, walkers praising the countryside, players praising their favorite game—praise of weather, wines, dishes, actors, motors, horses, colleges, countries, historical personages, children, flowers, mountains, rare stamps, rare beetles, even sometimes politicians or scholars. I had not noticed how the humblest, and at the same time most balanced

and capacious, minds praised most, while the cranks, misfits and malcontents praised least....

I had not noticed either that just as men spontaneously praise whatever they value, so they spontaneously urge us to join them in praising it: "Isn't she lovely? Wasn't it glorious? Don't you think that magnificent?" The Psalmists in telling everyone to praise God are doing what all men do when they speak of what they care about. My whole, more general, difficulty about the praise of God depended on my absurdly denying to us, as regards the supremely Valuable, what we delight to do, what indeed we can't help doing, about everything else we value.

I think we delight to praise what we enjoy because the praise not merely expresses but completes the enjoyment; it is its appointed consummation. It is not out of compliment that lovers keep on telling one another how beautiful they are; the delight is incomplete till it is expressed.[12]

There is the solution! We praise what we enjoy because the delight is incomplete until it is expressed in praise. If we were not allowed to speak of what we value and celebrate what we love and praise what we admire, our joy would not be full. So if God loves us enough to make our joy full, He must not only give us Himself; He must also win from us the praise of our hearts—not because He needs to shore up some weakness in Himself or compensate for some deficiency, but because He loves us and seeks the fullness of our joy that can be found only in knowing and praising Him, the most magnificent of all Beings. If He is truly for us, He must be for Himself!

God is the one Being in all the universe for whom seeking His own praise is the ultimately loving act. For Him, self-exaltation is the highest virtue. When He does all things "for the praise of His glory," He preserves for us and offers to us the only thing in all the world that can satisfy our longings. God is for us!

---

12. C. S. Lewis, *Reflections on the Psalms* (New York: Harcourt, Brace & World, 1958), 93–5.

And the foundation of this love is that God has been, is now, and always will be for Himself.

SUMMARY

God is absolutely sovereign. "Our God is in the heavens; he does all that he pleases" (Psalm 115:3). Therefore He is not frustrated. He rejoices in all His works when He contemplates them as colors of the magnificent mosaic of redemptive history. He is an unshakably happy God.

His happiness is the delight He has in Himself. Before creation, He rejoiced in the image of His glory in the person of His Son. Then the joy of God "went public" in the works of creation and redemption. These works delight the heart of God because they reflect His glory. He does everything He does to preserve and display that glory, for in this His soul rejoices.

All the works of God culminate in the praises of His redeemed people. The climax of His happiness is the delight He takes in the echoes of His excellence in the praises of the saints. This praise is the consummation of our own joy in God. Therefore, God's pursuit of praise from us and our pursuit of pleasure in Him are the same pursuit. This is at the heart of the great gospel! This is the foundation of Christian Hedonism.

"Not everyone who says to me, 'Lord, Lord,'
will enter the kingdom of heaven."

MATTHEW 7:21

"The kingdom of heaven is like a treasure hidden in a field,
which a man found and covered up.
Then in his joy he goes and sells all that he has
and buys that field."

MATTHEW 13:44

If I were to ask you why you have believed in Christ,
why you have become Christians, every man will answer truly,
"For the sake of happiness."

AUGUSTINE

CHAPTER 2

CONVERSION
The Creation of a Christian Hedonist

"THE GATE IS NARROW"

If everyone were bound to enter the kingdom of heaven, we might not have to speak of conversion. But not everyone is bound to enter: "For the gate is narrow and the way is hard that leads to life, and those who find it are few" (Matthew 7:14).

Chapter 1 ended with the discovery that God's pursuit of praise from us and our pursuit of pleasure in Him are one and the same pursuit. God's quest to be glorified and our quest to be satisfied reach their goal in this one experience: our delight in God, which overflows in praise. For God, praise is the sweet echo of His own excellence in the hearts of His people. For us, praise is the summit of satisfaction that comes from living in fellowship with God.

The stunning implication of this discovery is that all the omnipotent energy that drives the heart of God to pursue His own glory also drives Him to satisfy the hearts of those who seek their joy in Him. The good news of the Bible is that God is not at all disinclined to satisfy the hearts of those who hope in Him. Just the opposite: The very thing that can make us happiest is what God delights in with all His heart and with all His soul:

> "I will make with them an everlasting covenant, that I will not turn away from doing good to them.... I will rejoice in doing them good...with all my heart and all my soul." (Jeremiah 32:40–41)

With all His heart and with all His soul, God joins us in the pursuit of our everlasting joy because the consummation of that joy in Him redounds to the glory of His own infinite worth. All who cast themselves on God find that they are carried into endless joy by God's omnipotent commitment to His own glory:

"For my own sake, for my own sake, I do it, for how should my name be profaned? My glory I will not give to another." (Isaiah 48:11)

Yes, Omnipotent Joy pursues the good of all who cast themselves on God! "The LORD takes pleasure in those who...hope in his steadfast love (Psalm 147:11). But this is not everyone.

"For *those who love God* all things work together for good, for those who are called according to his purpose" (Romans 8:28)—but not for everyone. There are sheep and there are goats (Matthew 25:32). There are wise and there are foolish (Matthew 25:2). There are those who are being saved and those who are perishing (1 Corinthians 1:18). And the difference is that one group has been converted and the other hasn't.

The aim of this chapter is to show the necessity of conversion and to argue that it is nothing less than the creation of a Christian Hedonist. I don't mean you have to use this phrase, or even like this phrase. I mean that no one is a Christian who does not embrace Jesus gladly as his most valued treasure, and then pursue the fullness of that joy in Christ that honors Him.

WHY NOT JUST SAY, "BELIEVE"?

Someone may ask, "If your aim is conversion, why don't you just use the straightforward, biblical command 'Believe in the Lord Jesus, and you will be saved' (Acts 16:31)? Why bring in this new terminology of Christian Hedonism?"

My answer has two parts. First, we are surrounded by unconverted people who think they *do* believe in Jesus. Drunks on the street say they believe. Unmarried couples sleeping together say they believe. Elderly people who haven't sought worship or fellowship for forty years say they believe. All kinds of lukewarm, world-loving church attenders say they believe. The world abounds with millions of unconverted people who say they believe in Jesus.

It does no good to tell these people to believe in the Lord Jesus. The phrase is empty. My responsibility as a preacher of the gospel and a teacher in the church is not to preserve and repeat cherished biblical sentences, but to pierce the heart with biblical truth. In my neighborhood, every drunk on the street "believes" in Jesus. Drug dealers "believe" in Jesus. Panhandlers who haven't been to church in forty years "believe" in Jesus. So I use different words to unpack what *believe* means. In recent years I have asked, "Do you receive Jesus as your *Treasure?*" Not just *Savior* (everybody wants out of hell, but not to be with Jesus). Not just *Lord* (they might submit begrudgingly). The key is: Do you treasure Him more than everything? Converts to Christian Hedonism say with Paul, "I count everything as loss because of the surpassing worth of knowing Christ Jesus my Lord" (Philippians 3:8).

This leads to the second part of my answer. There are other straightforward biblical commands besides "Believe in the Lord Jesus, and you will be saved." The reason for introducing the idea of Christian Hedonism is to force these commands to our attention.

Could it be that today the most straightforward biblical command for conversion is not, "Believe in the Lord," but, "Delight yourself in the LORD"? And might not many slumbering hearts be stabbed broad awake by the words "Unless a man be born again *into a Christian Hedonist* he cannot see the kingdom of God"?

SIX CRUCIAL TRUTHS TO SUMMARIZE OUR NEED AND GOD'S PROVISION

Why is conversion so crucial? What is there about God and man that makes it necessary? And what has God done to meet our desperate need? And what must we do to enjoy the benefits of His provision? These are huge questions. I attempt a summary answer with the following six truths from Scripture.

HOW HAVE WE FAILED?

1.   God created us for His glory.

"Bring my sons from afar and my daughters from the end of the earth, everyone who is called by my name, whom I created for my glory." (Isaiah 43:6–7)

The proper understanding of everything in life begins with God. No one will ever understand the necessity of conversion who does not know why God created us. He created us "in His image" so that we would image forth His glory in the world. We were made to be prisms refracting the light of God's glory into all of life. Why God should want to give us a share in shining with His glory is a great mystery. Call it grace or mercy or love—it is an unspeakable wonder. Once we were not. Then we existed—for the glory of God!

2.   Therefore, it is the duty of every person to live for the glory of God.

So, whether you eat or drink, or whatever you do, do all to the glory of God. (1 Corinthians 10:31)

If God made us for His glory, it is clear that we should live for His glory. Our duty comes from God's design.

What does it mean to glorify God?

It does not mean to make Him more glorious. It means to acknowledge His glory, to value it above all things, and to make it known. It implies heartfelt gratitude: "The one who offers thanksgiving as his sacrifice glorifies me" (Psalm 50:23). It also implies trust: Abraham "grew strong in his faith as he gave glory to God" (Romans 4:20).

Glorifying God is the duty not only of those who have heard the preaching of the gospel, but also of peoples who have only the witness of nature and their own conscience:

His invisible attributes, namely, his eternal power and divine nature, have been clearly perceived, ever since the creation of the world, in the things that have been made. So they are without excuse. For although they knew God, they did not honor him as God or give thanks to him. (Romans 1:20–21)

God will not judge anyone for failing to perform a duty if the person had no access to the knowledge of that duty. But even without the Bible, all people have access to the knowledge that we are created by God and therefore are dependent on Him for everything, thus owing Him the gratitude and trust of our hearts. Deep within us we all know that it is our duty to glorify our Maker by thanking Him for all we have, trusting Him for all we need, and obeying all His revealed will.

HOW DESPERATE IS OUR CONDITION?

3.   Yet all of us have failed to glorify God as we ought.

All have sinned and fall short of the glory of God. (Romans 3:23)

What does it mean to "fall short" of the glory of God? It does not mean that we are supposed to be as glorious as God is and that we have fallen short. We ought to fall short in that sense! The best explanation of Romans 3:23 is Romans 1:23. It says that those who did not glorify or thank God became fools "and exchanged the glory of the immortal God for images." This is the way we "fall short" of the glory of God: We exchange it for something of lesser value. All sin comes from not putting supreme value on the glory of God—this is the very essence of sin.

And we have all sinned. "None is righteous, no, not one" (Romans 3:10). None of us has trusted God the way we should. None of us has felt the depth and consistency of gratitude we owe Him. None of us has obeyed Him according to His wisdom and right. We have exchanged and dishonored His glory again and again. We have trusted ourselves. We have taken credit for His gifts. We have turned away from the path of His commandments because we thought we knew better.

In all this we have held the glory of the Lord in contempt. The exceeding evil of sin is not the harm it does to us or to others (though that is great!). The wickedness of sin is owing to the implicit disdain for God. When David committed adultery with Bathsheba, and even had her husband killed, what did God say to him through the prophet Nathan? He did not remind the king that marriage is inviolable or that human life is sacred. He said, "'You have despised *me*'" (2 Samuel 12:10).

But this is not the whole account of our condition. We not only choose to sin; we *are* sinful. The Bible describes our heart as blind (2 Corinthians 4:4) and hard (Ezekiel 11:19; 36:26) and dead (Ephesians 2:1, 5) and unable to submit to the law of God (Romans 8:7–8). By nature we are "children of wrath" (Ephesians 2:3).

4.   Therefore, all of us are subject to eternal condemnation by God.

The wages of sin is death. (Romans 6:23)

They shall suffer the punishment of eternal destruction, away from the presence of the Lord and from the glory of his might. (2 Thessalonians 1:9)

Having held the glory of God in contempt through ingratitude and distrust and disobedience, we are sentenced to be excluded from the enjoyment of that glory forever and ever in the eternal misery of hell.

The word *hell (gehenna)* occurs in the New Testament twelve times—eleven on the lips of Jesus. It is not a myth created by dismal and angry preachers. It is the solemn warning of the Son of God who died to deliver sinners from its curse. We ignore it at great risk.

Hell is a place of torment. It is not merely the absence of pleasure. It is not annihilation.[1] Jesus repeatedly describes it as an experience of fire. "Whoever says, 'You fool!' will be liable to the hell of fire" (Matthew 5:22). "It is better for

---

1.   For the biblical support against annihilationism and in support of hell as eternal conscious torment, see John Piper, *Let the Nations Be Glad: The Supremacy of God in Missions*, 3rd ed., revised and expanded (Grand Rapids, Mich.: Baker, 2010), chapter 4, and the bibliography cited therein.

you to enter life with one eye than with two eyes to be thrown into the hell of fire" (Matthew 18:9). "It is better for you to enter the kingdom of God with one eye than with two eyes to be thrown into hell, where their worm does not die and the fire is not quenched" (Mark 9:47–48). He warned often that there would be "weeping and gnashing of teeth" (Matthew 8:12; 22:13; 24:51; 25:30).

Not only is it a place of torment; it is also everlasting. Hell is not remedial, contrary to what many popular writers are saying these days.[2] Jesus closes the Parable of the Last Judgment with these words: "'Depart from me, you cursed, into the eternal fire prepared for the devil and his angels.' …These will go away into eternal punishment, but the righteous into eternal life" (Matthew 25:41, 46). The "punishment" is eternal the same way the "life" is eternal.

Another evidence that hell is everlasting is the teaching of Jesus that there is sin that will not be forgiven in the age to come: "Whoever speaks against the Holy Spirit will not be forgiven, either in this age or in the age to come" (Matthew 12:32). If hell is remedial and will someday be emptied of all sinners, then they would have to be forgiven. But Jesus says there is sin that will never be forgiven.

John sums up the terrible realities of torment and endlessness in Revelation 14:11: "And the smoke of their torment goes up forever and ever, and they have no rest, day or night."

Therefore, hell is just. Some have objected that an everlasting punishment is out of proportion to the seriousness of the sin committed. But this is not true,

---

2. Among evangelicals, the reputation of George MacDonald's works has promoted this notion of hell as remedial and not eternal. For example, MacDonald's sermon "Justice," in *Creation in Christ*, ed. Rolland Hein (Wheaton, Ill.: Harold Shaw, 1976), 63–81, argues vehemently against the orthodox view of hell:

> Mind I am not saying it is not right to punish [wicked people]; I am saying that justice is not, never can be, satisfied by suffering—nay, cannot have any satisfaction in or from suffering.… Such justice as Dante's keeps wickedness alive in its most terrible forms. The life of God goes forth to inform, or at least give a home to, victorious evil. Is He not defeated every time that one of these lost souls defies Him? God is triumphantly defeated, I say, throughout the hell of his vengeance. Although against evil, it is but the vain and wasted cruelty of a tyrant.… Punishment is for the sake of amendment and atonement. God is bound by His love to punish sin in order to deliver His creature: He is bound by his justice to destroy sin in His creation. (71–2)

J. I. Packer discusses the contemporary forms of this view in "Good Pagans and God's Kingdom," *Christianity Today* 17 (17 January 1986), 22–5 and in "The Problem of Eternal Punishment," in *The J. I. Packer Collection*, selected and introduced by Alister McGrath (Downers Grove, Ill.: InterVarsity, 2000), 210–26.

because the seriousness of our sin is infinite. Consider the explanation of Jonathan Edwards:

> The crime of one being despising and casting contempt on another, is proportionably more or less heinous, as he was under greater or less obligations to obey him. And therefore if there be any being that we are under infinite obligations to love, and honor, and obey, the contrary towards him must be infinitely faulty.
>
> Our obligation to love, honor, and obey any being is in proportion to his loveliness, honorableness, and authority.... But God is a being infinitely lovely, because he hath infinite excellency and beauty....
>
> So sin against God, being a violation of infinite obligations, must be a crime infinitely heinous, and so deserving infinite punishment.... The eternity of the punishment of ungodly men renders it infinite...and therefore renders no more than proportionable to the heinousness of what they are guilty of.[3]

When every human being stands before God on the day of judgment, God would not have to use one sentence of Scripture to show us our guilt and the appropriateness of our condemnation. He would need only to ask three questions: (1) Was it not plain in nature that everything you had was a gift and that you were dependent on your Maker for life and breath and everything? (2) Did not the judicial sentiment[4] in your own heart always hold other people guilty when they lacked

---

3. Jonathan Edwards, "The Justice of God in the Damnation of Sinners," in *The Works of Jonathan Edwards,* vol. 1 (Edinburgh: Banner of Truth, 1974), 669.

4. I want to express gratitude and deep admiration for Edward John Carnell's penetrating analysis of "the judicial sentiment" and its relation to the existence of God. The judicial sentiment is the moral faculty that is duly offended when we are mistreated. Here is a taste of his words from the profound and beautiful book *Christian Commitment* (New York: Macmillan, 1957):

> Whereas conscience accuses the self the judicial sentiment accuses others. The direction of accusation is the important thing. Conscience monitors one's own moral conduct, while the judicial sentiment monitors the moral conduct of others.
>
> Furthermore, conscience is subject to social and cultural conditioning, whereas the judicial sentiment is not. All normal men, past, present, and future, experience an aroused judicial sentiment whenever they are personally mistreated. (110)
>
> An aroused judicial sentiment is merely heaven's warning that the image of God is being outraged. Cultural conditioning may alter the direction of the judicial sentiment, but is does not alter the faculty itself. (112)
>
> The voice of the judicial sentiment is the voice of God. (136)

the gratitude they should have had in response to a kindness you performed? (3) Has your life been filled with gratitude and trust toward Me in proportion to My generosity and authority? Case closed.

WHAT HAS GOD DONE TO SAVE US FROM HIS WRATH?

5.   Nevertheless, in His great mercy, God sent His Son, Jesus Christ, to save sinners by dying in their place on the cross and rising bodily from the dead.

> The saying is trustworthy and deserving of full acceptance, that Christ Jesus came into the world to save sinners. (1 Timothy 1:15) [Jesus] was delivered up for our trespasses and raised for our justification. (Romans 4:25)

Over against the terrifying news that we have fallen under the condemnation of our Creator and that He is bound by His own righteous character to preserve the worth of His glory by pouring out eternal wrath on our sin, there is the wonderful news of the gospel. This is a truth no one can ever learn from nature. It has to be told to neighbors and preached in churches and carried by missionaries.

The good news is that God Himself has decreed a way to satisfy the demands of His justice without condemning the whole human race. Hell is one way to settle accounts with sinners and uphold His justice. But there is another way. The wisdom of God has ordained a way for the love of God to deliver us from the wrath of God without compromising the justice of God.

And what is this wisdom?

The death of the Son of God for sinners! "We preach Christ crucified, a stumbling block to Jews and folly to the Gentiles, but to those who are called, both Jews and Greeks, Christ the power of God and the wisdom of God" (1 Corinthians 1:23–24).

The death of Christ is the wisdom of God by which the love of God saves sinners from the wrath of God, all the while upholding and demonstrating the righteousness of God in Christ. Romans 3:25–26 may be the most important verses in the Bible:

> God put [Christ] forward as a propitiation[5] by his blood, to be received by faith. This was to show God's righteousness, because in his divine forbearance he had passed over former sins. It was to show his righteousness at the present time, so that he might be just and the justifier of the one who has faith in Jesus.

Not either/or! Both! God is wholly just! *And* He justifies the ungodly! He acquits the guilty, but is not guilty in doing so. This is the greatest news in the world![6]

> [God] made [Christ] to be sin who knew no sin, so that in him we might become the righteousness of God. (2 Corinthians 5:21)

> By sending his own Son in the likeness of sinful flesh and for sin, he condemned sin in the flesh. (Romans 8:3)

> [Christ] bore our sins in his body on the tree. (1 Peter 2:24)

> Christ also suffered once for sins, the righteous for the unrighteous, that he might bring us to God. (1 Peter 3:18)

> If we have been united with him in a death like his, we shall certainly be united with him in a resurrection like his. (Romans 6:5)

---

5. *Propitiation* is a rare word today. It has been replaced in many translations with more common words *(expiation, sacrifice of atonement)*. I keep it in order to stress the original meaning, namely, that what Christ did by dying on the cross for sinners was to appease the wrath of God against sinners. By requiring of His Son such humiliation and suffering for the sake of God's glory, He openly demonstrated that He does not sweep sin under the rug. All contempt for His glory is duly punished, either on the cross, where the wrath of God is propitiated for those who believe, or in hell, where the wrath of God is poured out on those who don't.

6. This truth of the justification of the ungodly by faith alone is worthy of a book all on its own. I was so gripped by the glory of it and so disturbed by the assault on it that I wrote *Counted Righteous in Christ* (Wheaton, Ill.: Crossway, 2002). If you want to understand the doctrine of justification as the imputation of Christ's righteousness to us, or see a modern defense of it, I commend this book to you.

If the most terrifying news in the world is that we have fallen under the condemnation of our Creator and that He is bound by His own righteous character to preserve the worth of His glory by pouring out His wrath on our sin, then the best news in all the world (the gospel!) is that God has decreed a way of salvation that also upholds the worth of His glory, the honor of His Son, and the eternal salvation of His elect. He has given His Son to die for sinners and to conquer their death by His own resurrection.

WHAT MUST WE DO TO BE SAVED?

6. The benefits purchased by the death of Christ belong to those who repent and trust in Him.

   "Repent therefore, and turn again, that your sins may be blotted out." (Acts 3:19)

   "Believe in the Lord Jesus, and you will be saved." (Acts 16:31)

Not everybody is saved from God's wrath just because Christ died for sinners. There is a condition we must meet in order to be saved.[7] I want to try to show that the condition, summed up here as repentance and faith, is conversion and that conversion is nothing less than the creation of a Christian Hedonist.

WHAT IS CONVERSION?

Conversion[8] is used in the Bible only once, in Acts 15:3. Paul and Barnabas "passed through both Phoenicia and Samaria, describing in detail the conversion of the Gentiles, and brought great joy to all the brothers." This conversion involved repentance and faith, as the other reports in Acts show.

---

7. In using the word *condition* for what we must do, I do not in any way want to minimize the truth that Jesus fulfilled the divine demand for our righteousness as the ground of our justification. What is required of us is not that we in any way improve on Christ's righteousness as the ground of our right standing with God. Rather, what is required of us is a "condition" in a different sense: We must receive as a treasure what Christ has done for us and all the promises and joyful fellowship with God that He purchased.

8. The verb form of *conversion* (convert) is used in the Authorized Version of the New Testament in Matthew 13:15 (= Mark 4:12 = John 12:40 = Acts 28:27); 18:3; Luke 22:32; Acts 3:19; and James 5:19–20.

For example, in Acts 11:18 the apostles respond to Peter's testimony about Gentile conversions like this: "Then to the Gentiles also God has granted *repentance* that leads to life." And in Acts 14:27, Paul and Barnabas report the conversion of the Gentiles by saying that "God...had opened a door of *faith* to the Gentiles."

Conversion, then, involves repentance (turning from sin and unbelief) and faith (trusting in Christ alone for salvation).[9] They are really two sides of the same coin. One side is tails—turn tail on the fruits of unbelief. The other side is heads—head straight for Jesus and trust His promises. You can't have the one without the other any more than you can face two ways at once or serve two masters.

This means that saving faith in Christ always involves a profound change of heart. It is not merely agreement with the truth of a doctrine. *Satan* agrees with true doctrine (James 2:19). Saving faith is far deeper and more pervasive than that.

CONVERSION IS A GIFT OF GOD

We get an inkling of something awesome behind repentance and faith when we see hints in the book of Acts that conversion is the gift of God. "God has granted repentance that leads to life" (11:18). "God exalted [Christ] at his right hand...to give repentance to Israel" (5:31). God "opened a door of faith to the Gentiles" (14:27). "The Lord opened [Lydia's] heart to pay attention to what was said by Paul" (16:14).

We will never fully appreciate what a deep and awesome thing conversion is until we own up to the fact that it is a miracle. It is a gift of God. Recall again the point that we not only sin, but we also *are* sinful—blind, hard, dead, unable to submit to the law of God. And so when we hear the gospel, we will never respond positively unless God performs the miracle of regeneration.[10]

---

9. For further elaboration, see Wayne Grudem, *Systematic Theology: An Introduction to Biblical Doctrine* (Grand Rapids, Mich.: Zondervan, 1994), 709–21.

10. *Regeneration* is a big word for the new birth. It occurs in Greek *(palingenesia)* only once in the New Testament in reference to the new birth of a person (Titus 3:5) (also once in reference to the rebirth of the creation in the age to come, Matthew 19:28). For more on regeneration, see John Piper, *Finally Alive: What Happens When We Are Born Again* (Christian Focus, 2009).

FAITH IS OUR ACT, BUT IS POSSIBLE BECAUSE OF GOD'S ACT

Repentance and faith are our work. But we will not repent and believe unless God does His work to overcome our hard and rebellious hearts. This divine work is called *regeneration.* Our work is called *conversion.*[11]

Conversion does indeed include an act of will by which we renounce sin and submit ourselves to the authority of Christ and put our hope and trust in Him. We are responsible to do this and will be condemned if we don't. But just as clearly, the Bible teaches that, owing to our hard heart and willful blindness and spiritual insensitivity, we cannot do this.[12]

We must first experience the regenerating work of the Holy Spirit. The Scriptures promised long ago that God would devote Himself to this work in order to create for Himself a faithful people:

> "And the LORD your God will circumcise your heart and the heart of your offspring, so that you will love the LORD your God with all your heart and with all your soul, that you may live." (Deuteronomy 30:6)

> "I will give them a heart to know that I am the LORD, and they shall be my people and I will be their God, for they shall return to me with their whole heart." (Jeremiah 24:7)

---

11. "In conversion man is active, and it wholly consists in his act; but in regeneration the Spirit of God is the only active cause." Samuel Hopkins, "Regeneration and Conversion," in *Introduction to Puritan Theology,* ed. Edward Hindson (Grand Rapids, Mich.: Baker, 1976), 180. I recommend this entire essay as an excellent statement on the relationship between regeneration (new birth) and conversion (repentance and faith).

12. This is a great stumbling block for many people—to assert that we are responsible to do what we are morally unable to do. The primary reason for asserting it is not that it springs obviously from our normal use of reason, but that the Bible so plainly teaches it. It may help, however, to consider that the inability we speak of is not owing to a physical handicap, but to moral corruption. Our inability to believe is not the result of a physically damaged brain, but of a morally perverted will. Physical inability would remove accountability. Moral inability does not. We cannot come to the light, because our corrupt and arrogant nature hates the light. So when someone does come to the light, "it is clearly seen that his deeds have been *wrought by God*" (John 3:21). The best treatment of this difficult subject I know of is Jonathan Edwards's *Freedom of the Will* (Morgan, Penn.: Soli Deo Gloria, 1998, original 1754); also found in *The Works of Jonathan Edwards,* vol. 1. For an excellent summary of Edwards's argument, see C. Samuel Storms, "Jonathan Edwards on the Freedom of the Will," *Trinity Journal* 3 (Fall 1982): 131–69.

"And I will give them one heart, and a new spirit I will put within them. I will remove the heart of stone from their flesh and give them a heart of flesh, that they may walk in my statutes and keep my rules and obey them. And they shall be my people, and I will be their God." (Ezekiel 11:19–20)

"And I will give you a new heart, and a new spirit I will put within you. And I will remove the heart of stone from your flesh and give you a heart of flesh. And I will put my Spirit within you, and cause you to walk in my statutes and be careful to obey my rules." (Ezekiel 36:26–27)

These great promises from the Old Testament describe a work of God that changes a heart of stone into a heart of flesh and causes people to "know" and "love" and "obey" God. Without this spiritual heart transplant, people will not know and love and obey God. This prior work of God is what we mean by regeneration.

WE ARE "CALLED" THE WAY JESUS CALLED LAZARUS: DEATH TO LIFE

In the New Testament, God is clearly active, creating a people for Himself by calling[13] them out of darkness and enabling them to believe the gospel and walk in the light. John teaches most clearly that regeneration precedes and enables faith.

Everyone who believes that Jesus is the Christ *has been* born of God. (1 John 5:1)

---

13. The Bible requires that we speak of God's "call" in at least two distinct senses. One call is the general or external call that goes out in the preaching of the gospel. Everyone who hears a gospel message or reads the Bible is called in this sense. But God calls in another sense to some who hear the gospel. This is God's internal or effectual call. It changes a person's heart so that faith is secured. It is like the call "Let there be light!" or "Lazarus, come forth!" It creates what it demands. The key passage that demands this distinction is 1 Corinthians 1:23–24: "We preach Christ crucified [general call], a stumbling block to Jews and folly to Gentiles, but to those who are called [effectual call], both Jews and Greeks, Christ the power of God and the wisdom of God." Among the "generally called," there is a group who are "called" in such a way that they are enabled to esteem the gospel as wisdom and power. The change caused by the effectual call is none other than the change of regeneration. For more on effectual calling, see Piper, *Finally Alive*.

The verb tenses make John's intention unmistakable: "Everyone who goes on believing [*pisteuōn*, present, continuous action] that Jesus is the Christ has been born [*gennēsanta*, perfect, completed action with abiding effects] of God." Faith is the effect of new birth, not the cause of it. This is consistent with John's whole book (cf. 1 John 2:29; 3:9; 4:2–3; 4:7).

Since faith and repentance are possible only because of the regenerating work of God, both are called the gift of God:

Even when we were dead in our trespasses, [God] made us alive together with Christ—by grace you have been saved.... By grace you have been saved through faith. And this[14] is not your own doing; it is the gift of God. (Ephesians 2:5, 8)

The Lord's servant must not be quarrelsome but kind to everyone, able to teach, patiently enduring evil, correcting his opponents with gentleness. *God may perhaps grant them repentance* leading to a knowledge of the truth, and they may escape from the snare of the devil, after being captured by him to do his will. (2 Timothy 2:24–26)

CONVERSION IS A CONDITION OF SALVATION AND A MIRACLE OF GOD

This meditation on the nature and origin of conversion clarifies two things. One is the sense in which conversion is a condition for salvation. Continuous confusion is caused at this point by failing to define salvation precisely.

If *salvation* refers to new birth, conversion is *not* a condition of it. New birth comes first and enables the repentance and faith of conversion. Before new birth we are dead, and dead men don't meet conditions. Regeneration is totally

---

14. The words for *grace (chariti)* and *faith (piste-os)* are feminine in the original Greek. The word for *this (touto)* is neuter. Some have used this lack of agreement to say that the gift here is not faith. But this ignores the implication of verse 5: "Even when we were dead." Grace is grace because it saved us even when we were dead. But it saves "through faith." How does it save the dead through faith? By awakening the dead into the life of faith. That is why faith is a gift in Ephesians 2:5–8. *This* refers to the whole event of salvation by grace through faith and therefore does include faith as a gift. (Cf. Acts 18:27: "When he arrived, he greatly helped those who *through grace* had believed.")

unconditional. It is owing solely to the free grace of God. "It depends not on human will or exertion, but on God, who has mercy" (Romans 9:16).[15] We get no credit. He gets all the glory.

But if *salvation* refers to justification, there is one clear condition we must meet: faith in Jesus Christ (Romans 3:28; 4:4–5; 5:1). And if *salvation* refers to our future deliverance from the wrath of God at the judgment and our entrance into eternal life, then not only does the New Testament say we must "believe," but also that this faith must be so real that it produces the fruit of obedience. There must be faith and the fruit of faith. "Faith by itself, if it does not have works, is dead" (James 2:17; cf. v. 26). "In Christ Jesus neither circumcision nor uncircumcision counts for anything, but only faith working through love" (Galatians 5:6). "Strive for peace with everyone, and for the holiness without which no one will see the Lord" (Hebrews 12:14).

When we cry, "What must I do to be saved?" the answer depends on what we are asking: how to be born again, how to be justified, or how to be finally welcomed into heaven. When we say that the answer is "Become a Christian Hedonist," we mean God's work in new birth, our faith in Christ, and the work of God in our lives by faith to help us obey Christ. This is the fullest meaning of conversion.

Which brings us to the second thing that has become clear from our discussion. Conversion, understood as the coming into being of a new nature (a Christian Hedonist) that will obey Christ, is no mere human decision. It *is* a human decision—but, oh, so much more! Repentant faith (or believing repentance) is based on an awesome miracle performed by the sovereign God. It is the breath of a new creature in Christ.

Saving faith has in it various elements. The nature of these elements makes

---

15. Some have tried to argue that Romans 9 has nothing to do with individuals and their eternal destiny. But I have tried, in turn, to show that this is precisely what Paul has in mind because the problem he is wrestling with in this chapter is how individual Jews within God's chosen people, Israel, can be accursed and God's Word still stand (see Romans 9:3–6). I wrote an entire book to demonstrate this interpretation: *The Justification of God: An Exegetical and Theological Study of Romans 9:1–23*, 2nd ed. (Grand Rapids, Mich.: Baker, 1993). See also Thomas R. Schreiner, "Does Romans 9 Teach Individual Election unto Salvation?" in *Still Sovereign: Contemporary Perspectives on Election, Foreknowledge, and Grace*, ed. Thomas R. Schreiner and Bruce A. Ware (Grand Rapids, Mich.: Baker, 2000), 89–106.

faith a very powerful thing that produces changes in our lives. Unless we see this, the array of conditions for present and final salvation in the New Testament will be utterly perplexing. Consider the following partial list.

What must I do to be saved?

The answer in Acts 16:31 is "Believe in the Lord Jesus, and you will be saved."

The answer in John 1:12 is that we must receive Christ: "To all who did receive him…he gave the right to become children of God."

The answer in Acts 3:19 is "Repent therefore, and turn again, that your sins may be blotted out."

The answer in Hebrews 5:9 is obedience to Christ. Christ "became the source of eternal salvation to all who obey him." So also in John 3:36, "Whoever does not obey the Son shall not see life."

Jesus Himself answered the question in a variety of ways. For example, in Matthew 18:3 He said that childlikeness is the condition for salvation: "Truly, I say to you, unless you turn and become like children, you will never enter the kingdom of heaven."

In Mark 8:34–35 the condition is self-denial: "If anyone would come after me, let him deny himself and take up his cross and follow me. For whoever would save his life will lose it, but whoever loses his life for my sake and the gospel's will save it."

In Matthew 10:37, Jesus lays down the condition of loving Him more than anyone else: "Whoever loves father or mother more than me is not worthy of me; and whoever loves son or daughter more than me is not worthy of me." The same thing is expressed in 1 Corinthians 16:22: "If anyone has no love for the Lord, let him be accursed."

And in Luke 14:33 the condition for salvation is that we be free from the love of our possessions: "Any one of you who does not renounce all that he has cannot be my disciple."

These are just some of the conditions that the New Testament says we must meet in order to be saved in the fullest and final sense. We must believe in Jesus and receive Him and turn from our sin and obey Him and humble ourselves like little children and love Him more than we love our family, our possessions, or our own life. This is what it means to be converted to Christ. This alone is the way of life everlasting.

But what is it that holds all these conditions together and gives them unity?[16] And what keeps them from becoming a way of earning salvation by works? One answer is the awesome reality of saving faith—trusting in the pardon of God, the promises of Christ, and the power of the Holy Spirit, not ourselves. This is the unifying key that not only unites us to Christ for justification, but also empowers us for sanctification.

Yes, but what is it about saving faith that unifies and changes so much of our lives?

THE CREATION OF A CHRISTIAN HEDONIST

Jesus pointed to the answer in the little parable of Matthew 13:44:

> "The kingdom of heaven is like a treasure hidden in a field, which a man found and covered up. Then in a [literally, *from*] his joy he goes and sells all that he has and buys that field."

This parable describes how someone is converted and brought into the kingdom of heaven. A person discovers a treasure and is impelled by joy to sell all that he has in order to have this treasure. The kingdom of heaven is the abode of the King. The longing to be there is not the longing for heavenly real estate, but for camaraderie with the King. The treasure in the field is the fellowship of God in Christ.

I conclude from this parable that we must be deeply converted in order to enter the kingdom of heaven and that we are converted when Christ becomes for us a Treasure Chest of holy joy—a crucified and risen Savior who pardons all our sins, provides all our righteousness, and becomes in His own fellowship our greatest pleasure.

---

16. For a more extended treatment of the conditions of salvation and how they all resolve into faith and love, see John Piper, *The Purifying Power of Living by Faith in Future Grace* (Sisters, Ore.: Multnomah, 1995), chapters 19 and 20, especially pp. 255–9.

THE CREATION OF A NEW TASTE

How then does this arrival of joy relate to saving faith? The usual answer is that joy is the fruit of faith. And in one sense it is: "May the God of hope fill you with all joy and peace *in believing*" (Romans 15:13). It is "in believing" that we are filled with joy. Confidence in the promises of God overcomes anxiety and fills us with peace and joy. Paul even calls it the "joy of faith" (Philippians 1:25, literal translation).

But there is a different way of looking at the relationship of joy and faith. In Hebrews 11:6 the writer says, "Without faith it is impossible to please him, for whoever would draw near to God must believe that he exists and that he rewards those who seek him." In other words, the faith that pleases God is a confidence that God will reward us when we come to Him. But surely this does not mean that we are to be motivated by material things. Surely the reward we long for is the glory of God Himself and the perfected companionship of Christ (Hebrews 2:10; 3:6; 10:34; 11:26; 12:22–24; 13:5). We will sell everything to have the treasure of Christ Himself.

So the faith that pleases God is the assurance that when we turn to Him, we will find the all-satisfying Treasure. We will find our heart's eternal delight. But do you see what this implies? It implies that something has happened in our hearts *before* the act of faith. It implies that beneath and behind and in the act of faith that pleases God, a new taste has been created—a taste for the glory of God and the beauty of Christ. Behold, a kind of joy has been born!

Once we had no delight in God, and Christ was just a vague historical figure. What we enjoyed was food and friendships and productivity and investments and vacations and hobbies and games and reading and shopping and sex and sports and art and TV and travel…but not God. He was an idea—even a good one—and a topic for discussion; but He was not a treasure of delight.

Then something miraculous happened. It was like the opening of the eyes of the blind during the golden dawn. First the stunned silence before the unspeakable beauty of holiness. Then the shock and terror that we had actually loved the darkness. Then the settling stillness of joy that this is the soul's end.

The quest is over. We would give anything if we might be granted to live in the presence of this glory forever and ever.

And then, faith—the confidence that Christ has made a way for me, a sinner, to live in His glorious fellowship forever, the confidence that if I come to God through Christ, He will give me the desire of my heart to share His holiness and behold His glory.

But before the confidence comes the craving. Before the decision comes the delight. Before trust comes the discovery of Treasure.

We Come to Christ When We Love the Light

Is not this the teaching of John 3:18–20?

> "Whoever believes in [the Son of God] is not condemned, but whoever does not believe is condemned already, because he has not believed in the name of the only Son of God. And this is the judgment: the light has come into the world, and people loved the darkness rather than the light because their deeds were evil. For everyone who does wicked things hates the light and does not come to the light, lest his deeds should be exposed."

The reason people do not come to the light is because they do not love it. Love for the light is not caused by coming to the light. We come because we love it. Otherwise, our coming is no honor to the light. Could there be any holy motivation to believe in Christ where there is no taste for the beauty of Christ? To be sure, we could be motivated by the desire to escape hell or the desire to have material riches or the desire to rejoin a departed loved one. But how does it honor the light when the only reason we come to the light is to find those things that we loved in the dark?

Is this saving faith?

Christ Died to Give Us Our Heart's Desire: God

Saving faith is the cry of a new creature in Christ. And the newness of the new creature is that it has a new taste. What was once distasteful or bland is now craved. Christ Himself has become a Treasure Chest of holy joy. The tree of faith grows only in the heart that craves the supreme gift that Christ died to give: not health, not wealth, not prestige—but God![17] Test yourself here. There are many professing Christians who delight in God's gifts, but not God. Would you want to go to heaven if God were not there, only His gifts?[18]

"Christ...suffered once for sins...that he might bring us to *God*" (1 Peter 3:18). "Through him we...have access in one Spirit to *the Father*" (Ephesians 2:18). "Through him we have...obtained access by faith into this grace...and we rejoice in hope of the glory of *God*.... We...rejoice in *God* through our Lord Jesus Christ" (Romans 5:2, 11).

A NEW PASSION FOR THE PLEASURE OF GOD'S PRESENCE

The pursuit of joy in God is not optional. It is not an "extra" that a person might grow into after he comes to faith. It is not simply a way to "enhance" your walk with the Lord. Until your heart has hit upon this pursuit, your "faith" cannot please God. It is not saving faith.

Saving faith is the confidence that if you sell all you have and forsake all sinful pleasures, the hidden treasure of holy joy will satisfy your deepest desires. Saving faith is the heartfelt conviction not only that Christ is reliable, but also that He is desirable. It is the confidence that He will come through with His promises *and* that what He promises is more to be desired than all the world.

We may speak of the "joy of faith" at three levels. First, there is the new spiritual taste created by the Spirit of God for the glory of God. This new taste is the seed and root of joy. Thus, it is the "joy of faith" in embryo, as it were. Second, there is the shoot, the stem, of faith itself reaching out actively for all that God is

---

17. Recalling our discussion of the Trinity in chapter 1 (note 9), it is worth musing over the implications that the Holy Spirit is the divine Workman who gives us a new heart of faith and is Himself the personification of the joy that the Father and the Son have in each other. We might say the change that must occur in the human heart to make saving faith possible is permeation by the Holy Spirit, which is nothing less than a permeation by the very joy that God the Father and God the Son have in each other's beauty. In other words, the taste for God that begets saving faith is God's very taste for Himself, imparted to us in measure by the Holy Spirit.

18. For more on the great enjoyment of heaven being God Himself, see John Piper, *God Is the Gospel* (Wheaton Ill.: Crossway, 2005).

for us in Christ. The pith of this stem is joy in God. It is not possible for vital, genuine faith in the Fountain of Joy not to partake of that joy. Joyless embracing of the God of hope, for who He really is, is impossible. Third, there is the fruit of daily gladness that Paul speaks of in Romans 15:13: "May the God of hope fill you with all *joy* and peace *in believing.*" Here joy and peace flow out *from* faith into the whole of life (e.g., Galatians 5:22–23).

In conversion we find the hidden Treasure of the kingdom of God. We venture all on it. And year after year in the struggles of life, we prove the value of the treasure again and again, and we discover depths of riches we had never known. And so the joy of faith grows. When Christ calls us to a new act of obedience that will cost us some temporal pleasure, we call to mind the surpassing value of following Him, and by faith in His proven worth, we forsake the worldly pleasure. The result? More joy! More faith! Deeper than before. And so we go on from joy to joy and faith to faith.

Behind the repentance that turns away from sin, and behind the faith that embraces Christ, is the birth of a new taste, a new longing, a new passion for the pleasure of God's presence. This is the root of conversion. This is the creation of a Christian Hedonist.

"The hour is coming, and is now here, when the true worshipers will worship the Father in spirit and truth, for the Father is seeking such people to worship him. God is spirit, and those who worship him must worship in spirit and truth."

JOHN 4:23–24

CHAPTER 3

WORSHIP

The Feast of Christian Hedonism

SOUL HUNTER

Sometimes spiritual sleepers need to be shocked. If you want them to hear what you have to say, you might even need to scandalize them. Jesus is especially good at this. When He wants to teach us something about worship, He uses a whore!

"Go call your husband," he says to the Samaritan woman.

"I don't have a husband," she answers.

"That's right," Jesus says. "But you've had five, and the man you sleep with now is not your husband."

She is shocked. We're shocked! But Jesus simply sits there on the edge of the well with His hands folded, looking at the woman with razors in His eyes, ready to teach us about worship.

The first thing we learn is that worship has to do with real life. It is not a mythical interlude in a week of reality. Worship has to do with adultery and hunger and racial conflict.

Jesus is bone weary from the journey. He is hot and thirsty. He decides: "Yes, even now, just now, I will seek someone to worship the Father—a Samaritan adulteress. I will show My disciples how My Father seeks worship in the midst of real life from the least likely. She is a Samaritan. She is a woman.

She is a harlot. Yes, I will even show them a thing or two about how to make true worshipers out of the white harvest of harlots in Samaria."

LIFTING THE LEVEL OF AMAZEMENT

Let's back up to the beginning of the story. Jesus "had to pass through Samaria" on His way to Galilee. "So he came to a town of Samaria called Sychar.... Jacob's well was there; so Jesus, wearied as he was from his journey, was sitting beside the well. It was about the sixth hour" (John 4:4–6).

The Samaritans were leftovers from the northern Jewish kingdom who had intermarried with foreigners after the chiefs and nobles were taken into exile in 722 B.C. They had once built a separate worship place on their own Mount Gerizim. They rejected all of the Old Testament except their own version of the first five books of Moses. Their animosity toward Jews (such as Jesus) was centuries old.

Jesus walks right into this hostility, sits down, and asks for a drink. The woman is stunned that Jesus would even speak to her: "How is it that you, a Jew, ask for a drink from me, a woman of Samaria?" (v. 9).

Instead of answering her directly, Jesus shifts the focus of her amazement up a level. He says, "If you knew the gift of God, and who it is that is saying to you 'Give me a drink,' you would have asked him, and he would have given you living water" (v. 10). The really amazing thing is not that He asked her for a drink, but that she didn't ask Him! He has "living water," and He calls it the "gift of God."

But the woman doesn't rise very high. She simply says, "How can you give me water when you don't have a bucket?" She is not on Jesus' wavelength yet.

So Jesus again lifts the level of amazement. "Everyone who drinks of this water will be thirsty again, but whoever drinks of the water that I will give him will never be thirsty forever. The water that I will give him will become in him a spring of water welling up to eternal life" (vv. 13–14). The amazing thing is not that He can give her water without a bucket, but that His water satisfies forever. Even more: When you drink it, your soul becomes a spring. It is miracle water:

It buries itself in a sandy soul and bubbles up a spring of life.

What does this mean?

THE WATER THAT BECOMES A WELL

"The teaching of the wise is a fountain of life," says Proverbs 13:14. Perhaps, then, Jesus means that His teaching is a fountain of life. When thirsty people drink it, they revive and then give it to others. Did He not say, "The words that I have spoken to you are spirit and life" (John 6:63)?

But the closest parallel to the image of a soul becoming a spring is in John 7:37–39: "Jesus stood up and cried out, 'If anyone thirsts, let him come to me and drink. Whoever believes in me, as the Scripture has said, "Out of his heart will flow rivers of living water."' Now this he said about the Spirit, whom those who believed in him were to receive."

So the water Jesus gives is the Holy Spirit. The presence of God's Spirit in your life takes away the frustrated soul-thirst and turns you into a fountain where others can find life.

But probably both these meanings are true. Both the teaching of Jesus and the Holy Spirit satisfy the longing of our souls and make us into fountains for others. Jesus held the Word and the Spirit together.

For example, in John 14:26 He said, "The Holy Spirit, whom the Father will send in my name, he will teach you all things and bring to your remembrance all that I have said." The work of the Spirit of Christ is to make the Word of Christ clear and satisfying to the soul.

The water offered to the Samaritan adulteress was the Word of truth and the power of the Spirit. When we come to Christ to drink, what we drink is truth—not dry, lifeless, powerless truth, but truth soaked with the life-giving Spirit of God! The Word of promise and the power of the Spirit are the living water held out to the Samaritan harlot.

TO THE HEART THROUGH A WOUND

But again the woman misses the point. She cannot rise above her five senses. "Sir, give me this water, so that I will not be thirsty or have to come here to draw water" (John 4:15). Beware of giving up on people too soon, though. Jesus has set His saving sights on this woman. He aims to create a worshiper of God "in spirit and truth."

So now He touches the most sensitive and vulnerable spot in her life: "Go, call your husband" (v. 16). The quickest way to the heart is through a wound.

Why does Jesus strip open the woman's inner life like this? Because He had said in John 3:20, "Everyone who does wicked things hates the light and does not come to the light, lest his deeds should be exposed." Concealed sin keeps us from seeing the light of Christ.

Sin is like spiritual leprosy. It deadens your spiritual senses so that you rip your soul to shreds and don't even feel it. But Christ lays bare her spiritual leprosy: "You have had five husbands, and the man you are sleeping with now is not your husband."

A TRAPPED ANIMAL WILL CHEW OFF ITS LEG

Now watch the universal reflex of a person trying to avoid conviction. She has to admit that He has extraordinary insight: "Sir, I perceive that you are a prophet" (John 4:19). But instead of going the direction He pointed, she tries to switch to an academic controversy: "Our fathers worshiped on this mountain; but you Jews say that in Jerusalem is the place where people ought to worship. What's your position on this issue?"

A trapped animal will chew off its own leg to escape. A trapped sinner will mangle her own mind and rip up the rules of logic. "Why, yes, as long as we are talking about my adultery, what is Your stance on the issue of where people should worship?" This is standard evasive double-talk for trapped sinners.

But the great Soul Hunter is not so easily eluded. He does not insist that she stay on His path. He will follow her into the bush. Or could it be that He has circled around and is waiting there for her as she brings up the subject of worship? He never goes back to the issue of adultery. It was a thrust against the sealed door of her heart. But now His foot is in, and He is willing to deal with the issue of worship.

THE HOW AND WHOM OF WORSHIP

The woman raised the issue of *where* people ought to worship. Jesus responds by saying, "That controversy can't compare in importance with the issue of *how* and *whom* you worship."

First, He draws her attention to the how: "Jesus said to her, 'Woman, believe me, the hour is coming when neither on this mountain nor in Jerusalem will you worship the Father'" (John 4:21). In other words, don't get bogged down in unessential controversies. It is possible to worship God in vain both in your place and in ours! Did not God say, "This people...honor me with their lips, while their hearts are far from me" (Isaiah 29:13)? The issue is not where, but how.

Then He rivets her attention on whom: "You worship what you do not know; we worship what we know, for salvation is from the Jews" (v. 22). These are harsh words. But when life and death are at stake, there comes a point when you put the matter bluntly—like telling a person with lung disease to stop smoking.

The Samaritans rejected all the Old Testament except their own version of the first five books. Their knowledge of God was deficient. Therefore, Jesus tells the woman that Samaritan worship is deficient. It matters whether you know the One you worship!

How and *whom* are crucial, not *where*. Worship must be vital and real in the heart, and worship must rest on a true perception of God. There must be spirit and there must be truth. So Jesus says, "The hour is coming, and now is, when the true worshipers will worship the Father in spirit and truth." The two words *spirit* and *truth* correspond to the *how* and *whom* of worship.

Worshiping in spirit is the opposite of worshiping in merely external ways. It is the opposite of empty formalism and traditionalism. Worshiping in truth is the opposite of worship based on an inadequate view of God. Worship must have heart and head. Worship must engage emotions and thought.

Truth without emotion produces dead orthodoxy and a church full (or half-full) of artificial admirers (like people who write generic anniversary cards for a living). On the other hand, emotion without truth produces empty frenzy and cultivates shallow people who refuse the discipline of rigorous thought. But true worship comes from people who are deeply emotional and who love deep and sound doctrine. Strong affections for God rooted in truth are the bone and marrow of biblical worship.

FUEL, FURNACE, AND HEAT

Perhaps we can tie things together with this picture: The fuel of worship is the truth of God; the furnace of worship is the spirit of man; and the heat of worship is the vital affections of reverence, contrition, trust, gratitude, and joy.

But there is something missing from this picture. There is furnace, fuel, and heat, but no *fire*. The fuel of truth in the furnace of our spirit does not automatically produce the heat of worship. There must be ignition and fire. This is the Holy Spirit.

When Jesus says, "True worshipers will worship the Father in spirit and truth," some interpreters take this to refer to the Holy Spirit. I have taken it to mean our spirit. But maybe these two interpretations are not far apart in Jesus' mind. In John 3:6, Jesus connects God's Spirit and our spirit in a remarkable way.

He says, "That which is born of the Spirit is spirit." In other words, until the Holy Spirit quickens our spirit with the flame of life, our spirit is so dead and unresponsive it does not even qualify as spirit. Only that which is born of the Spirit is spirit. So when Jesus says that true worshipers worship the Father "in spirit," He must mean that true worship comes only from spirits made alive and sensitive by the quickening of the Spirit of God.

Now we can complete our picture. The fuel of worship is a true vision of the greatness of God; the fire that makes the fuel burn white hot is the quickening of the Holy Spirit; the furnace made alive and warm by the flame of truth is our renewed spirit; and the resulting heat of our affections is powerful worship, pushing its way out in confessions, longings, acclamations, tears, songs, shouts, bowed heads, lifted hands, and obedient lives.

FROM MATTERS OF FOOD TO MATTERS OF FAITH

Now back to Samaria for a moment. The disciples have gone into town for food. Jesus has been alone with the woman by the well. When the disciples return, they offer Jesus lunch. But He does the same thing with them that He had done with the woman—He jumps from matters of food to matters of faith: "I have food to eat that you do not know about" (John 4:32). Jesus has been eating the whole time they were gone. But what? "My food is to do the will of him who sent me and to accomplish his work" (v. 34). And what is the work of the Father? The Father is seeking people to worship Him in spirit and truth.

The whole interchange between Jesus and the Samaritan adulteress is the work of God to make a genuine worshiper. Then Jesus applies the episode to the disciples—and to us! "Do you not say, 'There are yet four months, then comes the harvest'? Look, I tell you, lift up your eyes, and see that the fields are white for harvest" (v. 35). He is saying, "There is a white harvest of harlots in Samaria. I have just made one into a worshiper of God. That is why the Father sent me—so send I you. God seeks people to worship Him in spirit and truth. Here comes the city of Sychar white unto harvest. If you love the glory of God, make ready to reap."

Christ has set a course for us in the rest of this chapter on worship. What does it really mean to worship "in spirit and truth"? What is the response of the Spirit-quickened spirit of man? What is the relationship of truth to this experience? That's our plan: to ponder the nature of worship as an affair of the heart, and then as an affair of the mind. Then at the end we will briefly consider the external form of worship.[1]

AN AFFAIR OF THE HEART

Almost everyone would agree that biblical worship involves some kind of outward act. The very word in Hebrew means to bow down. Worship is bowing, lifting hands, praying, singing, reciting, preaching, performing rites of eating, cleansing, ordaining, and so on.

But the startling fact is that all these things can be done in vain. They can be pointless and useless and empty. This is the warning of Jesus in Matthew 15:8–9 when He devastates the Pharisees with God's word from Isaiah 29:13:

---

1. To make it crystal clear, when I speak of worship, I do not limit what I mean to corporate events where Christians sing. That is one expression of worship. But you can sing and read the Scriptures and pray and *not* be worshiping, because worship is first and most essentially an act of the heart. It is a being satisfied with all that God is for us in Jesus. That satisfaction can be expressed in song or in visiting a prisoner.

"This people honors me with their lips, but their heart is far from me; in vain do they worship me."

First, notice that the parallel between the phrases "honor me" and "worship me" shows that worship is essentially a way of honoring God. Of course, that doesn't mean making Him honorable or increasing His honor. It means recognizing His honor and feeling the worth of it and ascribing it to Him in all the ways appropriate to His character.

Splendor and majesty are before him; strength and beauty are in his sanctuary. Ascribe to the LORD, O families of the peoples, ascribe to the LORD glory and strength! Ascribe to the LORD the glory due his name. (Psalm 96:6–8)

So the first thing to see in Jesus' words is that worship is a way of gladly reflecting back to God the radiance of His worth.

The reason for saying *gladly* is that even mountains and trees reflect back to God the radiance of His worth: "Praise the LORD from the earth…mountains and all hills, fruit trees and all cedars!" (Psalm 148:7, 9). Yet this reflection of God's glory in nature is not conscious. The mountains and hills do not willingly worship. In all the earth, only humans have this unique capacity.

If we do not gladly reflect God's glory in worship, we will nevertheless reflect the glory of His justice in our own condemnation: "Surely the wrath of man shall praise you" (Psalm 76:10). But this unwilling reflection of God's worth is *not* worship. Therefore, it is necessary to define worship not simply as a way of reflecting back to God the radiance of His worth, but, more precisely, as a way of doing it *gladly.*

The word *gladly* is liable to misunderstanding because (as we will see in a moment) worship at times involves contrition and brokenness, which we do not usually associate with gladness. But I keep the word because if we say only, for example, that worship is a "willing" reflection back to God of His worth, then we are on the brink of a worse misunderstanding; namely, that worship can be willed when the heart has no real desire, or as Jesus says, when the heart is "far from God." Moreover, I think we will see that in genuine biblical contrition there is at least a seed of gladness that comes from the awakening hope that God will "revive the heart of the contrite" (Isaiah 57:15).

HOW TO WORSHIP GOD IN VAIN

This leads to the second thing to see in Matthew 15:8, namely, that we can "worship" God in vain: "This people honors me with their lips, but their heart is far from me." An act of worship is vain and futile when it does not come from the heart. This was implied in the words of Jesus to the Samaritan adulteress: "True worshipers will worship the Father in spirit and truth, for the Father is

---

2. As I use them in this book, the words *feeling* and *emotion* and *affection* do not generally carry different meanings. If something distinct is intended in any given case, I will give some indication in the context. In general, I use the words synonymously and intend by them what Jonathan Edwards did in his great *Treatise Concerning the Religious Affections,* in *The Works of Jonathan Edwards,* vol. 1 (Edinburgh: Banner of Truth, 1974), 237.

Edwards defined the affections as "the more vigorous and sensible exercises of the inclination and will of the soul." To understand this we need to sum up briefly his view of the human soul or mind:

God has endued the soul with two principal faculties: The one, that by which it is capable of perception and speculation, or by which it discerns and judges of things; which is called the *understanding.* The other, that by which the soul is some way inclined with respect to the things it views or considers: or it is the faculty by which the soul beholds things—not as an indifferent unaffected spectator, but—either liking or disliking, pleased or displeased, approving or rejecting. This faculty is called by various names; it is sometimes called the *inclination;* and, as it respects the actions determined and governed by it, the *will;* and the *mind,* with regard to the exercises of this faculty, is often called the *heart....*

The will, and the affections of the soul, are not two faculties: the affections are not essentially distinct from the will, nor do they differ from the mere actings of the will and inclination, but only in the liveliness and sensibility of exercise...

As examples of the affections, Edwards mentions (among others) love, hatred, desire, joy, delight, grief, sorrow, fear, and hope. These are "the more vigorous and sensible [i.e., sensed or felt] exercises of the will." Edwards is aware that there is a profound and complex relationship between the body and the mind at this point:

Such seems to be our nature, and such the laws of the union of soul and body, that there never is in any case whatsoever, any lively and vigorous exercise of the inclination, without some effect upon the body.... But yet, it is not the body, but the mind only, that is the proper seat of the affections. The body of man is no more capable of being really the subject of love or hatred, joy or sorrow, fear or hope, than the body of a tree, or than the same body of man is capable of thinking and understanding. As it is the soul only that has ideas, so it is the soul only that is pleased or displeased with its ideas. As it is the soul only that thinks, so it is the soul only that loves or hates, rejoices or is grieved at, what it thinks of.

The biblical evidence for this is the fact that God, who has no body, nevertheless has many affections. Also Philippians 1:23 and 2 Corinthians 5:8 teach that after a Christian's death, and before the resurrection of the body, the Christian will be with the Lord and capable of joys "far better" than what we have known here.

seeking such people to worship him" (John 4:23). Now what is this experience of the spirit? What goes on in the heart when worship is *not* in vain?

Worship is more than an act of mere willpower. All the outward acts of worship are performed by acts of will. But that does not make them authentic. The will can be present (for all kinds of reasons) while the heart is not truly engaged (or, as Jesus says, is "far way"). The engagement of the heart in worship is the coming alive of the feelings and emotions and affections of the heart.[2] Where feelings for God are dead, worship is dead.

THE AFFECTIONS THAT MAKE WORSHIP AUTHENTIC

Now let's be specific. What are these feelings or affections that make the outward acts of worship authentic? For an answer, we turn to the inspired psalms and hymns of the Old Testament. An array of different and intertwined affections may grip the heart at any time. So the extent and order of the following list is not intended to limit the possibilities of pleasure in anyone's heart.

Perhaps the first response of the heart at seeing the majestic holiness of God is stunned silence: "Be still, and know that I am God" (Psalm 46:10). "The LORD is in his holy temple; let all the earth keep silence before him" (Habakkuk 2:20).

In the silence rises a sense of awe and reverence and wonder at the sheer magnitude of God: "Let all the earth fear the LORD; let all the inhabitants of the world stand in awe of him!" (Psalm 33:8).

And because we are all sinners, there is in our reverence a holy dread of God's righteous power. "The LORD of hosts, him you shall regard as holy. Let him be your fear, and let him be your dread" (Isaiah 8:13). "I will bow down toward your holy temple in the fear of you" (Psalm 5:7).

But this dread is not a paralyzing fright full of resentment against God's absolute authority. It finds release in brokenness and contrition and grief for our ungodliness: "The sacrifices of God are a broken spirit; a broken and contrite heart, O God, you will not despise" (Psalm 51:17). "Thus says the One who is high and lifted up, who inhabits eternity, whose name is Holy: 'I dwell in the high and holy place, and also with him who is of a contrite and lowly spirit, to revive the spirit of the lowly, and to revive the heart of the contrite'" (Isaiah 57:15).

Mingled with the feeling of genuine brokenness and contrition, there arises a longing for God: "As a deer pants for flowing streams, so pants my soul for you, O God. My soul thirsts for God, for the living God" (Psalm 42:1–2). "Whom have I in heaven but you? And there is nothing on earth that I desire besides you. My flesh and my heart may fail, but God is the strength of my heart and my portion forever" (Psalm 73:25–26). "O God, you are my God; earnestly I seek you; my soul thirsts for you; my flesh faints for you, as in a dry and weary land where there is no water" (Psalm 63:1).

God is not unresponsive to the contrite longing of the soul. He comes and lifts the load of sin and fills our heart with gladness and gratitude. "You have turned for me my mourning into dancing; you have loosed my sackcloth and clothed me with gladness, that my glory may sing your praise and not be silent. O LORD my God, I will give thanks to you forever!" (Psalm 30:11–12).

But our joy does not just rise from the backward glance in gratitude. It also rises from the forward glance in hope: "Why are you cast down, O my soul, and why are you in turmoil within me? Hope in God; for I shall again praise him, my salvation and my God" (Psalm 42:5–6). "I wait for the LORD, my soul waits, and in his word I hope" (Psalm 130:5).

In the end the heart longs not for any of God's good gifts, but for God Himself. To see Him and know Him and be in His presence is the soul's final feast. Beyond this there is no quest. Words fail. We call it pleasure, joy, delight. But these are weak pointers to the unspeakable experience: "One thing have I asked of the LORD, that will I seek after: that I may dwell in the house of the LORD all the days of my life, to gaze upon the beauty of the LORD and to inquire in his temple" (Psalm 27:4). "In your presence there is fullness of joy; at your right hand are pleasures forevermore" (Psalm 16:11). "Delight yourself in the LORD" (Psalm 37:4).

These are some of the affections of the heart that keep worship from being "in vain." Worship is a way of gladly reflecting back to God the radiance of His worth. It is not a mere act of willpower by which we perform outward acts. Without the engagement of the heart, we do not really worship. The engagement of the heart in worship is the coming alive of the feelings and emotions and affections of the heart. *Where feelings for God are dead, worship is dead.*

True worship must include inward feelings that reflect the worth of God's glory. If this were not so, the word *hypocrite* would have no meaning. But there is such a thing as hypocrisy—going through outward motions (like singing, praying, giving, reciting) that signify affections of the heart that are not there. "This people honors me with their lips, but their heart is far from me."

TESTING A COMMON SLOGAN: "FACT! FAITH! FEELING!"

The virtue of slogans is brevity. Their vice is ambiguity. So they are risky ways of communicating. They are powerful and perilous. So we should exploit the power and explain the peril. I would like to venture a corrective explanation to the slogan "Fact! Faith! Feeling!"

It's an old and common evangelical slogan. F. B. Meyer, A. T. Pearson, and L. E. Maxwell all preached sermons by this title. Today a Campus Crusade booklet uses it powerfully. The point of the slogan is the order. First, the facts about Christ. Second, the response of faith. Third, the feelings that may or may not follow.

So what's the ambiguity? There are two: Changed "feelings" may be essential to true Christian conversion, not incidental; and "faith" may not be completely distinct from feeling.

In one well-known booklet the slogan appears as a train: The locomotive is "fact." The coal car is "faith." The caboose is "feeling." The explanation reads: "The train will run with or without the caboose. However, it would be futile to attempt to pull the train by the caboose." But what are the "feelings" the train of Christian living can run without? Do "feelings" refer merely to physical experiences like sweaty palms, knocking knees, racing heart, trembling lips, tearful eyes? If so, the slogan is clear and accurate.

But most people don't think of feelings that way. Feelings include things like gratitude, hope, joy, contentment, peacefulness, desire, compassion, fear, hate, anger, grief. None of these is merely physical. Angels, demons, and departed saints without bodies can have these "feelings."

I think that apart from the Bible, Jonathan Edwards has written the most important book on feelings in the Christian life. It's called *The Religious Affections*. The definition of these "affections" (or what most people today mean by feelings) is: "the more vigorous and sensible exercises of the inclination and will of the soul." In other words, the feelings that really matter are not mere physical sensations. They are the stirring up of the soul with some perceived treasure or threat.

There is a connection between the feelings of the soul and the sensations of the body. This is owing, Edwards says, to "the laws of union which the Creator has fixed between the soul and the body."[3] In other words, heartfelt gratitude can make you cry. Fear of God can make you tremble. The crying and the trembling are in themselves spiritually insignificant. The train can run without them. That's the truth in the slogan. But the gratitude and the fear are not optional in the Christian life. Yet these are what most people call feelings. That is the peril of the slogan. It seems to make optional what the Bible makes essential.

Minimizing the importance of transformed feelings makes Christian conversion less supernatural and less radical. It is humanly manageable to make decisions of the will for Christ. No supernatural power is required to pray prayers, sign cards, walk aisles, or even stop sleeping around. Those are good. They just don't prove that anything spiritual has happened. Christian conversion, on the other hand, is a supernatural, radical thing. The heart is changed. And the evidence of it is not just new decisions, but new affections, new feelings.

Negatively, the apostle Paul says that those who go on in the same old way of "hostility," "jealousy," "rage," and "envy" "will not inherit the kingdom of God" (see Galatians 5:20–21). These are all feelings. They must change. The train won't get to heaven unless they do. Positively, Christians are commanded to have God-honoring feelings. We are commanded to feel joy (Philippians 4:4), hope (Psalm 42:5), fear (Luke 12:5), peace (Colossians 3:15), zeal (Romans 12:11), grief (Romans 12:15), desire (1 Peter 2:2), tenderheartedness (Ephesians 4:32), and brokenness and contrition (James 4:9).

---

3. Jonathan Edwards, *Religious Affections*, in *The Works of Jonathan Edwards*, vol. 2, ed. John E. Smith (New Haven: Yale University Press, 1959), 96.

Moreover, faith itself has in it something that most people would call feeling. Saving faith means "receiving Christ": "To all who did *receive* him, who believed in his name, he gave the right to become children of God" (John 1:12). But receive as what? We usually say, "as Lord and Savior." That's right. But something more needs to be said. Saving faith also receives Christ as our *Treasure.* A non-treasured Christ is a nonsaving Christ. Faith has in it this element of valuing, embracing, prizing, relishing Christ. It is like a man who finds a treasure hidden in a field and "from joy" sells all his treasures to have that field (Matthew 13:44).

Therefore, let us affirm the slogan when it means that physical sensations are not essential. But let us also make clear that the locomotive of fact is not headed for heaven if it is not followed by a faith that *treasures* Christ and if it is not pulling a caboose-load of new, though imperfect, affections.

WORSHIP AS AN END IN ITSELF

Now what does this imply about the feast of worship? Surprisingly, it implies that worship is an end in itself. We do not eat the feast of worship as a means to anything else. Happiness in God is the end of all our seeking. Nothing beyond it can be sought as a higher goal. John Calvin put it like this: "If God contains the fullness of all good things in himself like an inexhaustible fountain, nothing beyond him is to be sought by those who strike after the highest good and all the elements of happiness."[4]

If what transforms outward ritual into authentic worship is the quickening of the heart's affections, then true worship cannot be performed as a means to some other experience. Feelings are not like that. Genuine feelings of the heart cannot be manufactured as stepping stones to something else.

For example: My brother-in-law called me long-distance in 1974 to tell me my mother had just been killed. I recall his breaking voice as I took the phone from my wife: "Johnny, this is Bob, good buddy. I've got bad news… Your mother and dad were in a serious bus accident. Your mom didn't make it, and your dad is hurt bad."

---

4. John Calvin, *Institutes of the Christian Religion,* ed. John T. McNeill, trans. Ford Lewis Battles (Philadelphia: Westminster, 1960), 3.25.10.

One thing is for sure: When I hear news like that, I do not sit down and say, "Now to what end shall I feel grief?" As I pull my baby son off my leg and hand him to my wife and walk to the bedroom to be alone, I do not say, "What good end can I accomplish if I cry for the next half-hour?" The feeling of grief is an end in itself, as far as my conscious motivation is concerned.

It is there spontaneously. It is not performed as a means to anything else. It is not consciously willed. It is not decided upon. It comes from deep within, from a place beneath the conscious will. It will no doubt have many by-products—most of them good. But that is utterly beside the point as I kneel by my bed and weep. The feeling is there, bursting out of my heart. And it is an end in itself.

Grief is not the only example. If you have been floating on a raft without water for three days after a shipwreck on the ocean and a speck of land appears on the horizon, you do not say, "Now to what end shall I feel desire for that land? What good end should now prompt me to decide to feel hope?" Even though the longing in your heart may give you the renewed strength to get to land, you do *not* perform the act of desire and hope and longing in order to get there.

The longing erupts from deep in your heart because of the tremendous value of water (and life!) on that land. It is not planned and performed (like the purchase of a plane ticket) as a means to getting what you desire. It rises spontaneously in the heart. It is not a decision made in order to…anything! As a genuine feeling of the heart, it is an end in itself.

Or consider fear. If you are camping in the Boundary Waters of Minnesota and waken in the night to the sound of snorting outside and see in the moonlight the silhouette of a huge bear coming toward your tent, you do not say, "Now to what end shall I feel fear?" You do not calculate the good results that might come from the adrenaline that fear produces, and then decide that fear would be an appropriate and helpful emotion to have. It is just there!

When you stand at the edge of the Grand Canyon for the first time and watch the setting sun send the darkness down through the geological layers of time, you do not say, "Now to what end shall I feel awe and wonder before this beauty?"

When a little child on Christmas morning opens his first gift and finds his "most favoritest" rocket, which he has wanted for months, he does not think,

Now to what end shall I feel happy and thankful? We call a person an ingrate when words of gratitude are dutifully forced instead of coming spontaneously from the heart.

When a five-year-old enters kindergarten and starts getting picked on by some second-graders and his big fourth-grade brother comes over and takes his side, he does not "decide" to feel confidence and love welling up in his little heart. He just does.

All genuine emotion is an end in itself. It is not consciously caused as a means to something else. This does not mean we cannot or should not seek to have certain feelings. We should and we can. We can put ourselves in situations where the feeling may more readily be kindled. We may indeed prize some of the results of these feelings as well as the feelings themselves. But in the moment of authentic emotion, the calculation vanishes. We are transported (perhaps only for seconds) above the reasoning work of the mind, and we experience feeling without reference to logical or practical implications.

This is what keeps worship from being "in vain." Worship is authentic when affections for God arise in the heart as an end in themselves. In worship, God is the dreaded voice on the phone. God is the island on the horizon. God is the bear and the setting sun and the "most favoritest" rocket and the mother who gave it and the big, strong fourth-grade brother.

If God's reality is displayed to us in His Word or His world and we do not then feel in our heart any grief or longing or hope or fear or awe or joy or gratitude or confidence, then we may dutifully sing and pray and recite and gesture as much as we like, but it will not be real worship. We cannot honor God if our "heart is far from him."

Worship is a way of gladly reflecting back to God the radiance of His worth. This cannot be done by mere acts of duty. It can be done only when spontaneous affections arise in the heart. And these affections for God are an end in themselves. They are the essence of eternal worship. Augustine said it like this: The highest good is "that which will leave us nothing further to seek in order to be happy, if only we make all our actions refer to it, and seek it not for the sake of something else, but for its own sake."[5]

YOU MUST KISS ME, BUT NOT THAT KIND OF MUST

Consider the analogy of a wedding anniversary. Mine is on December 21. Suppose on this day I bring home a dozen long-stemmed roses for Noël. When she meets me at the door, I hold out the roses, and she says, "O Johnny, they're beautiful; thank you" and gives me a big hug. Then suppose I hold up my hand and say matter-of-factly, "Don't mention it; it's my duty."

What happens? Is not the exercise of duty a noble thing? Do not we honor those we dutifully serve? Not much. Not if there's no heart in it. Dutiful roses are a contradiction in terms. If I am not moved by a spontaneous affection for her as a person, the roses do not honor her. In fact, they belittle her. They are a very thin covering for the fact that she does not have the worth or beauty in my eyes to kindle affection. All I can muster is a calculated expression of marital duty.

Here is the way Edward John Carnell puts it:

Suppose a husband asks his wife if he must kiss her good night. Her answer is, "You must, but not that kind of a must." What she means is this: "Unless a spontaneous affection for my person motivates you, your overtures are stripped of all moral value."[6]

---

5. Augustine, *The City of God,* trans. Marcus Dods (New York: Modern Library, 1950), 8.8.
6. E. J. Carnell, *Christian Commitment* (New York: Macmillan, 1967), 160–1. Carnell's whole book resounds with this emphasis (pp. 162, 176, 196, 206, 213, 222, 289, 301). Consider this insightful section from p. 222:

    The more we make rectitude a calculated object of striving, the further we recede from moral fulfillment; for moral fulfillment is spontaneous, affectionate fulfillment. Love carries its own sense of compulsion. It is borne on the wings of the law of the spirit of life. When we must be motivated by either rational or legal necessity, love gives way to forecast, interest, and calculation. Suppose a mother rushes to help her terrified child. She acts out of spontaneous love. She would be offended by even the suggestion that she must help her child from a legal sense of duty....
    Moral striving is paradoxical because we shall never love God unless we make a conscious effort; and yet because we must strive for legal righteousness, we prove that we shall never be righteous. If our affections were a fruit of the moral and spiritual environment, we should fulfill the law with the same unconscious necessity with which we breathe.
    The paradox can perhaps be illustrated by a painter who deliberately tries to become great. Unless he strives, he will never be an artist at all, let alone a great artist. But since he makes genius a deliberate goal of striving, he proves that he is not, and never will be, a genius. A master artist is great without trying to be great. His abilities unfold like the petals of a rose before the sun. Genius is a gift of God. It is a fruit, not a work.
    So is worship!

The fact is, many of us have failed to see that duty toward God can never be restricted to outward action. Yes, we must worship Him. "But not that kind of must." What kind then? The kind C. S. Lewis described to Sheldon Vanauken: "It is a Christian duty, as you know, for everyone to be as happy as he can."[7]

The real duty of worship is not the outward duty to say or do the liturgy. It is the inward duty, the command: "Delight yourself in the LORD"! (Psalm 37:4). "Be glad in the LORD, and rejoice!" (Psalm 32:11).

The reason this is the real duty of worship is that it honors God, while the empty performance of ritual does not. If I take my wife out for the evening on our anniversary and she asks me, "Why do you do this?" the answer that honors her most is "Because nothing makes me happier tonight than to be with you."

"It's my duty" is a dishonor to her.

"It's my joy" is an honor.

There it is! The feast of Christian Hedonism. How shall we honor God in worship? By saying, "It's my duty"? Or by saying, "It's my joy"?

Worship is a way of reflecting back to God the radiance of His worth. Now we see that the mirror that catches the rays of His radiance and reflects them back in worship is the joyful heart. Another way of saying this is to say

The chief end of man is to glorify God
by
enjoying Him forever.

BEWARE OF GIVING TO GOD

Now it becomes clear why it is significant that worship is an end in itself. Worship is an end in itself because it is the final end for which we were created.

It also becomes clear why it is not idolatrous and man-centered to say that our emotions are ends in themselves. It is not man-centered because the emo-

7. From a letter to Sheldon Vanauken in Vanauken's book *A Severe Mercy* (New York: Harper & Row, 1977), 189.

tions of our worship are centered on *God.* We look away from ourselves to Him, and only then do the manifold emotions of our heart erupt in worship.[8]

Nor is it idolatrous to say our affections in worship are ends in themselves, because our affections for God glorify God, not us. Whoever thought he was glorifying himself and not the Grand Canyon when he stood at its edge for hours in silent awe? Whoever would accuse me of glorifying myself and not my wife when I tell her, "I delight to spend this evening with you"? Who would accuse a little child of self-centeredness on Christmas morning if he runs away from his new rocket to hug his mother and say thank you because he is bursting with joyful gratitude?

Someone might object that in making the joy of worship an end in itself, we make God a means to our end rather than our being a means to His end. Thus, we seem to elevate ourselves above God. But consider this question: Which glorifies God more—that is, which reflects back to God more clearly the greatness of His glory—(1) a worship experience that comes to climax with joy in the wonder of God? Or (2) an experience that comes to climax in a noble attempt to free itself from rapture in order to make a contribution to the goal of God?

This is a subtle thing. We strive against God's all-sufficient glory if we think we can become a means to *His* end without making joy in Him *our* end. Christian Hedonism does not put us above God when it makes the joy of worship its goal. It is precisely in confessing our frustrated, hopeless condition without Him that we honor Him. A patient is not greater than his doctor because he longs to be made well. A child is not greater than his father when he wants the fun of playing with him.

On the contrary, the one who actually sets himself above God is the person who presumes to come to God to give rather than get. With a pretense of self-denial, he positions himself as God's benefactor—as if the world and all it contains were not already God's (Psalm 50:12)!

No, the hedonistic approach to God in worship is the only humble

---

8. Christian Hedonism is aware that self-consciousness kills joy and therefore kills worship. As soon as you turn your eyes in on yourself and become conscious of experiencing joy, it's gone. The Christian Hedonist knows that the secret of joy is self-forgetfulness. Yes, we go to the art museum for the joy of seeing the paintings. But the counsel of Christian Hedonism is: Set your whole attention on the paintings, and not on your emotions, or you will ruin the whole experience. Therefore, in worship there must be a radical orientation on God, not ourselves.

approach because it is the only one that comes with empty hands. Christian Hedonism pays God the respect of acknowledging (and really feeling!) that He alone can satisfy the heart's longing to be happy. Worship is an end in itself because we glorify God *by* enjoying Him forever.

THREE STAGES OF WORSHIP

But this is liable to be misunderstood. It might give the impression that we cannot come to God in real worship unless we are overflowing with the affections of delight and joy and hope and gratitude and wonder and awe and reverence. I do not believe this is necessarily implied in what I have said.

I see three stages of movement toward the ideal experience of worship. We may experience all three in one hour, and God is pleased with all three—if indeed they are stages on the way to full joy in Him. I will mention them in reverse order.

1. There is a final stage in which we feel an unencumbered joy in the manifold perfection of God—the joy of gratitude, wonder, hope, admiration: "My soul will be satisfied as with fat and rich food, and my mouth will praise you with joyful lips" (Psalm 63:5). In this stage we are satisfied with the excellency of God, and we overflow with the joy of His fellowship. This is the feast of Christian Hedonism.

2. In a prior stage that we often taste, we do not feel fullness, but rather longing and desire. Having tasted the feast before, we recall the goodness of the Lord—but it seems far off. We preach to our souls not to be downcast, because we are sure we shall again praise the Lord (Psalm 42:5). Yet, for now, our hearts are not very fervent.

Even though this falls short of the ideal of vigorous, heartfelt adoration and hope, yet it is a great honor to God. We honor the water from a mountain spring not only by the satisfied "ahhh" after drinking our fill, but also by the unquenched longing to be satisfied while still climbing to it.

In fact, these two stages are not really separable in the true saint, because all satisfaction in this life is still shot through with longing and all genuine longing has tasted the satisfying water of life. David Brainerd expressed the paradox:

Of late God has been pleased to keep my soul hungry almost continually, so that I have been filled with a kind of pleasing pain. When I really enjoy God, I feel my desires of Him the more insatiable and my thirstings after holiness more unquenchable.[9]

3. The lowest stage of worship—where all genuine worship starts, and where it often returns for a dark season—is the barrenness of soul that scarcely feels any longing, and yet is still granted the grace of repentant sorrow for having so little love: "When my soul was embittered, when I was pricked in heart, I was brutish and ignorant; I was like a beast toward you" (Psalm 73:21–22).

E. J. Carnell points toward these same stages when he says,

Rectitude, we know, is met in one of two ways: either by a spontaneous expression of the good or by spontaneous sorrow for having failed. The one is a direct fulfillment; the other is indirect fulfillment.[10]

Worship is a way of gladly reflecting back to God the radiance of His worth. This is the ideal. For God surely is more glorified when we delight in His magnificence than when we are so unmoved by it that we scarcely feel anything and only wish we could. Yet He is also glorified by the spark of anticipated gladness that gives rise to the sorrow we feel when our hearts are lukewarm. Even in the miserable guilt we feel over our beastlike insensitivity, the glory of God shines. If God were not gloriously desirable, why would we feel sorrowful for not feasting fully on His beauty?

Yet even this sorrow, to honor God, must in one sense be an end in itself—not that it shouldn't lead on to something better, but that it must be real and spontaneous. The glory from which we fall short cannot be reflected in a calculated sorrow. As Carnell says, "Indirect fulfillment is stripped of virtue whenever it is made a goal of conscious striving. Whoever deliberately tries to be sorry will never be sorry. Sorrow cannot be induced by human effort."[11]

---

9. Quoted in E. M. Bounds, *The Weapon of Prayer* (Grand Rapids, Mich.: Baker, 1975), 136.
10. Carnell, *Christian Commitment*, 213.
11. Ibid., 213–4.

The Moral Enemy of Worship

I conclude from this meditation on the nature of worship that the revolt against hedonism has killed the spirit of worship in many churches and many hearts. The widespread notion that high moral acts must be free from self-interest is a great enemy of true worship. Worship is the highest moral act a human can perform, so the only basis and motivation for it that many people can conceive is the notion of morality as the disinterested performance of duty. But when worship is reduced to disinterested duty, it ceases to be worship. For worship is a feast.

Neither God nor my wife is honored when I celebrate the high days of our relationship out of a sense of duty. They are honored when I delight in them! Therefore, to honor God in worship, we must not seek Him disinterestedly for fear of gaining some joy in worship and so ruining the moral value of the act. Instead we must seek Him hedonistically, the way a thirsty deer seeks the stream—precisely for the joy of seeing and knowing Him! Worship is nothing less than obedience to the command of God: "Delight yourself in the LORD"!

Misguided virtue smothers the spirit of worship. The person who has the vague notion that it is virtue to overcome self-interest, and that it is vice to seek pleasure, will scarcely be able to worship. For worship is the most hedonistic affair of life and must not be ruined with the least thought of disinterestedness. The great hindrance to worship is not that we are a pleasure-seeking people, but that we are willing to settle for such pitiful pleasures.

The prophet Jeremiah put it like this:

"My people have changed their glory for that which does not profit. Be appalled, O heavens, at this; be shocked, be utterly desolate, declares the LORD, for my people have committed two evils: they have forsaken me, the fountain of living waters, and hewed out cisterns for themselves, broken cisterns that can hold no water." (Jeremiah 2:11–13)

The heavens are appalled and shocked when people give up soon on their quest for pleasure and settle for broken cisterns.

WE ARE FAR TOO EASILY PLEASED

One of the most important things I ever read on my pilgrimage toward Christian Hedonism was from a sermon preached by C. S. Lewis in 1941. He said:

> If there lurks in most modern minds the notion that to desire our own good and earnestly to hope for the enjoyment of it is a bad thing, I submit that this notion has crept in from Kant and the Stoics and is no part of the Christian faith. Indeed, if we consider the unblushing promises of reward and the staggering nature of the rewards promised in the Gospels, it would seem that our Lord finds our desires, not too strong, but too weak. We are half-hearted creatures, fooling about with drink and sex and ambition when infinite joy is offered us, like an ignorant child who wants to go on making mud pies in a slum because he cannot imagine what is meant by the offer of a holiday at the sea. We are far too easily pleased.[12]

That's it! The enemy of worship is not that our desire for pleasure is too strong, but too weak! We have settled for a home, a family, a few friends, a job, a television, a microwave oven, an occasional night out, a yearly vacation, and perhaps a new laptop. We have accustomed ourselves to such meager, short-lived pleasures that our capacity for joy has shriveled. And so our worship has shriveled. Many can scarcely imagine what is meant by "a holiday at the sea"—worshiping the living God!

THE SHRIVELING OF DARWIN'S SOUL

Through long drinking at the broken cistern of mud-pie pleasures, many have lost almost all capacity for delighting in God—not unlike what happened to Charles Darwin. Near the end of his life he wrote an autobiography for his children in which he expressed one regret:

---

12. C. S. Lewis, "The Weight of Glory," in *The Weight of Glory and other Essays* (Grand Rapids, Mich.: Eerdmans, 1965), 1–2.

Up to the age of 30 or beyond it, poetry of many kinds…gave me great pleasure, and even as a schoolboy I took intense delight in Shakespeare.… Formerly pictures gave me considerable, and music very great, delight. But now for many years I cannot endure to read a line of poetry: I have tried to read Shakespeare, and found it so intolerably dull that it nauseated me. I have also almost lost any taste for pictures or music.… I retain some taste for fine scenery, but it does not cause me the exquisite delight which it formerly did.… My mind seems to have become a kind of machine for grinding general laws out of large collections of facts, but why this should have caused the atrophy of that part of the brain alone, on which the higher tastes depend, I cannot conceive.… The loss of these tastes is a loss of happiness, and may possibly be injurious to the intellect, and more probably to the moral character, by enfeebling the emotional part of our nature.[13]

Worship services across the land bear the scars of this process. For many, Christianity has become the grinding out of general doctrinal laws from collections of biblical facts. But childlike wonder and awe have died. The scenery and poetry and music of the majesty of God have dried up like a forgotten peach at the back of the refrigerator.

And the irony is that we have aided and abetted the desiccation by telling people they ought not seek their own pleasure, especially in worship.[14] We have implied in a thousand ways that the virtue of an act diminishes to the degree you enjoy doing it and that doing something because it yields happiness is bad. The notion hangs like a gas in the Christian atmosphere.

---

13. Cited in Virginia Stem Owens, "Seeing Christianity in Red and Green as Well as Black and White," *Christianity Today* 27, no. 13 (2 September 1983): 38.

14. For example, Carl Zylstra wrote: "The question is whether worship really is supposed to be a time for self-fulfillment and enjoyment or whether it should be, first of all, a time of service and honor to God, a sacrifice of praise" ("Just Dial the Lord," *The Reformed Journal* [October 1984], 6). When the question is put like this, it cannot be answered truthfully. It is very misleading. Of course worship is a time to honor God. But we kill that possibility by warning people not to pursue their own enjoyment. We should be telling them again and again to pursue their own enjoyment—*in God!* If Zylstra means to warn us against seeking fulfillment by looking to ourselves or merely from the experience of music or fellowship, then his warning is well taken.

IMMANUEL KANT AND HEBREWS 11:6 IN COMBAT

C. S. Lewis thought Immanuel Kant (who died in 1804) was a culprit in this confusion. So did the atheist Ayn Rand. Her striking description of Kant's ethics, if not historically precise, is at least a good description of the paralyzing effects it seems to have had in the church:

> An action is moral, said Kant, only if one has no desire to perform it, but performs it out of a sense of duty and derives no benefit from it of any sort, neither material nor spiritual. A benefit destroys the moral value of an action. (Thus if one has no desire to be evil, one cannot be good; if one has, one can.)[15]

Ayn Rand equated this notion of virtue with Christianity and rejected the whole thing out of hand. But this is not Christianity! It was tragic for her, and it is tragic for the church, that this notion—that the pursuit of joy is submoral, if not immoral—pervades the air of Christendom.

Would that Ayn Rand had understood her Christian contemporary Flannery O'Connor:

> I don't assume that renunciation goes with submission or even that renunciation is good in itself. Always you renounce a lesser good for a greater; the opposite is what sin is.... The struggle to submit...is not a struggle to submit but a struggle to accept and with passion. I mean, possibly, with joy. Picture me with my ground teeth stalking joy—fully armed too as it's a highly dangerous quest.[16]

Amen!

Every Sunday morning at 11 A.M., Hebrews 11:6 enters combat with

---

15. Ayn Rand, *For the Intellectual* (New York: Signet, 1961), 32.
16. Flannery O'Connor, *The Habit of Being*, ed. Sally Fitzgerald (New York: Farrar, Straus, & Giroux, 1979), 126.

Immanuel Kant. "Without faith it is impossible to please [God], for whoever would draw near to God must believe that he exists and that *he rewards those who seek him."* You cannot please God if you do not come to Him for reward! Therefore, worship that pleases God is the hedonistic pursuit of God. He is our exceeding great reward! In His presence is fullness of joy, and at His right hand are *pleasures* forevermore. Worship is the feast of Christian Hedonism.

AN AFFAIR OF THE MIND

God seeks people to worship Him "in spirit and truth" (John 4:23). I put tremendous emphasis on the "spirit" of worship in the previous section. Now I must balance the scales and reassert that true worship always combines heart and head, emotion and thought, affection and reflection, doxology and theology.

"True worshipers will worship the Father in spirit and truth." True worship does not come from people whose feelings are like air ferns with no root in the solid ground of biblical doctrine. The only affections that honor God are those rooted in the rock of biblical truth.

Else what meaning have the words of the apostle: "They have a zeal for God, but not according to knowledge" (Romans 10:2)? And did not the Lord pray, "Sanctify them in the truth; your word is truth" (John 17:17)? And did He not say, "You will know the truth, and the truth will set you free" (John 8:32)? Holy freedom in worship is the fruit of truth. Religious feelings that do not come from a true apprehension of God are neither holy nor truly free, no matter how intense.

The pastoral testimony of Jonathan Edwards has therefore always seemed to me inescapably biblical. He was the foremost defender of the Great Awakening in New England in the early 1740s. It had come under severe criticism because of apparent emotional excesses.

Charles Chauncy, pastor of the old First Church in Boston, opposed the revival strenuously. He pointed out all of its excesses like the "swooning away and falling to the ground...bitter shriekings and screamings; convulsion-like tremblings and agitations, strugglings and tumblings."[17]

---

17. Cited in C. H. Faust and T. H. Johnson, eds., *Jonathan Edwards: Selections* (New York: Hill & Wang, 1962), xviii.

Edwards did not defend the excesses, but he earnestly defended the deep and genuine engagement of the affections based on truth. He argued with these carefully chosen words:

I should think myself in the way of my duty, to raise the affections of my hearers as high as I possibly can, provided they are affected with nothing but truth, and with affections that are not disagreeable to the nature of what they are affected with.[18]

Edwards was utterly convinced of the crucial importance of powerful affections in worship:

The things of religion are so great, that there can be no suitableness in the exercises of our hearts, to their nature and importance, unless they be lively and powerful. In nothing is vigor in the actings of our inclinations so requisite, as in religion; and in nothing is lukewarmness so odious.[19]

Yes, the only heat he valued in worship was the heat that comes with light. In 1744 he preached an ordination sermon from the text about John the Baptist, "He was a burning and a shining light" (John 5:35, KJV). There must be heat in the heart and light in the mind—and no more heat than justified by the light!

If a minister has light without heat, and entertains his [hearers] with learned discourses, without a savour of the power of godliness, or any appearance of fervency of spirit, and zeal for God and the good of souls, he may gratify itching ears, and fill the heads of his people with empty notions; but it will not be very likely to reach their souls. And if, on the other hand, he be driven on with a fierce and intemperate zeal, and vehement heat, without light, he will be likely to kindle the like

---

18. Jonathan Edwards, *Some Thoughts Concerning the Revival in the Great Awakening,* ed. C. C. Goen (New Haven: Yale University Press, 1972), 387.
19. Edwards, *Religious Affections,* 238.

unhallowed flame in his people, and to fire their corrupt passions and affections; but will make them never the better, nor lead them a step towards heaven, but drive them apace the other way.[20]

Strong affections for God, rooted in and shaped by the truth of Scripture—this is the bone and marrow of biblical worship.

Therefore Christian Hedonism is passionately opposed to all attempts to drive a wedge between deep thought and deep feeling. It rejects the common notion that profound reflection dries up fervent affection. It resists the assumption that intense emotion thrives only in the absence of coherent doctrine.

On the contrary, Christian Hedonists are persuaded with Edwards that the only affections that magnify God's value are those that come from true apprehensions of His glory. If the feast of worship is rare in the land, it is because there is a famine of the Word of God (Amos 8:11–12).

THE FORM OF WORSHIP

It follows that forms of worship should provide two things: channels for the mind to apprehend the truth of God's reality and channels for the heart to respond to the beauty of that truth—that is, forms to ignite the affections with biblical truth and forms to express the affections with biblical passion.

Of course, good forms do both. Good sermons and hymns and prayers express and inspire worship. And they do it best when they are unabashedly hedonistic and therefore God-centered.

Take preaching, for example. John Broadus was on target when he wrote a hundred years ago:

The minister may lawfully appeal to the desire for happiness and its negative counterpart, the dread of unhappiness. Those philosophers [Kant?] who insist that we ought always to do right simply and only because it is right are not philosophers at all, for they are either grossly

---

20. Edwards, "The True Excellency of a Gospel Minister," in *The Works of Jonathan Edwards*, 2:958.

ignorant of human nature [and I would add: Scripture] or else indulging in mere fanciful speculations.[21]

Or take hymns! How unabashedly hedonistic they are! Hymns are the voices of the church's lovers, and lovers are the least duty-oriented and most God-besotted people in the world.

Jesus, Thou joy of loving hearts
Thou fount of life, Thou light of men
From the best bliss that earth imparts
We turn unfilled to Thee again.
Bernard of Clairvaux

Jesus, priceless treasure
Source of purest pleasure,
Truest friend to me:
Long my heart hath panted,
'Til it well-nigh fainted,
Thirsting after Thee.
Thine I am,
O spotless Lamb,
I will suffer nought to hide Thee,
Ask for nought beside Thee.
Johann Franck

Jesus, I am resting, resting
In the joy of what Thou art;
I am finding out the greatness
Of Thy loving heart.
Thou hast bid me gaze upon Thee,

---

21. John Broadus, *On the Preparation and Delivery of Sermons*, 4th ed., rev. Vernon Stanfield (New York: Harper & Row, 1979), 117.

And Thy beauty fills my soul,
For by Thy transforming power,
Thou hast made me whole.
Jean Sophia Pigott

Knowing You, Jesus,
knowing You,
there is no greater thing,
You're my all,
You're the best,
You're my joy, my righteousness,
and I love You, Lord.
Graham Kendrick

And for the prayers of the church, what could suffice better than the inspired (hedonistic!) prayers of the psalmists?

You have put more joy in my heart than they have when their grain and wine abound. (Psalm 4:7)

Let all who take refuge in you rejoice; let them ever sing for joy, and spread your protection over them, that those who love your name may exult in you. (5:11)

I will be glad and exult in you; I will sing praise to your name, O Most High. (9:2)

As for me, I shall behold your face in righteousness; when I awake, I shall be satisfied with your likeness. (17:15)

"I delight to do Your will, O my God; Your Law is within my heart." (40:8, NASB)

Create in me a clean heart, O God, and renew a right spirit within me.... Restore to me the joy of your salvation, and uphold me with a willing spirit. (51:10, 12)

O God, you are my God; earnestly I seek you; my soul thirsts for you; my flesh faints for you, as in a dry and weary land where there is no water. So I have looked upon you in the sanctuary, beholding your power and glory. Because your steadfast love is better than life, my lips will praise you. (63:1–3)

Whom have I in heaven but you? And there is nothing on earth that I desire besides you. My flesh and my heart may fail, but God is the strength of my heart and my portion forever. (73:25–26)

When the people of God—and especially the lead worshipers—begin to pray in this hedonistically God-centered way, then the form will both express and inspire authentic worship.

But in the end, the form is not the issue. The issue is whether the excellency of Christ is seen. Worship will happen when the God who said "Let light shine out of darkness" shines in our hearts to give us "the light of the knowledge of the glory of God in the face of Jesus Christ" (2 Corinthians 4:6).

We must see and feel the incomparable excellency of the Son of God. Incomparable because in Him meet infinite glory and lowest humility, infinite majesty and transcendent meekness, deepest reverence toward God and equality with God, infinite worthiness of good and greatest patience to suffer evil, supreme dominion and exceeding obedience, divine self-sufficiency and child-like trust.[22]

The irony of our human condition is that God has put us within sight of the Himalayas of His glory in Jesus Christ, but we have chosen to pull down the

---

22. These pairs are from a sermon by Jonathan Edwards entitled "The Excellency of Christ." In it, Edwards meditates on the image of Christ in Revelation 5:5–6 as both the Lion of the tribe of Judah and the Lamb that was slain. The sermon is in *The Works of Jonathan Edwards*, 1:680–9. For my meditations on these diverse excellencies of Christ, see *Seeing and Savoring Jesus Christ* (Wheaton, Ill.: Crossway, 2004).

shades of our chalet and show slides of Buck Hill—even in church. We are content to go on making mud pies in the slums because we cannot imagine what is meant by the offer of a holiday at the sea.

AN EXHORTATION AND AN EXPERIENCE

I close this chapter with an exhortation and an experience. Don't let your worship decline to the performance of mere duty. Don't let the childlike awe and wonder be choked out by unbiblical views of virtue. Don't let the scenery and poetry and music of your relationship with God shrivel up and die. You have capacities for joy that you can scarcely imagine. They were made for the enjoyment of God. He can awaken them no matter how long they have lain asleep. Pray for His quickening power. Open your eyes to His glory. It is all around you: "The heavens declare the glory of God, and the sky above proclaims his handiwork" (Psalm 19:1).

I was flying at night from Chicago to Minneapolis, almost alone on the plane. The pilot announced that there was a thunderstorm over Lake Michigan and into Wisconsin. He would skirt it to the west to avoid turbulence. As I sat there staring out into the total blackness, suddenly the whole sky was brilliant with light, and a cavern of white clouds fell away four miles beneath the plane and then vanished. A second later, a mammoth white tunnel of light exploded from north to south across the horizon, and again vanished into blackness. Soon the lightning was almost constant, and volcanoes of light burst up out of cloud ravines and from behind distant white mountains. I sat there shaking my head almost in unbelief. *O Lord, if these are but the sparks from the sharpening of Your sword, what will be the day of Your appearing!* And I remembered the words of Christ:

> As the lightning flashes and lights up the sky
> from one side to the other,
> so will the Son of Man be in his day.
>
> (LUKE 17:24)

Even now as I recollect that sight, the word *glory* is full of feeling for me. I thank God that again and again He has awakened my heart to desire Him, to see Him, and to sit down to the feast of Christian Hedonism and worship the King of Glory. The banquet hall is very large.

The Spirit and the Bride say,
"Come."… Let the one who is thirsty come;
let the one who desires take the water of life without price.

(Revelation 22:17)

In some sense the most benevolent, generous person in the world
seeks his own happiness in doing good to others,
because he places his happiness in their good.
His mind is so enlarged as to take them, as it were, into himself.
Thus when they are happy, he feels it;
he partakes with them, and is happy in their happiness.
This is so far from being inconsistent with the freeness of beneficence,
that, on the contrary, free benevolence and kindness consists in it.

JONATHAN EDWARDS

God loves a cheerful giver.

THE APOSTLE PAUL

CHAPTER 4

LOVE

The Labor of Christian Hedonism

So far I have argued that disinterested benevolence toward God is evil. C. S. Lewis puts it well: "It would be a bold and silly creature that came before its Creator with the boast, 'I'm no beggar. I love you disinterestedly.'"[1] If you come to God dutifully offering Him the reward of your fellowship instead of thirsting after the reward of His fellowship, then you exalt yourself above God as His benefactor and belittle Him as a needy beneficiary—and that is evil.

The only way to glorify the all-sufficiency of God in worship is to come to Him because "in [His] presence there is fullness of joy; at [His] right hand are pleasures forevermore" (Psalm 16:11). This has been the main point so far, and we could call it *vertical Christian Hedonism.* Between man and God, on the vertical axis of life, the pursuit of pleasure is not just tolerable; it is mandatory: "Delight yourself in the LORD"! (Psalm 37:4). The chief end of man is to glorify God *by* enjoying Him forever.

But now what about *horizontal Christian Hedonism?* What about our relationship with other people? Is disinterested benevolence the ideal among men? Or is the pursuit of pleasure proper and indeed mandatory for every kind of human love that pleases God?

---

1. C. S. Lewis, *The Four Loves* (London: Geoffrey Bles, 1960), 12.

This chapter's answer is that the pursuit of pleasure is an essential motive for every good deed. Or, to put it another way: If you aim to abandon the pursuit of full and lasting pleasure, you cannot love people or please God.

DOES LOVE SEEKS ITS OWN?

This will take some explaining and defending! I plead your patience and openness. I am swimming against the current of a revered river in this chapter. When I preached on this once, a philosophy professor wrote a letter to me with the following criticism:

> Is it not the contention of morality that we should do the good because it is the good?... We should do the good and perform virtuously, I suggest, because it is good and virtuous; that God will bless it and cause us to be happy is a consequence of it, but not the motive for doing it.

Another popular writer says:

> For the Christian happiness is never a goal to be pursued. It is always the unexpected surprise of a life of service.

I regard these quotes as contrary to Scripture and contrary to love and, in the end (though unintentionally), dishonoring to God.

No doubt, biblical passages come to mind that seem to say exactly the opposite of what I am saying. For example, in the great love chapter, the apostle Paul says that love "does not seek its own" (1 Corinthians 13:5, NASB). Earlier in the same book, he admonished the church, "*Let no one seek his own good, but the good of his neighbor....* I try to please everyone in everything I do, *not seeking my own advantage,* but that of many, that they may be saved" (10:24, 33). In Romans 15:1–3 he says, "We who are strong have an obligation to bear with the failings of the weak, and *not to please ourselves.* Let each of us please his neighbor for his good, to build him up. For *Christ did not please himself.*"

An isolated and unreflective focus on texts like these gives the impression that the essence of Christian morality is to free ourselves of all self-interest when it comes to doing good deeds for other people. But there is good reason to think that this impression is wrong. It does not take all of the context into account, and it certainly cannot account for many other teachings in the New Testament.

Take the context of 1 Corinthians 13, for example. Verse 5 says love seeks not its own. But is this meant so absolutely that it would be wrong to enjoy being loving? First consider the wider biblical context.

SHOULD WE DELIGHT IN BEING MERCIFUL?

According to the prophet Micah, God has commanded us not simply to be merciful, but to "love kindness": "He has told you, O man, what is good; and what does the LORD require of you but to do justice, and to love kindness, and to walk humbly with your God?" (6:8). In other words, the command is not just to do acts of mercy, but *to delight* to be merciful or *to want* to be merciful. If you love being merciful, how can you keep from satisfying your own desire in doing acts of mercy? How can you keep from seeking your own joy in acts of love when your joy consists in being loving? Does obedience to the command to "love kindness" mean you must disobey the teaching of 1 Corinthians 13:5 that love should "seek not its own"?

No. The more immediate context gives several clues that the point of 1 Corinthians 13:5 is not to forbid the pursuit of the joy of loving. Jonathan Edwards gives the true sense:

[The error 1 Corinthians 13:5 opposes is not] the degree in which [a person] loves his own happiness, but in his placing his happiness where he ought not, and in limiting and confining his love. Some, although they love their own happiness, do not place that happiness in their own confined good, or in that good which is limited to them-selves, but more in the common good—in that which is the good of others, or in the good to be enjoyed in and by others.... And when it is said that Charity seeketh not her own, we are to understand it of her own private good—good limited to herself.[2]

DOES PAUL ASSUME
WE WILL WANT TO GAIN NOTHING?

One clue that this is in fact what Paul means is the way he tries to motivate genuine love in verse 3. He says, "If I give away all I have, and if I deliver up my body to be burned, but have not love, *I gain nothing.*" If genuine love dare not set its sights on its own gain, isn't it strange that Paul warns us that not having love will rob us of "gain"? But this is in fact what he says: "If you don't have real love, you won't have real gain."

Someone, no doubt, will say that the gain is a sure result of genuine love, but if it is the motive of love, then love is not really love. In other words, it is good for God to reward acts of love, but it is not good for us to be drawn into love by the promise of reward. But if this is true, then why did Paul tell us in verse 3 that we would lose our reward if we were not really loving? If longing for the "gain" of loving ruins the moral value of love, it is very bad pedagogy to tell someone to be loving lest he lose his "gain."

Giving Paul the benefit of the doubt, should we not rather say there is a kind of gain that is wrong to be motivated by (hence, "Love seeks not its own"), as well as a kind of gain that is right to be motivated by (hence, "If I do not have love, I gain nothing")? Edwards says the proper gain to be motivated by is the happiness one gets in the act of love itself or in the good achieved by it.

CAN DISINTERESTED LOVE REJOICE IN THE TRUTH?

The second clue that Edwards is on the right track is verse 6: "[Love] does not rejoice at wrongdoing, but rejoices with the truth." Love is not a bare choice or mere act. It involves the affections. It does not just *do* the truth. Nor does it just

---

2. Jonathan Edwards, *Charity and Its Fruits* (Edinburgh: Banner of Truth, 1969, orig. 1852), 164.

choose the right. It *rejoices* in the way of truth. So Micah 6:8 is not a strained parallel at all: We must "love kindness"!

But if love rejoices in the choices it makes, it cannot be disinterested. It cannot be indifferent to its own joy! To rejoice in an act is to get joy from it. And this joy is "gain." It may be that there is much more gain than this, or that this joy is in fact the firstfruits of an indestructible and eternal joy. At this point, though, the least we can say is that Paul does not think the moral value of an act of love is ruined when we are motivated to do it by the anticipation of our own joy in it and from it. If it were, then a bad man who hated the prospect of loving could engage in pure love, since he would take no joy in it; while a good man who delighted in the prospect of loving could not love, since he would "gain" joy from it and thus ruin it.

Therefore, 1 Corinthians 13:5 ("Love seeks not its own") does not stand in the way of the thesis that *the pursuit of pleasure is an essential motive for every good deed.* In fact, surprisingly, the context supports it by saying that "love *rejoices* with the truth" and by implying that one should be vigilant in love so as not to lose one's "gain"—the gain of joy that comes in being a loving person, both now and forever.

If this is Paul's intention in 1 Corinthians 13:5, the same thing can be said of 10:24 and 33. These are simply specific instances of the basic principle laid down in 13:5: "Love seeks not its own." When Paul says we should not seek our own advantage, but that of our neighbors so that they may be saved, he does not mean we should not *delight* in the salvation of our neighbors.

In fact, Paul said of his converts, "You are our glory and *joy*" (1 Thessalonians 2:20). In another place he said, "My heart's *desire* and prayer to God for them is that they may be saved" (Romans 10:1).

This is not the voice of disinterested benevolence. The salvation of others was the joy and passion of his life! When he denied himself comforts for this, he was a Christian Hedonist, not a dutiful stoic. So the point of 1 Corinthians 10:24 and 33 is that we should not count any private comfort a greater joy than the joy of seeing our labor lead to another's salvation.

This is also the point of Romans 15:1–3, where Paul says we should not please ourselves, but instead should please our neighbor for his good, to edify him. This too is an application of the principle "Love seeks not its own." He does not mean we shouldn't seek the joy of edifying others, but that we should let *this* joy free us from bondage to private pleasures that make us indifferent to the good of others. Love does not seek its own *private, limited* joy, but instead seeks its own joy in the good—the salvation and edification—of others.[3]

In this way, we begin to love the way God loves. He loves because He delights to love. He does not seek to hide from Himself the reward of love lest His act be ruined by the anticipated joy that comes from it.

> "I am the LORD who practices steadfast love, justice, and righteousness in the earth. *For in these things I delight,"* declares the LORD. (Jeremiah 9:24)

LOVE IS MORE THAN DEEDS

We turn now from defense to offense. There are texts that seem to be a problem, but many others point positively to the truth of Christian Hedonism. We can take 1 Corinthians 13:3 as a starting point: "If I give away all I have, and if I deliver up my body to be burned, but have not love, I gain nothing." This is a startling text. For Jesus Himself said, "Greater love has no one than this, that someone lays down his life for his friends" (John 15:13). How can Paul say that laying down your life may in fact be a loveless act?

One thing is for sure: Love cannot be equated with sacrificial action! It cannot be equated with *any* action! This is a powerful antidote to the common teaching that love is not what you feel, but what you do. The good in this popular teaching is the twofold intention to show (1) that mere warm feelings can never replace actual deeds of love (James 2:16; 1 John 3:18) and (2) that efforts of love must be made even in the absence of the joy that one might wish were present. But it is careless and inaccurate to support these two truths by saying

---

3. This passage in Romans includes the sentence "For Christ did not please himself, but, as it is written, 'The reproaches of those who reproached you fell on me'" (15:3). Concerning this, see the discussion of Hebrews 12:1–2 under the heading "Love Suffers for Joy" later in this chapter.

that love is simply what you do, and not what you feel.[4] (See Epilogue, Reason Four, for a further discussion of how to obey when you don't feel like it.)

The very definition of love in 1 Corinthians refutes this narrow conception of love. For example, Paul says love is not *jealous* and not easily *provoked* and that it *rejoices* in the truth and *hopes* all things (13:4–7). All these are *feelings!* If you feel things like unholy jealousy and irritation, you are not loving. And if you do not feel things like joy in the truth and hope, you are not loving. In other words, *yes*, love is more than feelings; but, *no*, love is not less than feelings.

This may help account for the startling statement that it is possible to give your body to be burned and yet not have love. Evidently, an act does not qualify as love unless it involves right motives. But isn't the willingness to die a sign of good motives? You would think so if the essence of love were disinterestedness. But someone might say that what ruined the self-sacrificing act of apparent love was the intention to inherit reward after death or to leave a noble memory on earth.

That may be part of the answer. But it is not complete. It does not distinguish what sort of reward after death might be appropriate to aim at in an act of love (if any!). Nor does it describe what feelings, if any, must accompany an outward "act" of love for it to be truly loving.

In answering these questions, we need to ask another: What does love to man have to do with our love for God and His grace toward us? Could it be that the reason a person could give his body to be burned and not have love is that his act had no connection to a genuine love for God? Could it be that Paul's conception of horizontal love between people is such that it is authentic only when it is the extension of a vertical love for God? It would be strange indeed if the apostle who said "Whatever does not proceed from faith is sin" (Romans 14:23) could define genuine love without reference to God.

---

4. For example, one popular book says, "Love isn't something you necessarily feel; it's something you do. Good feelings may accompany loving deeds, but we are commanded to love whether we feel like it or not. Jesus didn't feel like giving His life to redeem humankind (Matthew 26:38–39)." Josh McDowell and Norman Geisler, *Love Is Always Right: A Defense of the One Moral Absolute* (Dallas: Word, 1996), 73. It is an oversimplification to say that Jesus did not feel like giving His life to redeem mankind. Yes, He knew it would be excruciating, and, yes, He shrank back from the pain. But Hebrews 12:2 says it was "for the joy set before" Him that He endured the cross. The joy of the future flowed back into the present in Gethsemane, and the taste of it sustained Him. Yes, there are acts of love that are more pleasant than others. But that does not mean that there is no painful joy in the hard ones.

LOVE IS THE OVERFLOW OF JOY IN GOD

Second Corinthians 8:1–4, 8 shows that Paul thinks of genuine love only in relation to God:

> Now, brethren, we wish to make known to you the grace of God which has been given in the churches of Macedonia, that in a great ordeal of affliction their abundance of joy and their deep poverty overflowed in the wealth of their liberality. For I testify that according to their ability, and beyond their ability, they gave of their own accord, begging us with much urging for the favor of participation in the support of the saints.... I am not speaking this as a command, but as proving through the earnestness of others the sincerity of your love also. (NASB)

The reason Paul wants the Corinthians to know about this remarkable work of grace among the Macedonians is that he hopes the same will prove true among them. He is traveling among the churches collecting funds for the poor saints in Jerusalem (Romans 15:26; 1 Corinthians 16:1–4). He writes 2 Corinthians 8 and 9 to motivate the Corinthians to be generous. For our purpose, the crucial thing to notice is that in 8:8 he says this is a test of their *love:* "I say this not as a command, but to prove by the earnestness of others that your *love also* is genuine."

The clear implication of 8:8 (especially the word *also*) is that the Macedonians' generosity is a model of love that the Corinthians "also" should copy. By recounting the earnest love of the Macedonians, Paul aims to stir up the Corinthians *also* to genuine love. So here we have a test case to see just what the love of 1 Corinthians 13 looks like in real life. The Macedonians have given away their possessions, just as 1 Corinthians 13:3 says ("If I give away all I have"). But *here* it is real love, while *there* it was not love at all. What makes the Macedonian generosity a genuine act of love?

The nature of genuine love can be seen in four things.

First, it is a work of divine *grace:* "We want you to know, brothers, about the *grace* of God that has been given among the churches of

Macedonia" (2 Corinthians 8:1). The generosity of the Macedonians was not of human origin. Even though verse 3 says they gave "of their own accord," the willingness was a gift of God—a work of grace.

You can see this same combination of God's sovereign grace resulting in man's willingness in verses 16–17:

> Thanks be to *God, who put into the heart of Titus the same earnest care I have for you.* For he…is going to you of his own accord.

God put it in his heart. So he goes of his *own* accord. The willingness is a gift—a work of divine grace.

Second, this experience of God's grace filled the Macedonians with joy: "In a severe test of affliction, their abundance of joy and their extreme poverty have overflowed in a wealth of generosity" (v. 2). Note that their joy was not owing to the fact that God had prospered them financially. He hadn't! In "extreme poverty" they had joy. Therefore, the joy was a joy in God—in the experience of His grace.

Third, their joy in God's grace *overflowed* in generosity to meet the needs of others: "Their abundance of joy…*overflowed* in a wealth of generosity" (v. 2). Therefore, the generosity expressed horizontally toward men was an overflow of joy in God's grace.

Fourth, the Macedonians begged for the opportunity to sacrifice their meager possessions for the saints in Jerusalem: "Beyond their ability, they gave of their own accord, *begging us with much urging for the favor of participation in the support of the saints*" (8:3–4, NASB). In other words, the way their joy in God overflowed was in the joy of giving. They *wanted* to give. It was their joy!

Now we can give a definition of love that takes God into account and also includes the feelings that should accompany the outward acts of love: *Love is the overflow of joy in God that gladly meets the needs of others.*

Paul does not set up the Macedonians as a model of love just because they sacrificed in order to meet the needs of others. What he stresses is how they *loved* doing this (remember Micah 6:8!). It was the overflow of *joy!* They "begged earnestly" to give. They found their pleasure in channeling the grace of God through their poverty to the poverty in Jerusalem. It is simply astonishing!

This is why a person can give his body to be burned and not have love. Love is the overflow of joy—*in God!* It is not duty for duty's sake or right for right's sake. It is not a resolute abandoning of one's own good with a view solely to the good of the other person. It is first a deeply satisfying experience of the fullness of God's grace, and then a doubly satisfying experience of sharing that grace with another person.

When poverty-stricken Macedonians beg Paul for the privilege of giving money to other poor saints, we may assume that this is not just what they ought to do or have to do, but what they really long to do. It is their joy—an extension of their joy in God. To be sure, they are "denying themselves" whatever pleasures or comforts they could have from the money they give away, but the joy of extending God's grace to others is a far better reward than anything money could buy. The Macedonians have discovered the labor of Christian Hedonism: love! It is the overflow of joy in God that gladly meets the needs of others.

GOD LOVES A CHEERFUL GIVER

In 2 Corinthians 9:6–7 we get a confirmation that we are on the right track. Paul continues to motivate the Corinthians to be generous. He says:

> Whoever sows sparingly will also reap sparingly, and whoever sows bountifully will also reap bountifully. Each one must give as he has made up his mind, not reluctantly or under compulsion, for *God loves a cheerful giver.*

I take this to mean that God is not pleased when people act benevolently but don't do it gladly. When people don't find pleasure (Paul's word is *cheer*) in their acts of service, God doesn't find pleasure in them. He loves cheerful givers, cheerful servants. What sort of cheer? Surely the safest way to answer that question is to remember what sort of cheer moved the Macedonians to be generous. It was the overflow of joy in the grace of God. Therefore, the giver God loves is the one whose joy in Him overflows "cheerfully" in generosity to others.

Perhaps it is becoming clear why part of the thesis of this chapter is that if you try to abandon the pursuit of your full and lasting joy, you cannot love people or please God. If love is the overflow of joy in God that gladly meets the needs of others, then to abandon the pursuit of *this* joy is to abandon the pursuit of love. And if God is pleased by cheerful givers, then to abandon the pursuit of *this* cheerfulness sets you on a course in which God takes no delight. If we are indifferent to whether we do a good deed cheerfully, we are indifferent to what pleases God. For God loves a cheerful giver.

Therefore, it is essential that we be Christian Hedonists on the horizontal level in our relationships with other people, and not just on the vertical axis in our relationship with God. If love is the overflow of joy in God that gladly meets the needs of other people, and if God loves such joyful givers, then this joy in giving is a Christian duty, and the effort not to pursue it is sin.

LOVE REJOICES IN THE JOY OF THE BELOVED

Before we leave 2 Corinthians, consider one more passage that brims with implications about the nature of love. In 1:23–2:4, Paul writes about a visit he didn't make and a painful letter he had to send. He explains the inner workings of his heart in all this:

> But I call God to witness against me—it was to spare you that I refrained from coming again to Corinth. Not that we lord it over your faith, but we work with you *for your joy,* for you stand firm in your faith. For I made up my mind not to make another painful visit to you. For if I cause you pain, *who is there to make me glad* but the one whom I have pained? And I wrote as I did, so that when I came *I might not suffer pain* from those who should have *made me rejoice,* for I felt sure of all of you, that *my joy would be the joy of you all.* For I wrote to you out of much

affliction and anguish of heart and with many tears, not to cause you pain but to let you know *the abundant love that I have for you.*

Notice how Paul's pursuit of their joy and his own joy relates to love. In verse 2 he gives the reason he did not make another painful visit to Corinth: "For if I cause you pain, who is there to *make me glad* but the one whom I have pained?" In other words, Paul's motive here is to preserve his own joy. He says in effect: "If I destroy your joy, then my joy goes, too." Why? Because their joy is precisely what gives him joy!

It is clear from 1:24 that the joy in view is the joy of faith. It is the joy of knowing and resting in God's grace—the same joy that moved the Macedonians to be generous (8:1–3). When *this* joy abounds in his converts, Paul feels great joy himself, and he unashamedly tells them that the reason he does not want to rob them of their joy is that this would rob him of *his* joy. This is the way a Christian Hedonist talks.

In 2:3 he gives the reason he sent them a painful letter: "I wrote as I did, so that when I came I might not suffer pain from those who should have made me rejoice, for I felt sure of all of you, that *my joy would be the joy of you all.*" Here his motive is the same, up to a point. He says he did not want to be pained. He wants joy, not pain. He is a Christian Hedonist! But he goes a step further here than in verse 2. He says the reason he wants joy, not pain, is that he is confident that his joy is also their joy: "For I felt sure of all of you, that my joy would be the joy of you all."

So verse 3 is the converse of verse 2. In verse 2 the point is that *their* joy is his joy; that is, when they are glad, he feels glad in their gladness. And the point of verse 3 is that *his* joy is their joy; that is, when he is glad, they feel glad in his gladness.

Then verse 4 makes the connection with love explicit. He says the reason he had written them was "to let you know the abundant *love* that I have for you." So what is love? Love abounds between us when your joy is mine and my joy is yours. I am not loving just because I seek your joy, but because I seek it as *mine.*

Suppose I tell one of my sons, "Be nice to your brother; help him clean up the room; try to make him happy, not miserable." What if he does help his brother clean up the room, but pouts the whole time and generally exudes unhappiness? Is there virtue in his effort? Not much. What's wrong is that his brother's happiness is not his own happiness. When he helps his brother, he does not pursue his joy in his brother's happiness. He is not acting like a Christian Hedonist. His labor is not the labor of love. It is the labor of legalism—he acts out of mere duty to escape punishment.

LOVE DELIGHTS TO CAUSE AND CONTEMPLATE JOY IN OTHERS

Now consider the relationship between the images of love in 2 Corinthians 8 and 2. In chapter 8, love is the overflow of joy in God that gladly meets the needs of others. It is the impulse of a fountain to overflow. It originates in the grace of God, which overflows freely because it delights to fill the empty. Love shares the nature of that grace because it too delights to overflow freely to meet the needs of others.

In chapter 2, love is what exists between people when they find their joy in each other's joy. Is this in contradiction to the love of chapter 8, where joy comes from God and overflows to others? It sounds in chapter 2 like joy is coming from the joy of other people, not from God. How do these two ways of talking about love relate to each other?

I think the answer is that love not only delights to cause joy in those who are empty (2 Corinthians 8), but also delights to contemplate joy in those who are full (2 Corinthians 2). And these two delights are not at all in contradiction. The grace of God delights to grant repentance (2 Timothy 2:25), *and* it rejoices over one sinner who repents (Luke 15:7). Therefore, when our hearts are filled with joy in the grace of God, we want not only to cause the joy of others, but also to contemplate it when it exists in others.

So it is not inconsistent to say that love is the overflow of joy in God that gladly meets the needs of others *and* to say that love is finding your joy in the joy of another. If love is the *labor* of Christian Hedonism, which delights to beget its joy in others, then it is also the *leisure* of Christian Hedonism, which delights to behold this joy begotten in others.[5]

LOVE WEEPS

But Paul's words in 2 Corinthians 2 raise another question. In verse 4 he says he wrote "out of much affliction and anguish of heart and with many tears." Is this a heart of love? I have stressed so heavily that love is the overflow of joy that someone might think there is no place for grief or anguish in the heart of love and no place for tears on its face. That would be very wrong.

The contentment of a Christian Hedonist is not a Buddha-like serenity, unmoved by the hurts of others. It is a profoundly *dissatisfied contentment.* It is constantly hungry for more of the feast of God's grace. And even the measure of contentment that God grants contains an insatiable impulse to expand itself to others (2 Corinthians 8:4; 1 John 1:4). Christian joy reveals itself as dissatisfied contentment whenever it perceives human need. It starts to expand in love to fill that need and bring about the joy of faith in the heart of the other person. But since there is often a time lapse between our perception of a person's need and

---

5. Historically, ethicists have tended to distinguish these two forms of love as agape and eros, or benevolence and complacency. Not only is there no linguistic basis for such a distinction, but conceptually both resolve into one kind of love at the root.

God's agape does not "transcend" His eros, but expresses it. God's redeeming, sacrificial love for His sinful people is described by Hosea in the most erotic terms: "How can I give you up, O Ephraim? How can I hand you over, O Israel?… My heart recoils within me; my compassion grows warm and tender. I will not execute my burning anger…for I am God and not a man" (11:8–9). Concerning His exiled people who had sinned so grievously, God says later through Jeremiah, "I will *rejoice in doing them good,* and I will plant them in this land in faithfulness, *with all my heart and all my soul*" (32:41).

The divine motive of self-satisfying joy is seen also in Jesus' own ministry. When He was called to give an account of why He lowered Himself to eat with tax collectors and sinners (Luke 15:1–2), His answer was "There will be *more joy in heaven* over one sinner who repents than over ninety-nine righteous persons who need no repentance" (v. 7). Finally, we are told in Hebrews 12:2 by what power Jesus endured suffering: *"For the joy that was set before him* [He] endured the cross, despising the shame, and is seated at the right hand of the throne of God." Should we not infer that in the painful work of redeeming love, God is *very* interested in the satisfaction that comes from His efforts and that He *does* demand the pleasure of a great return on His sacrifice?

While there is a sense in which God has no need for creation at all (Acts 17:25) and is profoundly fulfilled and happy in the eternal fellowship of the Trinity, yet there is in joy an urge to increase, by expanding itself to others who, if necessary, must first be created and redeemed. This divine urge is God's desire for the compounded joy that comes from having others share the very joy He has in Himself.

It becomes evident therefore that one should not ask, "Does God seek His own happiness as a means to the happiness of His people, or does He seek their happiness as a means to His own?" For there is no either-or. They are one. This is what distinguishes a holy, divine eros from a fallen, human one: God's eros longs for and delights in the eternal and holy joy of His people.

our eventual rejoicing in the person's restored joy, there is a place for weeping in that interval. The weeping of compassion is the weeping of joy impeded in the extension of itself to another.

LOVE KEEPS THE REWARD OF LOVE IN MIND

Another tearful experience comes when Paul uncovers his commitment to Christian Hedonism. In Acts 20 he gathers for the last time with elders of the church of Ephesus. There are many tears and much embracing as Paul finishes his farewell address (20:37). But these tears only accent the poignancy of affection the elders have for one who taught them the joy of ministry.

In verse 35, Paul says, "In all things I have shown you that by working hard in this way we must help the weak and *remember* the words of the Lord Jesus, how he himself said, 'It is more blessed to give than to receive.'" The last thing Paul left ringing in their ears on the beach at Miletus was the ministerial charge of Christian Hedonism: "It is more blessed to give than to receive."

Most people do not feel the hedonistic force of these words because they do not meditate on the meaning of the word *remember*. Literally, Paul says, "In all things I have shown you that, so laboring, it is necessary to help the weak and to *remember* the words of the Lord Jesus, that he himself said, 'It is more blessed to give than to receive.'"

In other words, Paul says that two things are *necessary*: (1) to help the weak and (2) to remember that Jesus said it is more blessed to give than to receive. Why are both of these things necessary? Why not just help the weak? Why must one also remember that giving brings blessing?

Most Christians today think that while it is true that giving brings blessing, it is not true that one should "remember" this. Popular Christian wisdom says that blessing will come *as a result* of giving, but that if you keep this fact before you as a motive, it will ruin the moral value of your giving and turn you into a mercenary. The word *remember* in Acts 20:35 is a great obstacle to this popular wisdom. Why would Paul tell church elders to *keep in mind* the benefits of ministry, if in fact their doing so would turn ministers into mercenaries?

Christian Hedonism's answer is that it is necessary to keep in mind the *true* rewards of ministry so we will *not* become mercenaries. C. S. Lewis sees this clearly:

> We must not be troubled by unbelievers when they say that this promise of reward makes the Christian life a mercenary affair. There are different kinds of reward. There is the reward which has no natural connection with the thing you do to earn[6] it, and is quite foreign to the desires that ought to accompany those things. Money is not the natural reward of love; that is why we call a man mercenary if he married a woman for the sake of her money. But marriage is the proper reward for a real lover, and he is not mercenary for desiring it. A general who fights well in order to get a peerage is mercenary; a general who fights for victory is not, victory being the proper reward of battle as marriage is the proper reward of love. The proper rewards are not simply tacked on to the activity for which they are given, but are the activity itself in consummation.[7]

I do not see how anyone can honor the word *remember* in Acts 20:35 and still think it is wrong to pursue the reward of joy in the ministry. On the contrary, Paul thinks it is necessary to keep the joy set firmly before us. This is the last and perhaps most important thing he has to say to the Ephesian elders before he departs. "*Remember!* It is more blessed to give than to receive."

LOVE ENJOYS MINISTRY

Nor is Paul the only apostle who counseled elders to remember and pursue the blessedness of ministry. In 1 Peter 5:1–2, Peter writes:

> I exhort the elders among you, as a fellow elder…shepherd the flock of God that is among you, exercising oversight, not under compulsion,

---

6. I would never use the word *earn* for the way Christians come to enjoy the rewards of love. *Earn* implies the exchange of value from one to another that obligates the other to pay because of the value he has received. But in truth, everything Christians "give" to God is simply a rebound of God's gift to them. All our service is done "in the strength that God supplies" (1 Peter 4:11), so that it is in fact God who "earns" the reward for us and through us. But this does not diminish the helpfulness of Lewis's comment on the nature of rewards.

7.   C. S. Lewis, *The Weight of Glory and Other Addresses* (Grand Rapids, Mich.: Eerdmans, 1965), 2.

but willingly, as God would have you; not for shameful gain, but eagerly.

In other words, "God loves a cheerful pastor." Notice how hedonistic these admonitions are. Peter does not admonish pastors to simply do their work, come what may. Perseverance through the hard times is good. It is essential! But it is not all that is commanded of pastors. We are commanded to enjoy our work!

Peter condemns two motives. One is "compulsion." Don't do your work under constraint. This means the impulse should come gladly from within, not oppressively from without. Parental pressure, congregational expectations, fear of failure or divine censure—these are not good motives for staying in the pastoral ministry. There should be an inner willingness. We should *want* to do the ministry. It should be our joy. Joy in ministry is a duty—a light burden and an easy yoke.

The other motive Peter condemns is the desire for money ("not for shameful gain, but eagerly"). If money is the motive, your joy comes not from the ministry, but from the stuff you can buy with your salary. This is what Lewis calls mercenary. The "eagerness" of ministry should not come from the extrinsic reward of money, but from the intrinsic reward of seeing God's grace flow through you to others.

John gives a good example of this joy in 3 John 1:4: "I have no greater joy than to hear that my children are walking in the truth." When this kind of reward creates joyful eagerness in ministry, *Christ* is honored (since He is the "truth" that our people follow) and *the people* are loved (since they can receive no greater benefit than the grace to follow Christ).

So the command of the apostle Peter is to pursue joy in the ministry. It is not optional. It is not a mere unexpected result. It is a duty! To say that you are indifferent to what the apostle commands you to experience is to be indifferent to the will of God. And that is sin.

Phillips Brooks, an Episcopalian pastor in Boston a hundred years ago, caught the spirit of Peter's counsel to pastors:

I think, again, that it is essential to the preacher's success that he should thoroughly enjoy his work. I mean in the actual doing of it, and not only in its idea. No man to whom the details of his task are repulsive can do his task well constantly, however full he may be of its spirit. He may make one bold dash at it and carry it over all his disgusts, but he cannot work on at it year after year, day after day. Therefore, count it not merely a perfectly legitimate pleasure, count it an essential element of your power, if you can feel a simple delight in what you have to do as a minister, in the fervor of writing, in the glow of speaking, in standing before men and moving them, in contact with the young. The more thoroughly you enjoy it, the better you will do it all.

This is all true of preaching. Its highest joy is in the great ambition that is set before it, the glorifying of the Lord and saving of the souls of men. No other joy on earth compares with that. The ministry that does not feel that joy is dead. But in behind that highest joy, beating in humble unison with it, as the healthy body thrills in sympathy with the deep thoughts and pure desires of the mind and soul, the best ministers have always been conscious of another pleasure which belonged to the very doing of the work itself. As we read the lives of all the most effective preachers of the past, or as we meet the men who are powerful preachers of the Word today, we feel how certainly and how deeply the very exercise of their ministry delights them.[8]

LOVE IS NOT EASILY PLEASED

Can we not then say that the hindrance to loving other people, whether through the pastoral ministry or any other avenue of life, is the same as the hindrance to worship we discovered in chapter 3? The obstacle that keeps us from obeying the first (vertical) commandment is the same obstacle that keeps us from obeying the second (horizontal) commandment. It is *not* that we are all trying to

---

8. Phillips Brooks, *Lectures on Preaching* (Grand Rapids, Mich.: Baker, 1969, orig. 1907), 53–4, 82–3.

please ourselves, but that we are all far too easily pleased. We do not believe Jesus when He says there is more blessedness, more joy, more lasting pleasure in a life devoted to helping others than there is in a life devoted to our material comfort. And therefore, the very longing for contentment that ought to drive us to simplicity of life and labors of love contents itself instead with the broken cisterns of prosperity and comfort.

The message that needs to be shouted from the houses of high finance is this: Secular man, you are not nearly hedonistic enough!

"Do not lay up for yourselves treasures on earth, where moth and rust destroy and where thieves break in and steal, but lay up for yourselves treasures in heaven, where neither moth nor rust destroys and where thieves do not break in and steal." (Matthew 6:19–20)

Quit being satisfied with the little 5 percent yields of pleasure that get eaten up by the moths of inflation and the rust of death. Invest in the blue-chip, high-yield, divinely insured security of heaven. Devoting a life to material comforts and thrills is like throwing money down a rat hole. But investing a life in the labor of love yields dividends of joy unsurpassed and unending:

"Sell your possessions, and give to the needy. [And *thus*] provide yourselves with moneybags that do not grow old, with a treasure in the heavens that does not fail." (Luke 12:33)

This message is very good news: Come to Christ, in whose presence are fullness of joy and pleasures forevermore. Join us in the labor of Christian Hedonism. For the Lord has spoken: It is more blessed to love than to live in luxury!

LOVE SUFFERS FOR JOY

Love is costly. It always involves some kind of self-denial. It often demands suffering. But Christian Hedonism insists that the gain outweighs the pain. It affirms that there are rare and wonderful species of joy that flourish only in the rainy atmosphere of suffering. "The soul would have no rainbow if the eye had no tears."9

The costly joy of love is illustrated repeatedly in Hebrews 10–12. Consider three examples.

Hebrews 10:32–35

> But recall the former days when, after you were enlightened, you endured a hard struggle with sufferings, sometimes being publicly exposed to reproach and affliction, and sometimes being partners with those so treated. For you had compassion on those in prison, and you *joyfully* accepted the plundering of your property, since you knew that you yourselves had a better possession and an abiding one. Therefore do not throw away your confidence, which has a great reward.

Based on my limited experience with suffering, I would have no right in myself to say such a thing is possible—to accept *joyfully* the plundering of my property. But the authority of Christian Hedonism is not in me; it is in the Bible. I have no right in myself to say, "Rejoice insofar as you share Christ's sufferings" (1 Peter 4:13). But Peter does because he and the other apostles were beaten for the gospel and "left the presence of the council, *rejoicing* that they were counted worthy to suffer dishonor for the name" (Acts 5:41).

And the Christians in Hebrews 10:32–35 have earned the right to teach us about costly love. The situation appears to be this: In the early days of their conversion, some of them were imprisoned for the faith. The others were confronted with a difficult choice: Shall we go underground and stay "safe," or shall we visit our brothers and sisters in prison and risk our lives and property? They chose the way of love and accepted the cost. "For you had compassion on those in prison, and you joyfully accepted the plundering of your property."

But were they losers? No. They lost property and gained *joy!* They joyfully

---

9. A Minquass proverb. See Guy A. Zona, ed., *The Soul Would Have No Rainbow If the Eye Had No Tears: And Other Native American Proverbs* (New York: TouchStone, 1994).

accepted the loss. In one sense they denied themselves. But in another they did not. They chose the way of joy. Evidently, these Christians were motivated for prison ministry the same way the Macedonians (of 2 Corinthians 8:1–9) were motivated to relieve the poor. Their joy in God overflowed in love for others.

They looked at their own lives and said, "The steadfast love of the Lord is better than life" (see Psalm 63:3). They looked at all their possessions and said, "We have a possession in heaven that is better and lasts longer than any of this" (Hebrews 10:34). Then they looked at each other and said:

> Let goods and kindred go,
> This mortal life also;
> The body they may kill;
> God's truth abideth still,
> His kingdom is forever.
> *Martin Luther*

With *joy* they "renounced all they had" (Luke 14:33) and followed Christ into the prison to visit their brothers and sisters. Love is the overflow of joy in God that meets the needs of others.

Hebrews 11:24–26

To drive the point home, the author of Hebrews gives Moses as an example of this sort of Christian Hedonism. Notice how similar his motivation is to that of the early Christians in chapter 10:

> By faith Moses, when he was grown up, refused to be called the son of Pharaoh's daughter, choosing rather to be mistreated with the people of God than to enjoy the fleeting pleasures of sin. He considered the reproach of Christ greater wealth than the treasures of Egypt, for he [looked] to the reward.

In 10:34 the author said that the desire of the Christians for a better and lasting possession overflowed in joyful love, which cost them their property.

Here in chapter 11, Moses is a hero for the church because his delight in the promised reward overflowed in such joy that he counted the pleasures of Egypt rubbish by comparison and was bound forever to God's people in love.

There is nothing here about ultimate self-denial. He was given eyes to see that the pleasures of Egypt were "fleeting," not eternal. He was granted to see that suffering for the cause of the Messiah was "greater wealth than the treasures of Egypt." As he considered these things, he was constrained to give himself to the labor of Christian Hedonism—love. And he spent the rest of his days channeling the grace of God to the people of Israel. His joy in God overflowed in a lifetime of service to a recalcitrant and needy people. He chose the way of maximum joy, not the way of "fleeting pleasures."

Hebrews 12:1–2

We raised the question earlier whether the example of Jesus contradicts the principle of Christian Hedonism; namely, that love is the way of joy and that one should choose it for that very reason, lest one be found begrudging obedience to the Almighty or chafing under the privilege of being a channel of grace or belittling the promised reward. Hebrews 12:2 seems to say fairly clearly that Jesus did not contradict this principle:

> Therefore, since we are surrounded by so great a cloud of witnesses, let us lay aside every weight, and sin which clings so closely, and let us run with endurance the race that is set before us, looking to Jesus, the founder and perfecter of our faith, who *for the joy that was set before him* endured the cross, despising the shame, and is seated at the right hand of the throne of God.

The greatest labor of love that ever happened was possible because Jesus pursued the greatest imaginable joy, namely, the joy of being exalted to God's right hand in the assembly of a redeemed people: "For the joy that was set before him [He] endured the cross!"

Back in December of 1978, I was trying to explain some of these things to a college class. As usual, I found some of them quite skeptical. One of the more thoughtful wrote me a letter to express his disagreement. Since this is one of the most serious objections raised against Christian Hedonism, I think it will be helpful to others if I print Ronn's letter here and my response.

Dr. Piper:

I disagree with your position that love seeks or is motivated by its own pleasure. I suggest that all of your examples are true: You have cited many cases in which personal joy is increased and *may even* be the motivation for a person to love God or another human.

But you cannot establish a doctrine on the fact that some evidence supports it unless you can show that no evidence contradicts it.

Two examples of the second type:

Picture yourself in Gethsemane with Christ. He is about to perform the supreme act of love in all of history. Walking up to him, you decide to test your position on Christian Hedonism. Should not this supreme love bring great pleasure, abundant joy? Yet what is this you see? Christ is sweating terribly, in anguish, crying. Joy is nowhere to be found. Christ is praying. You hear him ask God if there is any way out. He tells God the upcoming act will be so hard, so painful. Can't there be a fun way?

Thank God that Christ chose the hard way.

My second example is not biblical, though there are many more of them. Are you familiar with Dorothy Day? She is a very old woman who has devoted her life to loving others, especially the poor, displaced, downtrodden. Her experience of loving when there was no joy has led her to say: "Love in action is a harsh and dreadful thing."

I could not agree more with her than I do.

I would like to know your response to these thoughts. In truth, I do feel this presentation is too simplistic. But it is sincere.

Ronn

I responded to Ronn the same week. Since then, Dorothy Day has died, but I will leave the references as they were back then. Incidentally, to this day I count Ronn a friend and a sharp thinker about the Christian worldview.

Ronn,

Thanks very much for your concern to have a fully biblical stance on this matter of Christian Hedonism—a stance which honors all the evidence. This is my concern, too. So I must ask whether your two examples (Christ in Gethsemane and Dorothy Day in painful service of love) contradict or confirm my position.

(1) Take Gethsemane first. For my thesis to stand I need to be able to show that in spite of the horror of the cross, Jesus' decision to accept it was motivated by his conviction that this way would bring him more joy than the way of disobedience. Hebrews 12:2 says, "For the joy that was set before him Christ endured the cross, despising the shame." In saying this, the writer means to give Jesus as another example, along with the saints of Hebrews 11, of those who are so eager for, and confident in, the joy God offers that they reject the "fleeting pleasures of sin" (11:25) and choose ill-treatment in order to be aligned with God's will. It is not unbiblical, therefore, to say that what sustained Christ in the dark hours of Gethsemane was the hope of joy beyond the cross.

This does not diminish the reality and greatness of his love for us, because the joy in which he hoped was the joy of leading many sons to glory (Hebrews 2:10). His joy is in *our* redemption, which redounds to *God's* glory. To abandon the cross and thus to abandon us and the Father's will was a prospect so horrible in Christ's mind that he repulsed it and embraced death.

But my essay on "Dissatisfied Contentment" [this is what Ronn was responding to; its content has been incorporated into this chapter] suggests even more: namely, that in some profound sense there must be joy in the very act of love, if it is to be pleasing to God.

You have shown clearly that if this is true in the case of Jesus' death, there must be a radical difference between joy and "fun." But we all know that there is.

It is not fair when you shift from saying there is no "fun way" in Gethsemane, to saying "Joy is nowhere to be found." I know that at those times in my life when I have chosen to do the most costly good deeds, I have (with and under the hurts) felt a very deep joy at doing good.

I think that when Jesus rose from his final prayer in Gethsemane with the resolve to die, there flowed through his soul a glorious sense of triumph over the night's temptation. Did he not say, "My food is to do the will of him who sent me and to accomplish his work" (John 4:34)? Jesus cherished his Father's will like we cherish food. To finish his Father's work was what he fed upon; to abandon it would be to choose starvation. I think there was joy in Gethsemane as Jesus was led away— not fun, not sensual pleasure, not laughter, in fact not anything that this world can offer. *But there was a good feeling deep in Jesus' heart that his action was pleasing to his Father, and that the reward to come would outweigh all the pain.* This profoundly good feeling is the joy that enabled Jesus to do for us what he did.

(2) You say of Dorothy Day: "Her experience of loving [the poor, displaced, downtrodden] when there was no joy has led her to say this: 'Love in action is a harsh and dreadful thing.'" I will try to respond in two ways.

First, don't jump to the conclusion that there is no joy in things that are "harsh and dreadful." There are mountain climbers who have spent sleepless nights on the faces of cliffs, have lost fingers and toes in sub-zero temperatures, and have gone through horrible misery to reach a peak. They say, "It was harsh and dreadful." But if you ask them why they do it, the answer will come back in various forms: "There is an exhilaration in the soul that feels so good it is worth all the pain."

If this is how it is with mountain climbing, cannot the same be true of love? Is it not rather an indictment of our own worldliness that we are more inclined to sense exhilaration at mountain climbing than at conquering the precipices of un-love in our own lives and in society? Yes, love is often a "harsh and dreadful" thing, but I do not see how a person who cherishes what is good and admires Jesus can help but sense a joyful exhilaration when (by grace) he is able to love another person.

Now let me approach Dorothy Day's situation in another way. Let's pretend that I am one of the poor that she is trying to help at great cost to herself. I think a conversation might go like this:

Piper: Why are you doing this for me, Miss Day?

Day: Because I love you.

Piper: What do you mean, you love me? I don't have anything to offer. I'm not worth loving.

Day: Perhaps. But there are no application forms for my love. I learned that from Jesus. What I mean is, I want to *help* you because Jesus has helped me so much.

Piper: So you are trying to satisfy your "wants"?

Day: I suppose so, if you want to put it like that. One of my deepest wants is to make you a happy and purposeful person.

Piper: Does it upset you that I *am* happier and that I feel more purposeful since you've come?

Day: Heavens, no! What could make me happier?

Piper: So you really spend all those sleepless nights here for what makes you happy, don't you?

Day: If I say yes, someone might misunderstand me. They might think I don't care for *you* at all, but only for myself.

Piper: But won't you say it at least for me?

Day: Yes, I'll say it for you: I work for what brings me the greatest joy: your joy.

Piper: Thank you. Now I know that you love me.

Love's Deed and Reward
Are Organically Related

One thing touched on briefly in this letter that might need some elaboration is the question concerning the relationship between the joy that comes in the actual deed of love and the joy that comes from the reward promised in the more distant future. The reason I think this question is important is that the motivation of receiving a future reward could turn love into a mercenary affair (as we have seen) if the hoped-for reward were not somehow organically related to the act one is doing to get the reward.

If the nature of the deed did not partake of the nature of the reward, you could do things you thought were stupid or evil to get the reward you considered wise or good. But it would be stretching the word *love* beyond biblical limits to say that one is loving when he does a thing he thinks is stupid or evil. A loving act (even if very painful) must be approved by our conscience.

So to say that it is right and good to be motivated by the hope of reward (as Moses and the early Christians and Jesus were, according to Hebrews 11:26 and 10:34 and 12:2) does not mean that this view to the future nullifies the need to choose acts that in their nature are organically related to the hoped-for reward.

What I mean by "organically related" is this: Any act of love we choose for the sake of a holy reward must compel us because we see in that act the moral traits of that promised reward. Or to put it the other way around, the only fitting reward for an act of love is the experience of divine glory whose moral dimension is what made the chosen act attractive.

The reward to which we look as Christian Hedonists for all the good we are commanded to do is distilled for us in Romans 8:29: "Those whom he foreknew he also predestined to be conformed to the image of his Son, in order that he might be the firstborn among many brothers." There are two goals of our predestination mentioned here: one highlighting *our* glory and one highlighting *Christ's*.

The first goal of our predestination is to be like Christ. This includes new resurrection bodies of glory like His (Philippians 3:21; 1 Corinthians 15:49).

But most importantly, it includes spiritual and moral qualities and capacities like Christ's (1 John 3:2–3).

The second and more ultimate goal of our predestination is "that Christ might be the firstborn among many brothers." In other words, God aims to surround His Son with living images of Himself so that the preeminent excellency of the original will shine the more brightly in His images. The goals of predestination are (1) our delight in becoming holy as He is holy and (2) His delight in being exalted as preeminent over all in the midst of a transformed, joyful people.

But if the reward we long for is to behold and be like the preeminent Christ, then it would be a contradiction if the actions we choose were not morally consistent with the character of Christ. If we really are being attracted by the reward of being made holy as He is holy, then we will be attracted to those acts that partake of His holiness. If we delight in the prospect of knowing Christ even as we are known, we will delight in the sorts of acts and attitudes that reflect His moral character.

So in true Christian Hedonism there is an organic relationship between the love Christ commands and the reward He promises. It is never a mercenary affair in which we do what we despise to get what we enjoy. Jesus illustrates this connection between act and reward in Luke 6:35:

> "Love your enemies, and do good, and lend, expecting nothing in return, *and your reward will be great,* and you will be sons of the Most High, for he is kind to the ungrateful and the evil."

Even though we should not care about human reward ("expecting nothing in return"), the Lord Himself gives us an incentive to love by promising His reward, namely, that we will be sons of the Most High. This sonship implies likeness ("for he is kind to the ungrateful"). So the command and the reward are one piece of fabric. The command is to love. The reward is to become like one who loves.

So it is important to emphasize, on the one hand, that the reward a Christian Hedonist pursues is the incomparable delight of being like God and loving what He loves with an intensity approaching His own (John 17:26). And it is important to emphasize, on the other hand, that the acts of love a Christian Hedonist performs are themselves therefore delightful in measure because they have about them the aroma of this final reward. This, as we saw, was also C. S. Lewis's point when he spoke of an activity's "proper rewards," which "are the activity in itself in consummation."

LOVE LONGS FOR THE POWER OF GRACE

One last question belongs to this chapter. I have defined love as the overflow of joy in God that meets the needs of others. It will be practically helpful in conclusion to ask how this actually works in experience. What is the psychological process that moves us from joy in God to the actual deed of love?

We start with a miracle; namely, that I, a sinner, should delight in God! Not just in His material rewards, but in Him, in all His manifold excellencies! This conversion experience, as we saw, is the "creation" of a Christian Hedonist. Now how does practical love emerge from this heart of joy in God?

When the object of our delight is moral beauty, the longing to *behold* is inseparable from the longing to *be*. When the Holy Spirit awakens the heart of a person to delight in the holiness of God, an insatiable desire is born not only to *behold* that holiness, but also to *be* holy as God is holy. Our joy is incomplete if we can only stand outside beholding the glory of God, but are not allowed to share it. It is one thing for a little boy to cheer in the grandstands at a football game. But his joy is complete if he can go home and get a team together and actually play the game.

We don't want to just *see* the grace of God in all its beauty, saving sinners and sanctifying saints. We want to share the power of that grace. We want to feel it saving.

We want to feel it conquer temptation in *our* lives. We want to feel it using *us* to save others. But why? Because our joy in God is insatiably hungry. The more we have, the more we want. The more we see, the more we want to see. The more we feel, the more we want to feel.

This means that the holy hunger for joy in God that wants to see and feel more and more manifestations of His glory will push a person into love. My desire to feel the power of God's grace conquering the pride and selfishness in my life inclines me to behavior that demonstrates the victory of grace, namely, love. Genuine love is so contrary to human nature that its presence bears witness to an extraordinary power. The Christian Hedonist pursues love because he is addicted to the experience of that power. He wants to feel more and more of the grace of God reigning in his life.

CONQUERING THE INTERNAL MOUNTAIN OF PRIDE

There is an analogy here to a powerful motive that exists in unbelieving hearts as well. Virtually all people outside Christ are possessed by the desire to find happiness by overcoming some limitation in their lives and having the sensation of power. Heinrich Harrer, a member of the first team to climb the north wall of the Eiger in the Swiss Alps, confessed that his reason for attempting such a climb was to overcome a sense of insecurity. "Self-confidence," he said, "is the most valuable gift a man can possess…but to possess this true confidence it is necessary to have learned to know oneself at moments when one was standing at the very frontier of things…. On the 'Spider' in the Eiger's North Face, I experienced such borderline situations, while the avalanches were roaring down over us, endlessly."[10]

The all-important difference between the non-Christian and the Christian Hedonist in this pursuit of joy is that the Christian Hedonist has discovered that self-confidence will never satisfy the longing of his heart to overcome finitude.

He has learned that what we are really made for is not the thrill of feeling our own power increase, but the thrill of feeling God's power increase, conquering the precipices of un-love in our sinful hearts.

As I said in the letter to my friend Ronn, it is an indictment of our own worldliness that we feel more exhilaration when we conquer an external mountain of granite in our own strength than when we conquer the internal mountain of pride in God's strength. The miracle of Christian Hedonism is that over-

---

10. Quoted in Daniel P. Fuller, *Hermeneutics* (Pasadena, Calif.: Fuller Theological Seminary, 1969), 7:4–5.

coming obstacles to love by the grace of God has become more enticing than every form of self-confidence. The joy of experiencing the power of God's grace defeating selfishness is an insatiable addiction.

JOY DOUBLED IN THE JOY OF ANOTHER

But there is another way of describing the psychological process that leads from delight in God to labors of love. When a person delights in the display of the glorious grace of God, that person will want to see as many displays of it as possible in other people. If I can be God's means of another person's miraculous conversion, I will count it all joy, because what would I rather see than another display of the beauty of God's grace in the joy of another person? My joy is doubled in his.

When the Christian Hedonist sees a person without hope or joy, that person's need becomes like a low-pressure zone approaching the high-pressure zone of joy in God's grace. In this spiritual atmosphere, a draft is created from the Christian Hedonist's high-pressure zone of joy to the low-pressure zone of need, as joy tends to expand to fill the need. That draft is called love.

Love is the overflow of joy in God that meets the needs of others. The overflow is experienced consciously as the pursuit of our joy in the joy of another. We double our delight in God as we expand it in the lives of others. If our ultimate goal were anything less than joy in God, we would be idolaters and no eternal help to anyone. Therefore, the pursuit of pleasure is an essential motive for every good deed. And if you aim to abandon the pursuit of full and lasting pleasure, you cannot love people or please God.

The precepts of the LORD *are right, rejoicing the heart.... More to be desired*
are they than gold, even much fine gold; sweeter also than honey
and drippings of the honeycomb. Moreover by them is your servant warned;
in keeping them there is great reward.

PSALM 19:8, 10–11

I saw more clearly than ever, that the first great and primary business
to which I ought to attend every day was, to have my soul happy in the Lord.
The first thing to be concerned about was not, how much I might serve
the Lord, how I might glorify the Lord; but how I might get my soul into
a happy state, and how my inner man may be nourished....
I saw that the most important thing I had to do was to give myself
to the reading of the Word of God and to meditation on it.

GEORGE MÜLLER OF BRISTOL

CHAPTER 5

SCRIPTURE

Kindling for Christian Hedonism

Christian Hedonism is much aware that every day with Jesus is *not* "sweeter than the day before." Some days with Jesus our disposition is sour. Some days with Jesus, we are so sad we feel our heart will break open. Some days with Jesus, we are so depressed and discouraged that between the garage and the house we just want to sit down on the grass and cry.

Every day with Jesus is not sweeter than the day before. We know it from experience and we know it from Scripture. For David says in Psalm 19:7, "The law of the LORD is perfect, *reviving* the soul." If every day with Jesus were sweeter than the day before, if life were a steady ascent with no dips in our affection for God, we wouldn't need to be *re*-vived.

In another place, David extolls the Lord with similar words: "He leads me beside still waters. He *restores* my soul" (Psalm 23:2–3). This means David must have had bad days.

There were days when his soul needed to be restored. It's the same phrase used in Psalm 19:7: "The law of the LORD is perfect, *reviving the soul.*" Normal Christian life is a repeated process of restoration and renewal. Our joy is not static. It fluctuates with real life. It is vulnerable to Satan's attacks.

When Paul says in 2 Corinthians 1:24, "Not that we lord it over your faith, but we work with you for your joy," we should emphasize it this way: "We *work* with you for your joy." The preservation of our joy in God takes *work*. It is a fight. Our adversary the devil prowls around like a roaring lion (1 Peter 5:8), and he has an insatiable appetite to destroy one thing: the joy of faith. But the Holy Spirit has given us a sword called the Word of God (Ephesians 6:17) for the defense of our joy.

Or, to change the image, when Satan huffs and puffs and tries to blow out the flame of our joy, we have an endless supply of kindling in the Word of God. Even on days when every cinder in our soul feels cold, if we crawl to the Word of God and cry out for ears to hear, the cold ashes will be lifted and the tiny spark of life will be fanned. For "the law of the LORD is perfect, *reviving* the soul." The Bible is the kindling of Christian Hedonism.

My aim in this chapter is to help you wear the sword of the Spirit, the Word of God, and wield it to preserve your joy in God. There are three steps we need to climb together:

First, we need to know why we accept the Bible as the reliable Word of God.

Second, we need to see the benefits and power of Scripture and how it kindles our joy.

Third, we need to hear a practical challenge to renew our daily meditation in the Word of God and to bind that sword so closely around our waist that we are never without it.

HOW TRUSTWORTHY IS THE BIBLE?

Almost everybody in the world would agree that if the one and true God has spoken, then people who ignore His Word can have no lasting happiness. But not everyone really believes that the Bible is the Word of the living God. Nor should someone believe it without sufficient reasons.

Some who read this book will share my persuasion that the Bible is the Word of God. They will want to get on with the use of it. Others will be struggling with whether to give the Bible such a powerful place in their lives. They may want to hear me give a reasonable account of my persuasion. I have spoken and written extensively on this topic, and much of this material is available online at www.desiringgod.org.[1] I encourage review of these resources and believe they will help many to stand confidently on the Scriptures as the very Word of God.

If our quest for lasting happiness is to succeed, we must seek it in relationship with our Creator. We can do that only by listening to His Word. This we have in the Bible. And the best news of all is that what God has said in His book is the kindling of Christian Hedonism.

THE BENEFITS AND POWER OF HOLY SCRIPTURE

In the Bible are many confirmations that its purpose is to kindle, and not kill, our joy. We find them when we set our sights on the benefits of Scripture, which sustain and deepen our true happiness.

The Bible Is Your Life

Moses says in Deuteronomy 32:46–47, "Take to heart all the words by which I am warning you today, that you may command them to your children, that they may be careful to do all the words of this law. For it is no empty word for you, but *your very life.*" The Word of God is not a trifle; it is a matter of life and death. If you treat the Scriptures as a trifle or as empty words, you forfeit life.

Even our physical life depends on God's Word, because by His Word we were created (Psalm 33:6; Hebrews 11:3) and "He upholds the universe by the word of his power" (Hebrews 1:3). Our spiritual life begins by the Word of God: "Of his own will he brought us forth by the word of truth" (James 1:18). "You have been born again…through the living and abiding word of God" (1 Peter 1:23).

Not only do we *begin* to live by God's Word, but we also *go on* living by God's Word: "Man shall not live by bread alone, but by every word that comes from the mouth of God" (Matthew 4:4; Deuteronomy 8:3). Our physical life is created and upheld by the Word of God, and our spiritual life is quickened and sustained by the Word of God.

---

1. One such resource is entitled "Why We Believe the Bible, Part 1," available in video, audio, and text formats at http://www.desiringgod.org/resource-library/seminars/why-we-believe-the-bible-part-1.

How many stories could be gathered to bear witness to the life-giving power of the Word of God! Consider the story of "Little Bilney, an early English Reformer born in 1495. He studied law and was outwardly rigorous in his efforts at religion. But there was no life within. Then he happened to receive a Latin translation of Erasmus's Greek New Testament. Here is what happened:

> I chanced upon this sentence of St. Paul (O most sweet and comfortable sentence to my soul!) in 1 Timothy 1: "It is a true saying, and worthy of all men to be embraced, that Christ Jesus came into the world to save sinners; of whom I am the chief and principal." This one sentence, through God's instruction and inward working, which I did not then perceive, did so exhilarate my heart, being before wounded with the guilt of my sins, and being almost in despair, that…immediately I…felt a marvelous comfort and quietness, in so much that "my bruised bones leaped for joy." After this, the Scriptures began to be more pleasant to me than the honey or the honeycomb.[1]

Indeed, the Bible is "no empty word for you"—it is your life! The foundation of all joy is life. Nothing is more fundamental than sheer existence—our creation and our preservation. All this is owing to the Word of God's power. By that same power, He has spoken in Scripture for the creation and sustenance of our spiritual life. Therefore, the Bible is no empty word, but is your very life—the kindling of your joy!

Faith Comes by Hearing

The Word of God begets and sustains spiritual *life* because it begets and sustains *faith:* "These are written," John says, "so that you may *believe* that Jesus is the Christ, the Son of God, and that by *believing* you may have *life* in his name" (John 20:31). "Faith comes from hearing," writes the apostle Paul, "and hearing

---

1. From a letter cited in Norman Anderson, *God's Word for God's World* (London: Hodder & Stoughton, 1981), 25.

through the word of Christ" (Romans 10:17). The faith that starts our life in Christ and by which we go on living comes from hearing the Word of God.

And there is no true joy without faith: "May the God of hope fill you with all joy and peace *in believing*" (Romans 15:13). "I know that I shall abide and continue with you all for your furtherance and *joy of faith*" (Philippians 1:25, KJV). How else can we sustain our joy in dark hours except by the promises of God's Word that He will work it all together for our good (Romans 8:28)?

A great testimony to the power of the Word to beget and sustain faith is found in the story of the conversion and execution of Tokichi Ichii—a man who was hanged for murder in Tokyo in 1918. He had been sent to prison more than twenty times and was known for being as cruel as a tiger. On one occasion, after attacking a prison official, he was gagged and bound, and his body was suspended in such a way that his toes barely reached the ground. But he stubbornly refused to say he was sorry for what he had done.

Just before being sentenced to death, Tokichi was sent a New Testament by two Christian missionaries, Miss West and Miss McDonald. After a visit from Miss West, he began to read the story of Jesus' trial and execution. His attention was riveted by the sentence "Jesus said, 'Father forgive them, for they know not what they do.'" This sentence transformed his life.

> I stopped: I was stabbed to the heart, as if by a five-inch nail. What did the verse reveal to me? Shall I call it the love of the heart of Christ? Shall I call it His compassion? I do not know what to call it. I only know that with an unspeakably grateful heart I believed.

Tokichi was sentenced to death and accepted it as "the fair, impartial judgment of God." Now the Word that had brought him to faith also sustained his faith in an amazing way. Near the end, Miss West directed him to the words of 2 Corinthians 6:8–10 concerning the suffering of the righteous. The words moved him very deeply, and he wrote:

"As sorrowing, yet always rejoicing." People will say that I must have a very sorrowful heart because I am daily awaiting the execution of the death sentence. This is not the case. I feel neither sorrow nor distress nor any pain. Locked up in a prison cell six feet by nine in size I am infinitely happier than I was in the days of my sinning when I did not know God. Day and night…I am talking with Jesus Christ.

"As poor, yet making many rich." This certainly does not apply to the evil life I led before I repented. But perhaps in the future, someone in the world may hear that the most desperate villain that ever lived repented of his sins and was saved by the power of Christ, and so may come to repent also. Then it may be that though I am poor myself, I shall be able to make many rich.

The Word sustained him to the end, and on the scaffold, with great humility and earnestness, he uttered his last words, "My soul, purified, today returns to the City of God."[2]

Faith is born and sustained by the Word of God, and out of faith grows the flower of joy.

God Supplies the Spirit Through the Hearing of Faith

We are commanded to be filled with the Holy Spirit: "Do not get drunk with wine, for that is debauchery, but be filled with the Spirit" (Ephesians 5:18). How does the Spirit come? In Galatians 3:2, Paul asks, "Did you receive the Spirit by works of the law or by hearing with faith?" The answer, of course, is "by hearing with faith." Hearing what? The Word of God!

The Spirit inspired the Word and therefore goes where the Word goes. The more of God's Word you know and love, the more of God's Spirit you will experience. Instead of being drunk on wine, we should be drunk on the Spirit. How? By setting our minds on the things of the Spirit: "Those who live according to the Spirit set their minds on the things of the Spirit" (Romans 8:5).

---

2. The story is recounted in Ibid., 38–41.

What are the things of the Spirit? When Paul said in 1 Corinthians 2:14, "The natural person does not accept the things of the Spirit," he was referring to his own Spirit-inspired teachings (2:13). Therefore, above all, the teachings of Scripture are the "things of the Spirit." We drink in the Spirit by setting our minds on the things of the Spirit, namely, the Word of God. And the fruit of the Spirit is joy (Galatians 5:22).

The Scriptures Give Hope

Sometimes faith and hope are virtual synonyms in Scripture: "Faith is the assurance of things *hoped* for" (Hebrews 11:1). Without this hope for the future, we get discouraged and depressed, and our joy drains away. Hope is absolutely essential to Christian joy: "We rejoice in our sufferings, knowing that suffering produces...hope" (Romans 5:3–4).

And how do we maintain hope? The psalmist puts it like this: "He established a testimony in Jacob and appointed a law in Israel, which he commanded our fathers to teach to their children...so that they should set their *hope* in God" (Psalm 78:5, 7). In other words, the "testimony" and the "law"—the Word of God—are kindling for the hope of our children.

Paul puts it so plainly: "Whatever was written in former days was written for our instruction, that through endurance and through the encouragement of the Scriptures we might have *hope*" (Romans 15:4). The whole Bible has this aim and this power: to create hope in the hearts of God's people. And when hope abounds, the heart is filled with joy.

The Truth Shall Make You Free

Another essential element of joy is freedom. None of us would be happy if we were not free from what we hate and free for what we love. And where do we find true freedom? Psalm 119:45 says, "I shall walk in freedom, for I sought your precepts" (author's translation). The picture is one of open spaces. The Word frees us from smallness of mind (1 Kings 4:29) and from threatening confinements (Psalm 18:19).

Jesus says, "You will know the truth, and the truth will set you *free*" (John

8:32). The freedom He has in mind is freedom from the slavery of sin (v. 34). Or, to put it positively, it is freedom for holiness. The promises of God's grace provide the power that makes the demands of God's holiness an experience of freedom rather than fear. Peter described the freeing power of God's promises like this: "Through [His precious and very great promises] you may become partakers of the divine nature, having escaped from the corruption that is in the world because of sinful desire" (2 Peter 1:4). In other words, when we trust the promises of God, we sever the root of corruption by the power of a superior promise.

Therefore we should pray for each other the way Jesus prays for us in John 17:17: "Sanctify them in the truth; your word is truth." There is no abiding joy without holiness, for the Scripture says, "Strive…for the holiness without which no one will see the Lord" (Hebrews 12:14). How important, then, is the truth that sanctifies! How crucial is the Word that breaks the power of counterfeit pleasures! And how vigilant we should be to light our paths and load our hearts with the Word of God! "Your word is a lamp to my feet and a light to my path" (Psalm 119:105). "I have stored up your word in my heart, that I might not sin against you" (v. 11; cf. v. 9).

The Testimony of the Lord Makes Wise the Simple

Of course, the Bible does not answer every question about life. Not every fork in the road has a biblical arrow. We need wisdom to know the path of lasting joy. But that, too, is a gift of Scripture: "The testimony of the LORD is sure, making *wise* the simple…. The commandment of the LORD is pure, *enlightening the eyes*" (Psalm 19:7–8; cf. 119:18). People whose minds are saturated with God's Word and submissive to His thoughts have a wisdom that in eternity will prove superior to all the secular wisdom in the world: "*Happy* is the man who finds wisdom, and the man who gets understanding" (Proverbs 3:13, RSV).

Written That You Might Have Assurance

Nevertheless, our perverted will and imperfect perceptions lead us time and again into foolish acts and harmful situations. The day this happens is not sweeter than the day before, and we need restoration and comfort. Where can we turn for comfort? We can follow the psalmist again: "This is my *comfort* in my affliction that thy *promise* gives me life.... When I think of thy ordinances from of old, I take comfort, O LORD" (Psalm 119:50, 52, RSV).

And when our failures and our afflictions threaten our assurance of faith, where do we turn to rebuild our confidence? John invites us to turn to the Word of God: "I *write* these things to you who believe in the name of the Son of God that you may *know* that you have eternal life" (1 John 5:13). The Bible is written to give us assurance of eternal life.

The Evil One Is Overcome by the Word of God

Satan's number-one objective is to destroy our joy of faith. We have one offensive weapon: the sword of the Spirit, the Word of God (Ephesians 6:17). But what many Christians fail to realize is that we can't draw the sword from someone else's scabbard. If we don't wear it, we can't wield it. If the Word of God does not abide in us (John 15:7), we will reach for it in vain when the enemy strikes. But if we do wear it, if it lives within us, what mighty warriors we can be! "I write to you, young men, because you are strong, and the word of God abides in you, and you have overcome the evil one" (1 John 2:14).

This has been the secret of God's great spiritual warriors. They have saturated themselves with the Word of God. Hudson Taylor, founder of the China Inland Mission, sustained himself through incredible hardships by a disciplined meditation on the Bible every day. Dr. and Mrs. Howard Taylor give us a glimpse of this discipline:

> It was not easy for Mr. Taylor in his changeful life, to make time for prayer and Bible study, but he knew that it was vital. Well do the writers remember traveling with him month after month in northern China, by cart and wheelbarrow with the poorest of inns at night. Often with only one large room for coolies and travelers alike, they would screen off a corner for their father and another for themselves, with curtains of some sort; and then, after sleep at last had brought a

measure of quiet, they would hear a match struck and see the flicker of candlelight which told that Mr. Taylor, however weary, was poring over the little Bible in two volumes always at hand. From two to four A.M. was the time he usually gave to prayer; the time he could be most sure of being undisturbed to wait upon God.[3]

The Sword of the Spirit is full of victory. But how few will give themselves to the deep and disciplined exercise of soul to take it up and wield it with joy and power!

An Earnest Exhortation

So the Bible is the Word of God. And the Word of God is no trifle. It is the source of life and faith and power and hope and freedom and wisdom and comfort and assurance and victory over our greatest enemy. Is it any wonder then that those who knew best said, "The precepts of the LORD are right, *rejoicing* the heart" (Psalm 19:8)? "I will *delight* in your statutes; I will not forget your word" (119:16). "Oh how I *love* your law! It is my meditation all the day" (v. 97). "Your testimonies are my heritage forever, for they are the *joy* of my heart" (v. 111). "Your words were found, and I ate them, and your words became to me a *joy* and the *delight* of my heart, for I am called by your name" (Jeremiah 15:16).

But are we to pursue this joy like Christian Hedonists? Are we to throw the kindling of God's Word every day on the fire of joy? Indeed, we are! Not only every day, but day and night: "Blessed is the man who walks not in the counsel of the wicked, nor stands in the way of sinners, nor sits in the seat of scoffers; but *his delight is in the law of the LORD, and on his law he meditates day and night"* (Psalm 1:1–2). This delight is the very design of our Lord in speaking to us: "These things I have *spoken* to you, *that my joy may be in you, and that your joy may be full"* (John 15:11). Not to pursue our joy every day in the Word of God is to abandon the revealed will of God. It is sin.

Oh, that we might not treat the Bible as a trifle! If we do, we oppose our-

---

3. Dr. and Mrs. Howard Taylor, *Hudson Taylor's Spiritual Secret* (Chicago: Moody, n. d., orig. 1932), 235.

selves and despise the saints who labored and suffered for the Word of God. Think of the courage of Martin Luther as he stood before the secular and ecclesiastical rulers of his day, who had the power to banish and even to execute him for his views of the Word of God. The Archbishop of Trier poses Luther the question one last time: "Do you or do you not repudiate yours books and the errors which they contain?"

Luther replies:

Since, then, Your Majesty and Your Lordships desire a simple reply, I will answer without horns and without teeth. Unless I am convicted by Scripture and plain reason—I do not accept the authority of popes and councils, for they have contradicted each other—my conscience is captive to the Word of God. I cannot and I will not recant anything, for to go against conscience is neither right nor safe. Here I stand, I cannot do otherwise. God help me.[4]

Luther disappeared abruptly after the edict of his condemnation was released. The great artist Albrecht Dürer reflected in his diary:

I know not whether he lives or is murdered, but in any case he has suffered for the Christian truth. If we lose this man, who has written more clearly than any other in centuries, may God grant his spirit to another.... O God, if Luther is dead, who will henceforth explain to us the gospel? What might he not have written for us in the next ten or twenty years?[5]

He was not dead. And he did keep writing—for another twenty-five years. And along with many other bold Reformers, he recovered for us the Word of God from the bondage of ecclesiastical tradition. Oh, that we might wield it the way they did! For them it was such a mighty sword against the enemy!

---

4. Quoted in Roland Bainton, *Here I Stand* (New York: Mentor, 1950), 144.
5. Ibid., 149.

Martin Luther knew as well as any man that *every* day with Jesus is *not* sweeter than the day before. And according to his biographer, Roland Bainton, he wrote these famous lines in the year of his deepest depression:

And though this world, with devils filled,
Should threaten to undo us,
We will not fear, for God has willed
His truth to triumph through us.
The prince of darkness grim,
We tremble not for him—
His rage we can endure,
For lo! His doom is sure:
One little word shall fell him.

To Wield It, We Must Wear It

But if we intend to wield it, we must wear it. We must be like Ezra: "The good hand of his God was on him. For *Ezra had set his heart to study the Law of the* LORD, and to do it and to teach his statues and rules in Israel" (Ezra 7:9–10). And we must get a heart like the saint who wrote the great love song to the law in Psalm 119: "Oh how I love your law! It is my meditation all the day" (v. 97). Let us labor to memorize the Word of God—for worship and for warfare. If we do not carry it in our heads, we cannot savor it in our hearts or wield it in the Spirit. If you go out without the kindling of Christian Hedonism, the fire of Christian happiness will be quenched before midmorning.

How George Müller Started His Day

I close this chapter with a testimony from a great man of prayer and faith. George Müller (1805–1898) is famous for establishing orphanages in England and for joyfully depending on God for all his needs. How did he kindle this joy and faith? In 1841 he made a life-changing discovery. The testimony of this from his autobiography has proved to be of tremendous value in my life, and I pray that it will also bear fruit in yours:

While I was staying at Nailsworth, it pleased the Lord to teach me a truth, irrespective of human instrumentality, as far as I know, the benefit of which I have not lost, though now…more than forty years have since passed away.

The point is this: I saw more clearly than ever, that the first great and primary business to which I ought to attend every day was, to have my soul happy in the Lord. The first thing to be concerned about was not, how much I might serve the Lord, how I might glorify the Lord; but how I might get my soul into a happy state, and how my inner man might be nourished. For I might seek to set the truth before the unconverted, I might seek to benefit believers, I might seek to relieve the distressed, I might in other ways seek to behave myself as it becomes a child of God in this world; and yet, not being happy in the Lord, and not being nourished and strengthened in my inner man day by day, all this might not be attended to in a right spirit.

Before this time my practice had been, at least for ten years previously, as an habitual thing, to give myself to prayer, after having dressed in the morning. *Now* I saw, that the most important thing I had to do was to give myself to the reading of the Word of God and to meditation on it, that thus my heart might be comforted, encouraged, warned, reproved, instructed; and that thus, whilst meditating, my heart might be brought into experimental, communion with the Lord. I began therefore, to meditate on the New Testament, from the beginning, early in the morning.

The first thing I did, after having asked in a few words the Lord's blessing upon His precious Word, was to begin to meditate on the Word of God; searching, as it were, into every verse, to get blessing out of it; not for the sake of the public ministry of the Word; not for the sake or preaching on what I had meditated upon; but for the sake of obtaining food for my own soul. The result I have found to be almost invariably this, that after a very few minutes my soul has been led to confession, or to thanksgiving, or to intercession, or to supplication; so that though I did not, as it were, give myself to *prayer*, but to *meditation*, yet it turned almost immediately more or less into prayer.

When thus I have been for awhile making confession, or intercession, or supplication, or have given thanks, I go on to the next words or verse, turning all, as I go on, into prayer for myself or others, as the Word may lead to it; but still continually keeping before me, that food for my own soul is the object of my meditation. The result of this is, that there is always a good deal of confession, thanksgiving, supplication, or intercession mingled with my meditation, and that my inner man almost invariably is even sensibly nourished and strengthened and that by breakfast time, with rare exceptions, I am in a peaceful if not happy state of heart. Thus also the Lord is pleased to communicate unto me that which, very soon after, I have found to become food for other believers, though it was not for the sake of the public ministry of the Word that I gave myself to meditation, but for the profit of my own inner man.

The difference between my former practice and my present one is this. Formerly, when I rose, I began to pray as soon as possible, and generally spent all my time till breakfast in prayer, or almost all the time. At all events I almost invariably began with prayer.... But what was the result? I often spent a quarter of an hour, or half an hour, or even an hour on my knees, before being conscious to myself of having derived comfort, encouragement, humbling of soul, etc.; and often after having suffered much from wandering of mind for the first ten minutes, or a quarter of an hour, or even half an hour, I only then began *really to pray*.

I scarcely ever suffer now in this way. For my heart being nourished by the truth, being brought into experimental fellowship with God, I speak to my Father, and to my Friend (vile though I am, and unworthy of it!) about the things that He has brought before me in His precious Word.

It often now astonished me that I did not sooner see this. In no book did I ever read about it. No public ministry ever brought the matter before me. No private intercourse with a brother stirred me up to this matter. And yet now, since God has taught me this point, it is as plain to me as anything, that the first thing the child of God has to do morning by morning is to *obtain food for his inner man.*

As the outward man is not fit for work for any length of time, except we take food, and as this is one of the first things we do in the morning, so it should be with the inner man. We should take food for that, as every one must allow. Now what is the food for the inner man: not *prayer,* but the *Word of God:* and here again not the simple reading of the Word of God, so that it only passes through our minds, just as water runs through a pipe, but considering what we read, pondering over it, and applying it to our hearts....

I dwell so particularly on this point because of the immense spiritual profit and refreshment I am conscious of having derived from it myself, and I affectionately and solemnly beseech all my fellow-believers to ponder this matter. By the blessing of God I ascribe to this mode the help and strength which I have had from God to pass in peace through deeper trials in various ways than I had ever had before; and after having now above forty years tried this way, I can most fully, in the fear of God, commend it. How different when the soul is refreshed and made happy early in the morning, from what is when, without spiritual preparation, the service, the trials and the temptations of the day come upon one![6]

---

6. *Autobiography of George Müller,* comp. Fred Bergen (London: J. Nisbet, 1906), 152–4.

"Until now you have asked nothing in my name.
Ask, and you will receive,
that your joy may be full."

JOHN 16:24

"But when you pray, go into your room and shut the door
and pray to your Father who is in secret.
And your Father who sees in secret will reward you."

MATTHEW 6:6

O what peace we often forfeit,
O what needless pain we bear,
All because we do not carry
Everything to God in prayer!

JOSEPH SCRIVEN

CHAPTER 6

PRAYER

The Power of Christian Hedonism

One common objection to Christian Hedonism is that it puts the interests of man above the glory of God—that it puts my happiness above God's honor. But Christian Hedonism most emphatically does *not* do this.

To be sure, we Christian Hedonists endeavor to pursue our interest and our happiness with all our might. We endorse the resolution of the young Jonathan Edwards: "Resolved: To endeavor to obtain for myself as much happiness in the other world as I possibly can, with all the power, might, vigor, and vehemence, yea violence, I am capable of, or can bring myself to exert, in any way that can be thought of."[1]

But we have learned from the Bible (and from Edwards!) that God's interest is to magnify the fullness of His glory by spilling over in mercy to us. Therefore, the pursuit of our interest and our happiness is never *above* God's, but always *in* God's. The most precious truth in the Bible is that God's greatest interest is to glorify the wealth of His grace by making sinners happy in Him—in *Him*!

When we humble ourselves like little children and put on no airs of self-sufficiency, but run happily into the joy of our Father's embrace, the glory of His

---

1. Edwards's resolutions have been published in a booklet: Stephen J. Nichols, *Jonathan Edwards' Resolutions, and Advice to Young Converts* (Phillipsburg, N.J.: Presbyterian & Reformed, 2002).

grace is magnified and the longing of our soul is satisfied. Our interest and His glory are one. Therefore, Christian Hedonists do not put their happiness above God's glory when they pursue happiness in *Him.*

WHY THE HEDONIST IS ON HIS KNEES

One piece of evidence that the pursuit of *our* joy and the pursuit of *God's* glory are meant to be one and the same is the teaching of Jesus on prayer in the Gospel of John. The two key sayings are in John 14:13 and 16:24. The one shows that prayer is the pursuit of God's glory. The other shows that prayer is the pursuit of our joy.

In John 14:13, Jesus says, "Whatever you ask in my name, this I will do, *that the Father may be glorified in the Son."* In John 16:24, He says, "Until now you have asked nothing in my name. Ask, and you will receive, *that your joy may be full."* The unity of these two goals—the glory of God and the joy of His children—is clearly preserved in the act of *prayer.* Therefore, Christian Hedonists will, above all, be people devoted to earnest prayer. Just as the thirsty deer kneels down to drink at the brook, so the characteristic posture of the Christian Hedonist is on his knees.

Let's look more closely at prayer as the pursuit of God's glory and the pursuit of our joy, in that order.

PRAYER AS THE PURSUIT OF GOD'S GLORY

Once again, hear Jesus' words in John 14:13: "Whatever you ask in my name, this I will do, *that the Father may be glorified in the Son."* Suppose you are totally paralyzed and can do nothing for yourself but talk. And suppose a strong and reliable friend promised to live with you and do whatever you needed done. How could you glorify your friend if a stranger came to see you? Would you glorify his generosity and strength by trying to get out of bed and carry him?

No! You would say, "Friend, please come lift me up, and would you put a pillow behind me so I can look at my guest? And would you please put my glasses on for me?" And so your visitor would learn from your requests that you are helpless and that your friend is strong and kind. You glorify your friend by needing him and asking him for help and counting on him.

In John 15:5 Jesus says, "I am the vine; you are the branches. Whoever abides in me and I in him, he it is that bears much fruit, for apart from me you can do nothing." So we really are paralyzed. Without Christ, we are capable of no good. As Paul says in Romans 7:18, "Nothing good dwells in me, that is, in my flesh."

But according to John 15:5, God intends for us to do something good— namely, bear fruit. So as our strong and reliable friend—"I have called you friends" (John 15:15)—He promises to do for us what we can't do for ourselves.

How then do we glorify Him? Jesus gives the answer in John 15:7: "If you abide in me, and my words abide in you, ask whatever you wish, and it will be done for you." We *pray!* We ask God to do for us through Christ what we can't do for ourselves—bear fruit. Verse 8 gives the result: "By this my Father is glorified, that you bear much fruit." So how is God glorified by prayer? Prayer is the open admission that without Christ we can do nothing. And prayer is the turning away from ourselves to God in the confidence that He will provide the help we need. Prayer humbles us as needy and exalts God as wealthy.

IF YOU KNEW HIM, YOU WOULD ASK!

In another text in John that shows how prayer glorifies God, Jesus asked a woman for a drink of water:

> The Samaritan woman said to him, "How is it that you, a Jew, ask for a drink from me, a woman of Samaria?" (For Jews have no dealings with Samaritans.) Jesus answered her, "If you knew the gift of God, and who it is that is saying to you, 'Give me a drink,' *you would have asked him, and he would have given you living water.*" (4:9–10)

If you were a sailor severely afflicted with scurvy, and a generous man came aboard ship with his pockets bulging with vitamin C and asked you for an orange slice, you might give it to him. But if you knew that he was generous and that he carried all you needed to be well, you would turn the tables and ask him for help.

Jesus says to the woman, "If you just knew the gift of God and who I am, you would ask Me—you would pray to Me!" There is a direct correlation between not knowing Jesus well and not asking much from Him. A failure in our prayer life is generally a failure to know Jesus. "If you knew who was talking to you, you would ask Me!" A prayerless Christian is like a bus driver trying alone to push his bus out of a rut because he doesn't know Clark Kent is on board. "If you knew, you would ask." A prayerless Christian is like having your room wallpapered with Saks Fifth Avenue gift certificates but always shopping at Goodwill because you can't read. "If you knew the gift of God and who it is that speaks to you, you would ask—*you would ask!*"

And the implication is that those who do ask—Christians who spend time in prayer—do it because they see that God is a great Giver and that Christ is wise and merciful and powerful beyond measure. And therefore their prayer glorifies Christ and honors His Father. The chief end of man is to glorify God. Therefore, when we become what God created us to be, we become people of prayer.

ROBINSON CRUSOE'S TEXT

Charles Spurgeon once preached a sermon on this very topic and called it "Robinson Crusoe's Text." He began like this:

> Robinson Crusoe has been wrecked. He is left on the desert island all alone. His case is a very pitiable one. He goes to his bed, and he is smitten with fever. This fever lasts upon him long, and he has no one to wait upon him—none even to bring him a drink of cold water. He is ready to perish. He had been accustomed to sin, and had all the vices of a sailor; but his hard case brought him to think. He opens a Bible which he finds in his chest, and he lights upon this passage, "Call upon me in the day of trouble: I will deliver thee, and thou shalt glorify me." That night he prayed for the first time in his life, and ever after there was in him a hope in God, which marked the birth of the heavenly life.[2]

---

2. Charles Spurgeon, *Twelve Sermons on Prayer* (Grand Rapids, Mich.: Baker, 1971), 105.

Robinson Crusoe's text was Psalm 50:15. It is God's way of getting glory for Himself—*Pray to Me! I will deliver you!* And the result will be that *you will glorify Me!*

Spurgeon's explanation is penetrating:

God and the praying man take shares.... First here is your share: "Call upon me in the day of trouble." Secondly, here is God's share: "I will deliver thee." Again, you take a share—for you shall be delivered. And then again it is the Lord's turn—"Thou shalt glorify me." Here is a compact, a covenant that God enters into with you who pray to him, and whom he helps. He says, "You shall have the deliverance, but I must have the glory...." Here is a delightful partnership: we obtain that which we so greatly need, and all that God getteth is the glory which is due unto his name.[3]

A delightful partnership indeed! Prayer is the very heart of Christian Hedonism. God gets the glory; we get the delight. He gets the glory precisely because He shows Himself full and strong to deliver us into joy. And we attain fullness of joy precisely because He is the all-glorious source and goal of life.

Here is a great discovery: We do not glorify God by providing His needs, but by praying that He would provide ours—and trusting Him to answer.

IS PRAYER SELF-CENTERED?

Someone may say that this is self-centered. But what does *self-centered* mean? If it means I passionately desire to be happy, then yes, prayer is self-centered.

But is this a bad thing, if what I cry for is that God's name be hallowed in my life? If my cry is for His reign to hold sway in my heart? If my cry is for His will to be done in my life as it is done by angels in heaven? If I crave the happiness of seeing and experiencing these things in my life, is that bad?

How is the will of God done in heaven? Sadly? Burdensomely? Begrudgingly?

---

3. Ibid., 115.

No! It is done gladly! If I then pray, *Thy will be done on earth as it is in heaven,* how can I not be motivated by a desire to be glad? It is a contradiction to pray for the will of God to be done in my life the way it is in heaven, and then to say that I am indifferent to whether I am glad or not. When the earth *rejoices* to do His will and does it perfectly, His will shall be done on earth as it is in heaven.

But surely we should not call this pursuit of happiness in prayer self-centered. It is radically God-centered. In my craving to be happy, I acknowledge that at the center of my life there is a gaping hole of emptiness without God. This hole constitutes my need and my rebellion at the same time. I want it filled, but I rebel at God's filling it with Himself. By grace I awake to the folly of my rebellion and see that if it is filled with God, my joy will be full. "Self-centered" is not a good way to describe this passion to be happy in God.

PRAYING LIKE AN ADULTERESS

But someone will say, "Yes, but not all prayers are prayers for God's name to be hallowed or for His kingdom to come. Many prayers are for food and clothing and protection and healing. Is this sort of praying not self-centered?"

It may be. James did condemn a certain kind of prayer. He said:

You ask and do not receive, because you ask wrongly, to spend it on your passions [literally: on your pleasures]. You adulterous people! Do you not know that friendship with the world is enmity with God? Therefore whoever wishes to be a friend of the world makes himself an enemy of God. Or do you suppose it is to no purpose that the Scripture says, "He yearns jealously over the spirit that he has made to dwell in us"? (James 4:3–5)

So there is a kind of praying that is wrong because it makes a cuckold out of God. We use our Husband's generosity to hire prostitutes for private pleasures. These are startling words. James calls us "adulterous people" if we pray like this.

He pictures the church as the wife of God. God has made us for Himself and has given Himself to us for our enjoyment. Therefore, it is adultery when we try to be "friends" with the world. If we seek from the world the pleasures we should seek in God, we are unfaithful to our marriage vows. And, what's worse, when we go to our heavenly Husband and actually pray for the resources with which to commit adultery with the world, it is a very wicked thing. It is as though we would ask our husband for money to hire male prostitutes to provide the pleasure we don't find in him!

So, yes, there is a kind of praying that is self-centered in an evil sense. Now the question becomes: What keeps all of our praying for "things" from being adulterous?

ENJOYING CREATION WITHOUT COMMITTING IDOLATRY

This is really part of a much larger question; namely, how is it possible for a creature to desire and enjoy the creation without committing idolatry (which is adultery)? This may seem like an irrelevant question to some. But for people who long to sing like the psalmists, it is very relevant. They sing like this:

Whom have I in heaven but you?
And there is nothing on earth that I desire besides you.
My flesh and my heart may fail,
But God is the strength of my heart and my portion forever.
(Psalm 73:25–26)

One thing have I asked of the LORD
that will I seek after:
that I may dwell in the house of the LORD,
all the days of my life,
to gaze upon the beauty of the LORD
and to inquire in his temple.
(Psalm 27:4)

If your heart longs to be this focused on God, then how to desire and enjoy "things" without becoming an idolater is a crucial question. How can prayer glorify God if it is a prayer for things? It seems to glorify things.

Of course, part of the answer was given in Robinson Crusoe's text, namely, that God gets glory as the all-sufficient Giver. But this is only part of the answer, because there can be a misuse of things even when we thank God as the Giver.

The rest of the answer is expressed by Thomas Traherne and Saint Augustine. Traherne said:

> You never Enjoy the World aright, till you see how a Sand Exhibiteth the Wisdom and Power of God: And Prize in every Thing the Service which they do you, by Manifesting His Glory and Goodness to your Soul, far more than the Visible Beauty on their Surface, or the Material Services, they can do your Body.[4]

And Augustine prayed the following words, which have proved immensely important in my effort to love God with *all* my heart:

> He loves Thee too little
> Who loves anything together with Thee,
> Which he loves not for Thy sake.[5]

In other words, if created things are seen and handled as gifts of God and as mirrors of His glory, they need not be occasions of idolatry—*if* our delight in them is always also a delight in their Maker.

C. S. Lewis put it like this in a "Letter to Malcolm":

> We can't—or I can't—hear the song of a bird simply as a sound. Its meaning or message ("That's a bird") comes with it inevitably—just as one

4. Thomas Traherne, *Centuries, Poems, and Thanksgivings* (London: Oxford University Press, 1958), 14.
5. Saint Augustine, *Confessions,* in *Documents of the Christian Church,* ed. Henry Bettenson (London: Oxford University Press, 1967), 54.

can't see a familiar word in print as a merely visual pattern. The reading is as involuntary as the seeing. When the wind roars I don't just hear the roar; I "hear the wind." In the same way it is possible to "read" as well as to "have" a pleasure. Or not even "as well as." The distinction ought to become, and sometimes is, impossible; to receive it and to recognize its divine source are a single experience. This heavenly fruit is instantly redolent of the orchard where it grew. This sweet air whispers of the country from whence it blows. It is a message. We know we are being touched by a finger of that right hand at which there are pleasures for evermore. There need be no question of thanks or praise as a separate event, something done afterwards. To experience the tiny theophany is itself to adore.[6]

If our experience of creation becomes an experience of the heavenly orchard, or the divine finger, then it may be worship, not idolatry. Lewis says it yet another way in his meditations on the Psalms:

By emptying Nature of divinity—or, let us say, of divinities—you may fill her with Deity, for she is now the bearer of messages. There is a sense in which Nature-worship silences her—as if a child or a savage were so impressed with the postman's uniform that he omitted to take in the letters.[7]

Therefore, it may or may not be idolatry to pray for the mailman to come. If we are only enamored by the short-term, worldly pleasures his uniform gives, it is idolatry. But if we consider the uniform a gracious bonus to the real delight of the divine messages, then it is not idolatry. If we pray for a spouse or job or physical healing or shelter for God's sake, then even here we are God-centered and not "self-centered." We are agreeing with the psalmist: "There is nothing on

6. C. S. Lewis, *Letters to Malcolm*, in *A Mind Awake: An Anthology of C. S. Lewis,* ed. Clyde Kilby (New York: Harcourt, Brace & World, 1968), 204.
7. C. S. Lewis, *Reflections on the Psalms* (New York: Harcourt, Brace and World, 1958), 82–3.

earth that I desire besides you"! That is, there is nothing I want more than You, and there is nothing I want that does not show me more of You.

GLORIFYING GOD NOT BY SERVING HIM, BUT BY BEING SERVED BY HIM

But now back to the main train of thought. I said a moment ago that Robinson Crusoe's text opened for us a great discovery. (And just then someone objected that all this is self-centered.) The discovery was that we do not glorify God by providing His needs, but by praying that He would provide ours—and trusting Him to answer. Here we are at the heart of the good news of Christian Hedonism.

God's insistence that we ask Him to give us help so that He gets glory (Psalm 50:15) forces on us the startling fact that we must *beware of serving God* and take special care to let Him serve us, lest we rob Him of His glory.

This sounds very strange. Most of us think serving God is a totally positive thing; we have not considered that serving God may be an insult to Him. But meditation on the meaning of prayer demands this consideration.

Acts 17:24–25 makes this plain:

The God who made the world and everything in it, being Lord of heaven and earth, does not live in temples made by man, nor is he served by human hands, as though he needed anything, since he himself gives to all mankind life and breath and everything.

This is the same reasoning as in Robinson Crusoe's text on prayer:

"If I were hungry, I would not tell you, for the world and its fullness are mine.... Call upon me in the day of trouble; I will deliver you, and you shall glorify me." (Psalm 50:12, 15)

Evidently, there is a way to serve God that would belittle Him as needy of our service. "The Son of Man came not to be served" (Mark 10:45). He aims to be the servant. He aims to get the glory as Giver.

STILL SERVANT AT THE SECOND COMING!

This is true, not just in the days of His earthly humiliation, but even in His glory at the close of the age. To me, the Bible's most astonishing image of Christ's second coming is in Luke 12:35–37, which pictures the return of a master from a marriage feast:

> "Stay dressed for action and keep your lamps burning, and be like men who are waiting for their master to come home from the wedding feast, so that they may open the door to him at once when he comes and knocks. Blessed are those servants whom the master finds awake when he comes. Truly, I say to you, he will dress himself for service and have them recline at table, and he will come and serve them."

HOW IS GOD DIFFERENT FROM ALL THE OTHER GODS?

To be sure, we are called servants—and that no doubt means we are to do exactly as we are told. But the wonder of this picture is that the "master" insists on "serving" even in the age to come when He appears in all His glory "with his mighty angels in flaming fire" (2 Thessalonians 1:7–8). Why? Because the very heart of His glory is the fullness of grace that overflows in kindness to needy people. Therefore, He aims "in the coming ages [to] show the immeasurable riches of his grace in kindness toward us in Christ Jesus" (Ephesians 2:7).

What is the greatness of our God? What is His uniqueness in the world? Isaiah answers:

> From of old no one has heard or perceived by the ear, no eye has seen a God besides thee, who works for those who wait for him. (Isaiah 64:4, RSV)

All the other so-called gods try to exalt themselves by making man work for them. In doing so, they only show their weakness. Isaiah derides the gods who need the service of their people:

Bel bows down; Nebo stoops; their idols are on beasts and livestock; these things you carry are borne as burdens on weary beasts. (46:1)

Jeremiah joins the derision:

Their idols are like scarecrows in a cucumber field, and they cannot speak; they have to be carried, for they cannot walk. (10:5)

God is unique: "For of old no one has heard or perceived by the ear..." And His uniqueness is that He aims to be the Workman for us, not vice versa. Our job is to "wait for Him."

God Works for Those Who Wait for Him

To wait! That means to pause and soberly consider our own inadequacy and the Lord's all-sufficiency and to seek counsel and help from the Lord and to hope in Him (Psalm 33:20–22; Isaiah 8:17). Israel is rebuked that "they did not wait for his counsel" (Psalm 106:13). Why? Because in not seeking and waiting for God's help, they robbed God of an occasion to glorify Himself.

For example, in Isaiah 30:15, 16 the Lord says to Israel, "In returning and rest you shall be saved; in quietness and in trust shall be your strength." But Israel refused to wait for the Lord and said, "No! We will flee upon horses."

Then in verse 18 the folly and evil of this self-initiated frenzy is revealed: "The LORD waits to be gracious to you, and therefore he exalts himself to show mercy to you. For the LORD is a God of justice; blessed are all those who wait for him." The folly of not waiting for God is that we forfeit the blessing of having God work for us. The evil of not waiting for God is that we oppose God's will to exalt Himself in mercy.

God aims to exalt Himself by working for those who wait for Him. Prayer is the essential activity of waiting for God—acknowledging our helplessness and His power, calling upon Him for help, seeking His counsel. Since His purpose in the world is to be exalted for His mercy, it is evident why prayer is so often commanded by God. Prayer is the antidote for the disease of self-confidence, which opposes God's goal of getting glory by working for those who wait for Him.

"The eyes of the LORD run to and fro throughout the whole earth, to give strong support to those whose heart is blameless toward him" (2 Chronicles 16:9). God is not looking for people to work for Him, so much as He is looking for people who will let Him work for them. The gospel is not a help-wanted ad. Neither is the call to Christian service. On the contrary, the gospel commands *us* to give up and hang out a help-wanted sign (this is the basic meaning of prayer). Then the gospel promises that God will work for us if we do. He will not surrender the glory of being the Giver.

But is there not anything we can give Him that won't belittle Him to the status of beneficiary? Yes—our anxieties. It's a command: "[Cast] all your anxieties on him" (1 Peter 5:7). God will gladly receive anything from us that shows our dependence and His all-sufficiency.

The Difference Between Uncle Sam and Jesus Christ

The difference between Uncle Sam and Jesus Christ is that Uncle Sam won't enlist you in his service unless you are healthy and Jesus won't enlist you unless you are sick: "Those who are well have no need of a physician, but those who are sick. I came not to call the righteous, but sinners" (Mark 2:17). Christianity is fundamentally convalescence ("Pray without ceasing" = Keep buzzing the nurse). Patients do not serve their physicians. They trust them for good prescriptions. The commands of the Bible are more like a doctor's health prescription than an employer's job description.

Therefore, our very lives hang on not working for God. "To one who works, his wages are not counted as a gift but as his due. And to the one who does not work but trusts him who justifies the ungodly, his faith is counted as righteousness" (Romans 4:4–5). Workmen get no gifts. They get their due. If we would have the gift of justification, we dare not work. God is the Workman in this affair. And what He gets is the trust of His client and the glory of being the benefactor of grace, not the beneficiary of service.

Nor should we think that after justification our labor for God's wages begins: "Did you receive the Spirit by works of the law, or by hearing with faith? Are you so foolish? Having begun by the Spirit, are you now being perfected by the flesh?" (Galatians 3:2–3). Working for wages only earns death. Trusting Jesus to work in you gets sanctification and its end, eternal life (Romans 6:22–23).

Religious "flesh" always wants to work for God (rather than humbling itself to realize that God must work for it in free grace). But "if you live according to the flesh you will die" (Romans 8:13). That is why our very lives hang on not working for God.

Then shall we not serve Christ? It is commanded: "Serve the Lord"! (Romans 12:11). Those who do not serve Christ are rebuked (16:18). Yes, we must serve Him. But we will beware of serving in a way that implies a deficiency on His part or exalts our indispensability.

SERVING GOD IS ALWAYS RECEIVING

How then shall we serve? Psalm 123:2 points the way: "Behold, as the eyes of servants look to the hand of their master, as the eyes of a maidservant to the hand of her mistress, so our eyes look to the LORD our God, till he has mercy upon us." The way to serve God so that He gets the glory is to look to Him for mercy. Prayer prevents service from being an expression of pride.

Any servant who tries to get off the divine dole and strike up a manly partnership with his heavenly Master is in revolt against the Creator. God does not barter. He gives the mercy of life to servants who will have it and the wages of death to those who won't. Good service is always and fundamentally receiving mercy, not rendering assistance. So there is no good service without prayer.

HOW DO YOU SERVE MONEY?

Matthew 6:24 gives another pointer toward good service: "No one can serve two masters, for either he will hate the one and love the other, or he will be devoted to the one and despise the other. You cannot *serve* God and money." How does a person serve money? He does not assist money. He does not enrich money. He is not the benefactor of money. How then do we serve money?

Money exerts a certain control over us because it seems to hold out so much promise of happiness. It whispers with great force, "Think and act so as to get into a position to enjoy my benefits." This may include stealing, borrowing, or working. Money promises happiness, and we serve it by believing the promise and walking by that faith. So we don't serve money by putting our power at its disposal for its good. We serve money by doing what is necessary so that money's power will be at our disposal for our good.

The same sort of service to God must be in view in Matthew 6:24, since Jesus put the two side by side: "You cannot serve God and money." So if we are going to serve God and not money, then we are going to have to open our eyes to the vastly superior promise of happiness God offers. Then God will exert a greater control over us than money does.

And so we will serve God by believing His promise of fullest joy and walking by that faith. We will not serve God by trying to put our power at His disposal for His good, but by doing what is necessary so that His power will be ever at our disposal for our good. And of course, God has appointed that His power be at our disposal through prayer: "Ask and you will receive"! So we serve by the power that comes through prayer when we serve for the glory of God.

Without doubt, this sort of serving also means obedience. That is what God works in us. "Work out your own salvation with fear and trembling, for it is God who works in you, both to will and to work for his good pleasure" (Philippians 2:12–13). "[T]he God of peace…[is] working in us that which is pleasing in his sight, through Jesus Christ" (Hebrews 13:20–21). In all our obedience, it is we who are the beneficiaries. God is ever the Giver. For it's the Giver who gets the glory.

THE GIVER GETS THE GLORY

First Peter 4:11 states the principle so well: "Whoever serves [must do so] as one who serves by the strength that God supplies—in order that in everything God may be glorified through Jesus Christ. To him belong glory and power forever and ever. Amen." The Giver gets the glory. So all serving that honors God must be a receiving. Which means that all service must be performed by prayer.

To be sure, let us work hard; but never let us forget that it is not we, but the grace of God that is with us (1 Corinthians 15:10). Let us obey now, as always, but never forget that it is God who works in us, both to will and to do His good pleasure (Philippians 2:13). Let us spread the gospel far and wide and spend ourselves for the sake of God's elect, but never venture to speak of anything except what Christ has wrought through us (Romans 15:18). Let us ever pray for His power and wisdom so that all our serving is the overflow of righteousness, joy, and peace from the Holy Spirit. "Whoever thus serves Christ is acceptable to God and approved by men" (Romans 14:18).

So the astonishing good news implied in the duty of prayer is that God will never give up the glory of being our Servant. "No eye has seen a God besides thee, who works for those who wait for him" (Isaiah 64:4, RSV).

PRAYER AS THE PURSUIT OF OUR JOY

Uniquely preserved in the act of prayer is the unity of two goals—the pursuit of God's glory and the pursuit of our joy. So far in this chapter, we have meditated on prayer as the pursuit of God's glory, with John 14:13 as our starting point: "Whatever you ask in my name, this I will do, that the Father may be glorified in the Son." Now we turn to Jesus' words in John 16:24: "Until now you have asked nothing in my name. Ask, and you will receive, *that your joy may be full.*"

Is this not a clear invitation to Christian Hedonism? Pursue the fullness of your joy! *Pray!*

From this sacred Word and from experience, we can draw a simple rule: Among professing Christians, prayerlessness produces joylessness. Why? Why is it that a deep life of prayer leads to fullness of joy, while a shallow life of prayerlessness produces joylessness? Jesus gives at least two reasons in the context of John 16:24.

PRAYER IS THE NERVE CENTER OF
FELLOWSHIP WITH JESUS

The first reason prayer leads to joy is given in John 16:20–22. Jesus alerts the disciples that they will grieve at His death, but then rejoice again at His resurrection:

"Truly, truly, I say to you, you will weep and lament, but the world will rejoice. You will be sorrowful, but your sorrow will turn into joy. When a woman is giving birth, she has sorrow because her hour has come, but when she has delivered the baby, she no longer remembers the anguish, for joy that a human being has been born into the world. So also you have sorrow now, but I will see you again and your hearts will rejoice."

Separation from Jesus means sadness. Restoration of fellowship means joy. Therefore, we learn that no Christian can have fullness of joy without a vital fellowship with Jesus Christ. Knowledge about Him will not do. Work for Him will not do. We must have personal, vital fellowship with Him; otherwise, Christianity becomes a joyless burden.

In his first letter, John wrote, "Our fellowship is with the Father and with his Son, Jesus Christ. And we are writing these things so that our joy may be complete" (1 John 1:3–4). Fellowship with Jesus shared with others is essential to fullness of joy.

The first reason, then, why prayer leads to fullness of joy is that prayer is the nerve center of our fellowship with Jesus. He is not here physically to see. But in prayer we speak to Him just as though He were. And in the stillness of those sacred times, we listen to His Word and we pour out to Him our longings.

Perhaps John 15:7 is the best summary of this two-sided fellowship of prayer: "If you abide in me, and my words abide in you, ask whatever you wish, and it will be done for you." When the biblical words of Jesus abide in our mind, we hear the very thoughts of the living Christ, for He is the same yesterday, today, and forever. And out of that deep listening of the heart comes the language of prayer, which is a sweet incense before God's throne. The life of prayer leads to fullness of joy because prayer is the nerve center of our vital fellowship with Jesus.

Jonathan Edwards gives us an account of his early years to illustrate the height and intensity to which this fellowship can rise:

I had vehement longing of soul after God and Christ, and after more holiness, wherewith my heart seemed to be full, and ready to break.... I spent most of my time in thinking of divine things, year after year; often walking alone in the words, and solitary places, for meditation, soliloquy, and prayer, and converse with God; and it was always my manner, at such times, to sing forth my contemplations. I was almost constantly in ejaculatory prayer, wherever I was. Prayer seemed to be natural to me, as the breath by which the inward burnings of my heart had vent.[8]

Prayer is God's appointed way to fullness of joy because it is the vent of the inward burnings of our heart for Christ. If we had no vent, if we could not commune with Him in response to His Word, we would be miserable indeed.

PRAYER EMPOWERS FOR THE MISSION OF LOVE

But there is a second reason prayer leads to joy's fullness: It provides the power to do what we love to do but can't do without God's help. The text says, "Ask, and you will receive, that your joy may be full." Receive what? What would bring us fullness of joy? Not a padded and protected and comfortable life. Rich people are as miserably unhappy as poor people. What we need in answer to prayer to fill our joy is the power to love. Or as John puts it, the power to bear fruit. Prayer is the fountain of joy because it is the source of power to love.

We see this twice in John 15. First in verses 7–8:

"If you abide in me, and my words abide in you, ask whatever you wish, and it will be done for you. By this my Father is glorified, that you bear much fruit."

The connection is clear between prayer and fruit-bearing. God promises to answer prayers for people who are pursuing fruit that abounds to His glory. Verses 16–17 point in the same direction:

---

8. Jonathan Edwards, "Personal Narrative," in *Jonathan Edwards: Representative Selections*, ed. C. H. Faust, T. H. Johnson (New York: Hill & Wang, 1962), 61.

"You did not choose me, but I chose you and appointed you that you should go and bear fruit and that your fruit should abide, so that whatever you ask the Father in my name, he may give it to you. These things I command you, so that you will love one another."

The logic here is crucial. Question: Why is the Father going to give the disciples what they ask in Jesus' name? Answer: Because they have been sent to bear fruit. The reason the Father gives the disciples the gift of prayer is because Jesus has given them a mission. In fact, the grammar of John 15:16 implies that the reason Jesus gives them their mission is so that they will be able to enjoy the power of prayer: "I send you to bear fruit...so that whatever you ask the Father...he may give you."

Isn't it plain that the purpose of prayer is to accomplish a mission? A mission of love: "This I command you, to love one another." It is as though the field commander (Jesus) called in the troops, gave them a crucial mission (go and bear fruit), handed each of them a personal transmitter coded to the frequency of the general's headquarters, and said, "Comrades, the General has a mission for you. He aims to see it accomplished. And to that end He has authorized Me to give each of you personal access to Him through these transmitters. If you stay true to His mission and seek His victory first, He will always be as close as your transmitter, to give tactical advice and to send in air cover when you need it."

CAN A WARTIME WALKIE-TALKIE
BE A DOMESTIC INTERCOM?

Could it be that many of our problems with prayer and much of our weakness in prayer come from the fact that we are not all on active duty, and yet we still try to use the transmitter? We have taken a wartime walkie-talkie and tried to turn it into a civilian intercom to call the servants for another cushion in the den.

There are other examples in Scripture of the wartime significance of prayer. In Luke 21:34–36, Jesus warned His disciples that times of great distress and opposition were coming. Then He said, "But stay awake at all times, praying that you may have strength to escape all these things that are going to take place, and to stand before the Son of man" (v. 36).

In other words, following Jesus will inevitably lead us into severe conflicts with evil. This evil will surround us and attack us and threaten to destroy our faith. So God has given us a transmitter. If we go to sleep, it will do us no good, but if we are alert and call for help in the conflict, the reinforcements will come, and the General will not let His faithful soldiers be denied their crown of victory before the Son of man.

Life is war. And "we do not wrestle against flesh and blood, but against the rulers, against the authorities, against the cosmic powers over this present darkness, against the spiritual forces of evil in the heavenly places." Therefore, Paul commands us to "take the helmet of salvation, and the sword of the Spirit, which is the word of God, praying at all times in the Spirit, *with all prayer* and supplication. To that end keep alert with all perseverance" (Ephesians 6:12, 17–18).

So we see repeatedly in Scripture that prayer is a walkie-talkie for warfare, not a domestic intercom for increasing our conveniences. The point of prayer is empowering for mission: "[Pray] for me, that words may be given to me in opening my mouth boldly to proclaim the mystery of the gospel" (Ephesians 6:19). "Pray also for us, that God may open to us a door for the word, to declare the mystery of Christ" (Colossians 4:3). "Strive together with me in your prayers to God on my behalf…that my service for Jerusalem may be acceptable to the saints" (Romans 15:30–31). "Pray for us, that the word of the Lord may speed ahead and be honored" (2 Thessalonians 3:1). "Pray earnestly to the Lord of the harvest to send out laborers into his harvest" (Matthew 9:38).

The fullness of joy we seek is the joy of overflowing love to other people. No amount of *getting* can satisfy the soul until it overflows in *giving*. And no sacrifice will destroy the soul-delights of an obedient people on a mission of love from God, for which prayer is His strategic provision. So the reason we pray is "that our joy may be full."

Fellowship with Jesus is essential to joy, but there is something about it that impels us outward, to share His life with others. A Christian can't be happy and stingy: "It is more blessed to give than to receive" (Acts 20:35). Therefore, the second reason a life of prayer leads to fullness of joy is that it gives us the power to love. If the pump of love runs dry, it is because the pipe of prayer isn't deep enough.

Love is the fruit of the Spirit (Galatians 5:22), and the Spirit is given in answer to prayer (Luke 11:13). Love is the outworking of faith (Galatians 5:6), and faith is sustained by prayer (Mark 9:24). Love is rooted in hope (Colossians 1:4–5), and hope is preserved by prayer (Ephesians 1:18). Love is guided and inspired by knowledge of the Word of God (Philippians 1:9; John 17:17), and prayer opens the eyes of the heart to the wonders of the Word (Psalm 119:18). If love is the path of fullest joy, then let us pray for the power to love "that our joy might be full"!

THE FINAL JOY OF GOD'S PEOPLE

What will be the final joy of God's people? Will it not be the day when the glory of the Lord fills the earth as the waters cover the sea? Will it not be the day when our mission is complete and the children of God are gathered in from every people and tongue and tribe and nation (John 11:52; Revelation 5:9; 7:9)— when all causes of sin and all evildoers are taken out of Christ's kingdom and the righteous shine like the sun in the kingdom of their Father (Matthew 13:42–43)?

And is not Frontier Missions[9] a road to that ultimate joy? And is not Frontier Missions quickened and carried by a movement of prayer? This was the conviction of the early church (Acts 1:14; 4:23–31; 7:4; 10:9; 12:5; 13:3; 14:23; and so on) and of the seventeenth-century Puritans[10] and of the eighteenth-century European Moravians[11] and American Evangelicals[12] and of the nineteenth-century student and laymen's movements.[13] It is also the deep conviction of mission leaders today.[14]

---

9. I use the term "Frontier Missions" to refer to those mission efforts that labor to break through a cultural barrier to plant the church in a people group for the first time, as distinct from mission efforts among those who already have a long established church, even though a person has crossed a culture to do it.
10. Iain H. Murray, *The Puritan Hope* (Edinburgh: Banner of Truth, 1971), 99–103.
11. Colin A. Grant, "Europe's Moravians: A Pioneer Missionary Church," in *Perspectives on the World Christian Movement*, 3rd ed., ed. Ralph Winter and Steven Hawthorne (Pasadena, Calif.: William Carey, 1999), 274–6.
12. Jonathan Edwards, *An Humble Attempt to Promote Explicit Agreement and Visible Union of God's People in Extraordinary Prayer for the Revival of Religion and the Advancement of Christ's Kingdom on Earth...*, in *Apocalyptic Writings*, ed. Stephen Stein (New Haven, Conn.: Yale University Press, 1977), 309–436.
13. David M. Howard, "Student Power in World Missions," in *Perspectives*, 277–86.
14. See especially David Bryant, *Concerts of Prayer* (Ventura, Calif.: Regal, 1984); idem, *Messengers of Hope: Becoming Agents of Revival for the 21st Century*, Dick Eastman, *The Hour that Changes the World* (Grand Rapids, Mich.: Baker, 1978); and Patrick Johnstone, *Operation World: When We Pray God Works* (Waynesboro, Ga.: Paternoster, 2001).

HOW A GREAT AWAKENING CAME

Rightly so. For history testifies to the power of prayer as the prelude to spiritual awakening and missions advance. One example from New York City history: Approaching the middle of the nineteenth century, the glow of earlier religious awakenings had faded. The city, like most of America, was prosperous and felt little need to call on God. Then came the late 1850s:

Secular and religious conditions combined to bring about a crash. The third great panic in American history swept away the giddy structure of speculative wealth. Thousands of merchants were forced to the wall as banks failed, and railroads went into bankruptcy. Factories were shut down and vast numbers thrown out of employment, New York City alone having 30,000 idle men. In October 1857, the hearts of the people were thoroughly weaned from speculation and uncertain gain, while hunger and despair stared them in the face.

On 1st July, 1857, a quiet and zealous businessman named Jeremiah Lanphier took up an appointment as a City Missionary in downtown New York. Lanphier was appointed by the North Church of the Dutch Reformed denomination. This church was suffering from depletion of membership due to the removal of the population from the downtown to the better residential headquarters, and the new City Missionary was engaged to make diligent visitation in the immediate neighborhood with a view to enlisting church attendance among the floating population of the lower city. The Dutch Consistory felt that it had appointed an ideal layman for the task in hand, and so it was.

Burdened so by the need, Jeremiah Lanphier decided to invite others to join him in a noonday prayer meeting, to be held on Wednesdays once a week. He therefore distributed a handbill:

How Often Shall We Pray?

*As often as the language of prayer is in my heart; as often as I
see my need of help; as often as I feel the power of temptation;
as often as I am made sensible of any spiritual declension or
feel the aggression of a worldly spirit.*

*In prayer we leave the business of time for that of eter-
nity, and intercourse with men for intercourse with God.*

*A day Prayer Meeting is held every Wednesday, from 12
to 1 o'clock, in the Consistory building in the rear of the
North Dutch Church, corner of Fulton and William Streets
(entrance from Fulton and Ann Streets).*

*The meeting is intended to give merchants, mechanics,
clerks, strangers, and businessmen generally an opportunity to
stop and call upon God and the perplexities incident to their
respective avocations. It will continue for one hour; but it is
also designed for those who may find it inconvenient to
remain more than five or ten minutes, as well as for those
who can spare the whole hour.*

Accordingly, at twelve noon, 23rd September, 1857 the door
opened and the faithful Lanphier took his seat to await the response to
his invitation.... Five minutes went by. No one appeared. The missionary paced the room in a conflict of fear and faith. Ten minutes elapsed.
Still no one came. Fifteen minutes passed.

Lanphier was yet alone. Twenty minutes; twenty-five; thirty; and then
at 12:30 a step was heard on the stairs, and the first person appeared, then
another, and another and another, until six people were present and the
prayer meeting began. On the following Wednesday...there were forty
intercessors.

Thus in the first week of October 1857, it was decided to hold a
meeting daily instead of weekly....

Within six months, ten thousand businessmen were gathering daily for prayer in New York, and within two years, a million converts were added to the American churches....

Undoubtedly the greatest revival in New York's colorful history was sweeping the city, and it was of such an order to make the whole nation curious. There was no fanaticism, no hysteria, simply an incredible movement of the people to pray.[15]

And the joy of Jeremiah Lanphier was very great. "Ask and you will receive, that your joy may be full."

SUMMARY AND EXHORTATION

The Bible plainly teaches that the goal of all we do should be to glorify God. But it also teaches that in all we do we should pursue the fullness of our joy. Some theologians have tried to force these two pursuits apart. But the Bible does not force us to choose between God's glory and our joy. In fact, it forbids us to choose. And what we have seen in this chapter is that prayer, perhaps more clearly than anything else, preserves the unity of these two pursuits.

Prayer pursues joy in fellowship with Jesus and in the power to share His life with others. And prayer pursues God's glory by treating Him as the inexhaustible reservoir of hope and help. In prayer we admit our poverty and God's prosperity, our bankruptcy and His bounty, our misery and His mercy. Therefore, prayer highly exalts and glorifies God precisely by pursuing everything we long for in Him, and not in ourselves. "Ask, and you will receive...that the Father may be glorified in the Son and...that your joy may be full."

I close this chapter with an earnest exhortation. Unless I'm badly mistaken, one of the main reasons so many of God's children don't have a significant life of prayer is not so much that we don't want to, but that we don't plan to. If you want to take a four-week vacation, you don't just get up one summer morning

---

15. J. Edwin Orr, *The Light of the Nations* (Grand Rapids, Mich.: Eerdmans, 1965), 103–5.

and say, "Hey, let's go today!" You won't have anything ready. You won't know where to go. Nothing has been planned.

But that is how many of us treat prayer. We get up day after day and realize that significant times of prayer should be a part of our life, but nothing's ever ready. We don't know where to go. Nothing has been planned. No time. No place. No procedure. And we all know that the opposite of planning is not a wonderful flow of deep, spontaneous experiences in prayer. The opposite of planning is the rut. If you don't plan a vacation, you will probably stay home and watch TV. The natural, unplanned flow of spiritual life sinks to the lowest ebb of vitality. There is a race to be run and a fight to be fought. If you want renewal in your life of prayer, you must *plan* to see it.

Therefore, my simple exhortation is this: Let us take time this very day to rethink our priorities and how prayer fits in. Make some new resolve. Try some new venture with God. Set a time. Set a place. Choose a portion of Scripture to guide you. Don't be tyrannized by the press of busy days. We all need midcourse corrections. Make this a day of turning to prayer—for the glory of God and for the fullness of your joy.

"Provide yourselves with moneybags that do not grow old."

Luke 12:33

"Make friends for yourselves by means of unrighteous wealth, so that when it fails they may receive you into the eternal dwellings."

Luke 16:9

CHAPTER 7

MONEY

The Currency of Christian Hedonism

M oney is the currency of Christian Hedonism. What you do with it—or desire to do with it—can make or break your happiness forever. The Bible makes clear that what you feel about money can destroy you:

> Those who desire to be rich fall into temptation, into a snare, into many senseless and harmful desires that plunge people into ruin and destruction. (1 Timothy 6:9)

Or what you do with your money can secure the foundation of eternal life:

> They are to do good, to be rich in good works, to be generous and ready to share, thus storing up treasure for themselves as a good foundation for the future, so that they may take hold of that which is truly life. (vv. 18–19)

These verses teach us to use our money in a way that will bring us the greatest and longest gain. That is, they advocate Christian Hedonism. They confirm that it is not only permitted, but commanded by God that we flee from destruction and pursue our full and lasting pleasure. They imply that all the evils in the world come not because our desires for happiness are too strong, but because they are so weak that we settle for fleeting pleasures that do not satisfy our deepest souls, but in the end destroy them. The root of all evil is that we are the kind of people who settle for the love of money instead of the love of God (1 Timothy 6:10).

BEWARE THE DESIRE TO BE RICH

This text in 1 Timothy 6 is so crucial that we should meditate on it in more detail. Paul is warning Timothy against false teachers:

> [They are] people who are depraved in mind and deprived of the truth, imagining that godliness is a means of gain. Now there is great gain in godliness with contentment, for we brought nothing into the world, and we cannot take anything out of the world. But if we have food and clothing, with these we will be content. But those who desire to be rich fall into temptation, into a snare, into many senseless and harmful desires that plunge people into ruin and destruction. For the love of money is the root of all evils. It is through this craving that some have wandered away from the faith and pierced themselves with many pangs. (vv. 5–10, author's translation)

Paul writes to Timothy a word of warning about slick deceivers who discovered they could cash in on the upsurge of godliness in Ephesus. According to verse 5, these puffed-up controversialists treat godliness as a means of gain. They are so addicted to the love of money that truth occupies a very subordinate place in their affections. They don't "rejoice in the truth." They rejoice in tax evasion. They are willing to use any new, popular interest to make a few bucks.

Nothing is sacred. If the bottom line is big and black, the advertising strategies are a matter of indifference. If godliness is in, then sell godliness.

This text is very timely. Ours are good days for profits in godliness. The godliness market is hot for booksellers and music makers and dispensers of silver crosses and fish buckles and olivewood letter openers and bumper stickers and lucky-water crosses with Jesus on the front and miracle water inside guaranteed to make you win at bingo or your money back in ninety days. These are good days for gain in godliness!

HE DIDN'T SAY, "DON'T LIVE FOR GAIN"

In his day or in ours, Paul could respond to this effort to turn godliness into gain by saying, "Christians don't live for gain. Christians do what's right for its own sake. Christians aren't motivated by profit." But that's *not* what Paul says. He says (in verse 6), "There is great gain in godliness with contentment."

Instead of saying Christians don't live for gain, he says Christians ought to live for greater gain than the slick money lovers do. Godliness is the way to get this great gain, but only if we are content with simplicity rather than greedy for riches. "Godliness *with contentment* is great gain."

If your godliness has freed you from the desire to be rich and has helped you be content with what you have, then your godliness is tremendously profitable: "For while bodily training is of some value, godliness is of value in every way, as it holds promise for the present life and also for the life to come" (1 Timothy 4:8). Godliness that overcomes the craving for material wealth produces great spiritual wealth. The point of 1 Timothy 6:6 is that it is very profitable not to pursue wealth.

What follows in verses 7–10 are three reasons why we should not pursue riches.

GETTING RAISES IS NOT THE SAME AS GETTING RICH

But first let me insert a clarification. We live in a society in which many legitimate businesses depend on large concentrations of capital. You can't build a new manufacturing plant without millions of dollars in equity. Therefore, financial officers in big businesses often have the responsibility to build reserves, for example, by selling shares to the community. When the Bible condemns the desire to get rich, it is not necessarily condemning a business that aims to expand and therefore seeks larger capital reserves. The officers of the business may be greedy for more personal wealth, or they may have larger, nobler motives of how their expanded productivity will benefit people.

Even when a competent person in business is offered a raise or a higher pay-ing job and accepts it, that is not enough to condemn him for the desire to be rich. He may have accepted the job because he craves the power and status and luxuries the money could bring. Or, content with what he has, he may intend to use the extra money for founding an adoption agency or giving a scholarship or sending a missionary or funding an inner-city ministry.

Working to earn money for the cause of Christ is not the same as desiring to be rich. What Paul is warning against is not the desire to earn money to meet our needs and the needs of others; he is warning against the desire to *have* more and more money and the ego boost and material luxuries it can provide.

THERE ARE NO U-HAULS BEHIND HEARSES

Let's look at the three reasons Paul gives in verses 7–10 for why we should not aspire to be rich.

1. In verse 7 he says, "For we brought nothing into the world, and we can-not take anything out of the world." There are no U-Hauls behind hearses.

Suppose someone passes empty-handed through the turnstile at a big-city art museum and begins to take the pictures off the wall and carry them impor-tantly under his arm. You come up to him and say, "What are you doing?"

He answers, "I'm becoming an art collector."

"But they're not really yours," you say, "and besides, they won't let you take any of those out of here. You'll have to go out just like you came in."

But he answers again, "Sure, they're mine. I've got them under my arm. People in the halls look at me as an important dealer. And I don't bother myself with thoughts about leaving. Don't be a killjoy."

We would call this man a fool! He is out of touch with reality. So is the person who spends himself to get rich in this life. We will go out just the way we came in.

Or picture 269 people entering eternity through a plane crash in the Sea of Japan. Before the crash, there are a noted politician, a millionaire corporate executive, a playboy and his playmate, and a missionary kid on the way back from visiting grandparents.

After the crash, they stand before God utterly stripped of Mastercards, checkbooks, credit lines, image clothes, how-to-succeed books, and Hilton reservations. Here are the politician, the executive, the playboy, and the missionary kid, all on level ground with nothing, absolutely nothing, in their hands, possessing only what they brought in their hearts. How absurd and tragic the lover of money will seem on that day—like a man who spends his whole life collecting train tickets and in the end is so weighed down by the collection that he misses the last train. Don't spend your precious life trying to get rich, Paul says, "for we brought nothing into the world, and we can take nothing out of the world."

SIMPLICITY IS POSSIBLE AND GOOD

2. Then in verse 8, Paul adds the second reason not to pursue wealth: "If we have food and clothing, with these we will be content." Christians can be and ought to be content with the simple necessities of life.

I'll mention three reasons why such simplicity is possible and good.

First, when you have God near you and for you, you don't need extra money or extra things to give you peace and security.

Keep your life free from love of money, and be content with what you have, for he has said, "I will never leave you nor forsake you." So we can confidently say, "The Lord is my helper; I will not fear; what can man do to me?" (Hebrews 13:5–6)

No matter which way the market is moving, God is always better than gold. Therefore, by God's help we can be, and we should be content, with the simple necessities of life.

Second, we can be content with simplicity because the deepest, most satisfying delights God gives us through creation are free gifts from nature and from loving relationships with people. After your basic needs are met, accumulated money begins to diminish your capacity for these pleasures rather than increase them. Buying things contributes absolutely nothing to the heart's capacity for joy.

There is a deep difference between the temporary thrill of a new toy and a homecoming hug from a devoted friend. Who do you think has the deepest, most satisfying joy in life, the man who pays $475 for a fortieth-floor suite downtown and spends his evenings in the half-lit, smoke-filled lounge impressing strange women with $10 cocktails, or the man who chooses the Motel 6 by a vacant lot of sunflowers and spends his evening watching the sunset and writing a love letter to his wife?

Third, we should be content with the simple necessities of life because we could invest the extra we make for what really counts. For example, the "Annual status of Global Mission 2010" reports that there are 2,026,696,000 unevangelized people in the world.[1] That means 29.3 percent of the world's population live in people groups that do not have indigenous evangelizing churches. This does not count the third of the world that does live in evangelized peoples but makes no profession of faith. If the unevangelized are to hear—and Christ commands that they hear—then crosscultural missionaries will have to be sent and paid for.

All the wealth needed to send this army of good news ambassadors is already in the church. And yet in 2007, the average Protestant gave 2.5 percent of his income to his church.[2]

According to the Status of Global Mission 2010[3]:

1. The total global church member annual income is *$28.8 trillion ($28,800 billion)*.
2. Of this, *$513 billion (1.73 percent)* is given to *Christian causes*.
3. Of this, *$29 billion (5.7 percent of the 1.73 percent)* goes to *Foreign Missions*.
4. Of this, *87 percent* goes for work among *those already Christian; 12 percent* goes for work among *already evangelized non-Christians, and one percent—$290 million*—goes to the unreached.

1. David B. Barrett and Todd M. Johnson, "Annual Statistical Table on Global Mission 2002," *International Bulletin of Missionary Research* 26 (January 2002):22–3.
2. See www.gordonconwell.edu/sites/default/files/IBMR2010.pdf.
3. See www.missionfrontiers.org/newslinks/statewe.html.

If we, like Paul, are content with the simple necessities of life, billions of dollars in the church would be released to take the gospel to the frontiers. The revolution of joy and freedom it would cause at home would be the best local witness imaginable. The biblical call is that you can and ought to be content with life's simple necessities.

HOW TO PIERCE YOURSELF WITH MANY PANGS

3. The third reason not to pursue wealth is that the pursuit will end in the destruction of your life. This is the point of verses 9 and 10:

> Those who desire to be rich fall into temptation and into a snare, and into many senseless and harmful desires that plunge people into ruin and destruction. For the love of money is the root of all evils. It is through this craving that some have wandered away from the faith and pierced themselves with many pangs. (author's translation)

No Christian Hedonist wants to plunge into ruin and destruction and be pierced with many pangs. Therefore, no Christian Hedonist desires to be rich.

Test yourself. Have you learned your attitude toward money from the Bible, or have you absorbed it from contemporary American merchandising? When you ride in an airplane and read the airline magazine, almost every page teaches and pushes a view of wealth exactly opposite from the view in 1 Timothy 6:9—that those desiring to be rich will fall into ruin and destruction. Paul makes vivid the peril of the same desire the airline magazines exploit and promote.

THE IMAGES OF WEALTH

I recall a full-page ad for a popular office chair that showed a man in a plush office. The ad's headline read, "His suits are custom tailored. His watch is solid gold. His office chair is _____." Below the man's picture was this quote:

I've worked hard and had my share of luck: my business is a success. I wanted my office to reflect this and I think it does. For my chair I chose a _____. It fits the image I wanted.... If you can't say this about your office chair, isn't it about time you sat in a _____? After all, haven't you been without one long enough?

The philosophy of wealth in those lines goes like this: If you've earned them, you would be foolish to deny yourself the images of wealth. If 1 Timothy 6:9 is true, and the desire to be rich brings us into Satan's trap and the destruction of hell, then this advertisement, which exploits and promotes that desire, is just as destructive as anything you might read in the sex ads of a big city daily.

Are you awake and free from the false messages of American merchandising? Or has the omnipresent economic lie so deceived you that the only sin you can imagine in relation to money is stealing? I believe in free speech and free enterprise because I have no faith whatsoever in the moral capacity of sinful civil government to improve upon the institutions created by sinful individuals. But, for God's sake, let us use our freedom as Christians to say *no* to the desire for riches and *yes* to the truth: There is great gain in godliness when we are content with the simple necessities of life.[4]

WHAT SHOULD THE RICH DO?

So far we have been pondering the words in 1 Timothy 6:6–10 addressed to people who are not rich but who may be tempted to want to be rich. In verses 17–19, Paul addresses a group in the church who are already rich. What should a rich person do with his money if he becomes a Christian? And what should a Christian do if God prospers his business so that great wealth is at his disposal? Paul answers like this:

> As for the rich in this present age, charge them not to be haughty, nor to set their hopes on the uncertainty of riches, but on God, who richly

---

4. For an explanation and qualification of what I mean by "the simple necessities of life," see the section later in this chapter entitled "Our Calling: A Wartime Lifestyle."

provides us with everything to enjoy. They are to do good, to be rich in good works, to be generous and ready to share, thus storing up treasure for themselves as a good foundation for the future, so that they may take hold of that which is truly life.

The words of verse 19 simply paraphrase Jesus' teaching. Jesus said:

"Do not lay up for yourselves treasures on earth, where moth and rust destroy and where thieves break in and steal, but lay up for yourselves treasures in heaven, where neither moth nor rust destroys and where thieves do not break in and steal. For where your treasure is, there your heart will be also." (Matthew 6:19–21)

Jesus is not against investment. He is against bad investment—namely, setting your heart on the comforts and securities that money can afford in this world. Money is to be invested for eternal yields in heaven: "Lay up for yourselves treasures in heaven!" How?

Luke 12:32–34 gives one answer:

"Fear not, little flock, for it is your Father's good pleasure to give you the kingdom. Sell your possessions, and give to the needy. Provide yourselves with moneybags that do not grow old, with a treasure in the heavens that does not fail, where no thief approaches and no moth destroys. For where your treasure is, there will your heart be also."

So the answer to how to lay up treasures in heaven is to spend your earthly treasures for merciful purposes in Christ's name here on earth. Give alms—that is, provide yourself with purses in heaven. Notice carefully that Jesus does not merely say that treasure in heaven will be the unexpected result of generosity on earth. No, He says we should *pursue* treasure in heaven. Lay it up! Provide yourselves with unfailing purses and treasures! This is pure Christian Hedonism.

YOU WILL BE REPAID AT THE RESURRECTION OF THE JUST

Another instance where Jesus tells us how to invest for eternal joy is Luke 14:13–14, where He is more specific about how to use our resources to lay up treasures in heaven: "When you give a reception, invite the poor, the crippled, the lame, the blind, and you will be blessed, since they do not have the means to repay you; for you will be repaid at the resurrection of the righteous" (NASB). This is virtually the same as saying, "Give to the needy; provide yourselves money-bags in heaven."

Don't seek the reward of an earthly tit for tat. Be generous. Don't pad your life with luxuries and comforts. Look to the resurrection and the great reward in God "in [whose] presence is fullness of joy; at [whose] right hand are pleasures forevermore" (Psalm 16:11).

BEWARE OF BEING WISER THAN THE BIBLE

Beware of commentators who divert attention from the plain meaning of these texts. What would you think, for example, of the following typical comment on Luke 14:13–14: "The promise of reward for this kind of life is there as a fact. You do not live this way for the sake of reward. If you do you are not living in this way but in the old selfish way."[5]

Is this true—that we are selfish and not loving if we are motivated by the promised reward? If so, why did Jesus entice us by mentioning the reward, even giving it as the basis ("for") of our action? And what would this commentator say concerning Luke 12:33, where we are not told that reward will result from our giving alms, but we are told to actively seek to get the reward—"provide yourselves with moneybags"?

And what would he say concerning the Parable of the Unrighteous Steward (Luke 16:1–13), where Jesus concludes, "Make friends for yourselves by means of unrighteous wealth, so that when it fails they may receive you into the eternal

---

5. T. W. Manson, *The Sayings of Jesus* (London: SCM, 1949), 280.

dwellings" (16:9)? The aim of this parable is to instruct the disciples in the right and loving use of worldly possessions. Jesus does not say that the result of such use is to receive eternal dwellings. He says to make it your aim to secure an eternal dwelling by the use of your possessions.

So it is simply wrong to say that Jesus does not want us to pursue the reward He promises. He commands us to pursue it (Luke 12:33; 16:9). More than forty times in the Gospel of Luke there are promises of reward and threats of punishment connected with the commands of Jesus.[6]

Of course, we must not seek the reward of earthly praise or material gain. This is clear not only from Luke 14:14, but also from Luke 6:35, "Love your enemies, and do good, and lend, expecting nothing in return, and *your reward will be great, and you will be sons of the Most High."* In other words, don't care about earthly reward; look to the heavenly reward—namely, the infinite joys of being a son of God!

Or, as Jesus put it in Matthew 6:3–4, don't care about human praise for your merciful acts. If that is your goal, that's all you will get, and it will be a pitiful reward compared to the reward of God. "When you give to the needy, do not let your left hand know what your right hand is doing, so that your giving may be in secret. And *your Father who sees in secret will reward you."*

LURING OTHERS TO THE REWARD
BY LOVING IT OURSELVES

The reason our generosity toward others is not a sham love when we are motivated by the longing for God's promise is that we are aiming to take those others with us into that reward. We know our joy in heaven will be greater if the people we treat with mercy are won over to the surpassing worth of Christ and join us in praising Him.

But how will we ever point them to Christ's infinite worth if we are not driven, in all we do, by the longing to have more of Him? It would only be unloving if we pursued our joy at the expense of others. But if our very pursuit

---

6. John Piper, *Love Your Enemies* (Cambridge: Cambridge University Press, 1979). I list and discuss these instances on pp. 163–5.

includes the pursuit of their joy, how is that selfish? How am I the less loving to you if my longing for God moves me to give away my earthly possessions so that my joy in Him can be forever doubled in your partnership of praise?

LAYING UP FOR YOURSELF A GOOD FOUNDATION

Paul's teaching to the rich in 1 Timothy 6:19 continues and applies these teachings of Jesus from the Gospels. He says rich people should use their money in such a way that they are "storing up treasure for themselves as a good foundation for the future, so that they may take hold of that which is truly life." In other words, there is a way to use your money that forfeits eternal life.[7]

We know Paul has eternal life in view because seven verses earlier he uses the same kind of expression in reference to eternal life: "Fight the good fight of the faith. Take hold of the eternal life to which you were called and about which you made the good confession in the presence of many witnesses" (1 Timothy 6:12).

The reason the use of your money provides a good foundation for eternal life is not that generosity earns eternal life, but that it shows where your heart is. Generosity confirms that our hope is in God, and not in ourselves or our money. We don't earn eternal life. It is a gift of grace (2 Timothy 1:9). We receive it by resting in God's promise. Then how we use our money confirms or denies the reality of that rest.

PRIDE OF POSSESSIONS

Paul gives three directions to the rich about how to use their money to confirm their eternal future.

First, don't let your money produce pride: "As for the rich in this present age, charge them not to be haughty" (1 Timothy 6:17). How deceptive our hearts are when it comes to money! Every one of us has felt the smug sense of

---

7. This does not contradict the biblical doctrine of the eternal security of God's chosen people who are truly born again, a doctrine firmly established by Romans 8:30. But it does imply that there is a change of heart if we have been born of God, and this includes evidences in the way we use our money. Jesus warned repeatedly of the false confidence that bears no fruit and will forfeit life in the end (Matthew 7:15–27; 13:47–50; 22:11–14). For more on eternal security and perseverance of the saints, see Wayne Grudem, *Systematic Theology: An Introduction to Biblical Doctrine* (Grand Rapids, Mich.: Zondervan, 1994), 788–809.

superiority that creeps in after a clever investment or a new purchase or a big deposit. Money's chief attractions are the power it gives and the pride it feeds. Paul says, Don't let this happen.

Why It Is hard for the Rich to Inherit Life

Second, he adds in verse 17, don't set your "hopes on the uncertainty of riches, but on God, who richly provides us with everything to enjoy." This is not easy for the rich to do. That's why Jesus said it is hard for a rich man to enter the kingdom of God (Mark 10:23). It is hard to look at all the earthly hope that riches offer and then turn away from that to God and rest all your hope on Him. It is hard not to love the gift instead of the Giver. But this is the only hope for the rich. If they can't do it, they are lost.

They must remember the warning Moses gave the people of Israel as they entered the Promised Land:

Beware lest you say in your heart, "My power and the might of my hand have gotten me this wealth." You shall remember the LORD your God, for it is he who gives you power to get wealth, that he may confirm his covenant that he swore to your fathers, as it is this day. (Deuteronomy 8:17–18)

The great danger of riches is that our affections will be carried away from God to His gifts.

Is This a Health-Wealth-and-Prosperity Teaching?

Before moving on to Paul's third exhortation for the rich, we must consider a common abuse of verse 17. The verse says that "God...richly provides us with everything to enjoy." This means, first, that God is usually generous in the provision He makes to meet our needs. He furnishes things "richly." Second, it means we need not feel guilty for enjoying the things He gives us. They are given "for enjoyment." Fasting, celibacy, and other forms of self-denial are right and good in the service of God, but they must not be elevated as the spiritual norm. The provisions of nature are given for our good and, by our Godward joy, can become occasions of thanksgiving and worship (1 Timothy 4:2–5).

But a wealth-and-prosperity doctrine is afoot today, shaped by the half-truth that says, "We glorify God with our money by enjoying thankfully all the things He enables us to buy. Why should a son of the King live like a pauper?" And so on. The true half of this is that we should give thanks for every good thing God enables us to have. That does glorify Him. The false half is the subtle implication that God can be glorified in this way by all kinds of luxurious purchases.[8]

If this were true, Jesus would not have said, "Sell your possessions, and give to the needy" (Luke 12:33). He would not have said, "Do not seek what you are to eat and what you are to drink" (Luke 12:29). John the Baptist would not have said, "Whoever has two tunics is to share with him who has none" (Luke 3:11). The Son of Man would not have walked around with no place to lay his head (Luke 9:58). And Zacchaeus would not have given half his goods to the poor (Luke 19:8).

God is not glorified when we keep for ourselves (no matter how thankfully) what we ought to be using to alleviate the misery of unevangelized, uneducated, unmedicated, and unfed millions. The evidence that many professional Christians have been deceived by this doctrine is how little they give and how much they own. God *has* prospered them. And by an almost irresistible law of consumer culture (baptized by a doctrine of health, wealth, and prosperity), they have bought bigger (and more) houses, newer (and more) cars, fancier (and more) clothes, better (and more) meat, and all manner of trinkets and gadgets and containers and devices and equipment to make life more fun.

WHY GOD PROSPERS MANY SAINTS

They will object: Does not the Old Testament promise that God will prosper His people? Indeed! God increases our yield so that by giving we can prove that

---

8. See *Let the Nations Be Glad,* 3rd ed., 2010, 19–32 for a critique of the prosperity gospel and twelve challenges to prosperity preachers.

our yield is not our god. God does not prosper a man's business so he can move from a Ford to a Cadillac. God prospers a business so that thousands of unreached peoples can be reached with the gospel. He prospers a business so that 20 percent of the world's population can move a step back from the precipice of starvation.

I am a pastor, not an economist. Therefore, I see my role today the way James Stewart saw his in Scotland thirty years ago.

> It is the function of economists, not the pulpit, to work out plans of reconstruction. But it is emphatically the function of the pulpit to stab men broad awake to the terrible pity of Jesus, to expose their hearts to the constraint of that divine compassion which halos the oppressed and the suffering, and flames in judgment against every social wrong.... There is no room for a preaching devoid of ethical directness and social passion, in a day when heaven's trumpets sound and the Son of God goes forth to war.[9]

OUR CALLING: A WARTIME LIFESTYLE

The mention of "war" is not merely rhetorical. What is specifically called for today is a "wartime lifestyle." I used the phrase "simple necessities of life" earlier in this chapter because Paul said in 1 Timothy 6:8, "If we have food and clothing, with these we will be content." But this idea of simplicity can be very misleading. I mean it to refer to a style of life that is unencumbered with nonessentials—and the criterion for "essential" should not be primitive "simplicity," but wartime effectiveness.

Ralph Winter illustrates this idea of a wartime lifestyle:

> The Queen Mary, lying in repose in the harbor at Long Beach, California, is a fascinating museum of the past. Used both as a luxury

---

9. James Stewart, *Heralds of God* (Grand Rapids, Mich.: Baker, 1972), 97.

liner in peacetime and a troop transport during the Second World War, its present status as a museum the length of three football fields affords a stunning contrast between the lifestyles appropriate in peace and war. On one side of a partition you see the dining room reconstructed to depict the peacetime table setting that was appropriate to the wealthy patrons of high culture for whom a dazzling array of knives and forks and spoons held no mysteries. On the other side of the partition the evidences of wartime austerities are in sharp contrast. One metal tray with indentations replaces fifteen plates and saucers. Bunks, not just double but eight tiers high, explain why the peace-time complement of 3000 gave way to 15,000 people on board in wartime. How repugnant to the peacetime masters this transformation must have been! To do it took a national emergency, of course. The survival of a nation depended on it. The essence of the Great Commission today is that the survival of many millions of people depends on its fulfillment.[10]

There is a war going on. All talk of a Christian's right to live luxuriantly "as a child of the King" in this atmosphere sounds hollow—especially since the King Himself is stripped for battle. It is more helpful to think of a wartime lifestyle than a merely simple lifestyle. Simplicity can be very inwardly directed and may benefit no one else. A wartime lifestyle implies that there is a great and worthy cause for which to spend and be spent (2 Corinthians 12:15).

Winter continues:

America today is a "save yourself" society if there ever was one. But does it really work? The underdeveloped societies suffer from one set of diseases: tuberculosis, malnutrition, pneumonia, parasites, typhoid, cholera, typhus, etc. Affluent America has virtually invented a whole new set of diseases: obesity, arteriosclerosis, heart disease, strokes, lung

---

10. Ralph Winter, "Reconsecration to a Wartime, Not a Peacetime, Lifestyle," in *Perspectives on the World Christian Movement*, 3rd ed., ed. Ralph Winter and Steven Hawthorne (Pasadena, Calif.: William Carey, 1999), 705.

cancer, venereal disease, cirrhosis of the liver, drug addiction, alcoholism, divorce, battered children, suicide, murder. Take your choice. Labor-saving machines have turned out to be body-killing devices. Our affluence has allowed both mobility and isolation of the nuclear family, and as a result, our divorce courts, our prisons and our mental institutions are flooded. In saving ourselves we have nearly lost ourselves.

How hard have we tried to save others? Consider the fact that the U.S. evangelical slogan, "Pray, give or go" allows people merely to pray, if that is their choice! By contrast the Friends Missionary Prayer Band of South India numbers 8,000 people in their prayer bands and supports 80 full-time missionaries in North India. If my denomination (with its unbelievably greater wealth per person) were to do that well, we would not be sending 500 missionaries, but 26,000. In spite of their true poverty, those poor people in South India are sending 50 times as many cross-cultural missionaries as we are![11]

The point here is to show that those who encourage Christians to pursue a luxuriant peacetime lifestyle are missing the point of all Jesus taught about money. He called us to lose our lives in order that we might gain them again (and the context is indeed money): "What does it profit a man to gain the whole world and forfeit his life?" (Mark 8:36). And the way He means for us to lose our lives is in fulfilling the mission of love He gave us.

BE RICH IN GOOD DEEDS

Which leads us to the final admonition Paul makes to the rich: "They are to do good, to be rich in good works, to be generous and ready to share" (1 Timothy 6:18). Once they are liberated from the magnet of pride and once their hope is set on God, not money, only one thing can happen: Their money will flow freely to multiply the manifold ministries of Christ.

---

11. Ibid., 706.

WHAT ABOUT THE LAKE HOME?

So what does a pastor say to his people concerning the purchase and ownership of two homes in a world where thirty-five thousand children starve to death every day and mission agencies cannot evangelize more unreached people for lack of funds? First, he may quote Amos 3:15: "I will strike the winter house along with the summer house, and the houses of ivory shall perish, and the great houses shall come to an end." Then he may read Luke 3:11, "Whoever has two tunics is to share with him who has none."

Then he might tell about the family in St. Petersburg, Florida, who caught a vision for the housing needs of the poor. They sold their second home in Ohio and used the funds to build houses for several families in Immokalee, Florida.

Then he will ask, "Is it wrong to own a second home that sits empty part of the year?" And he will answer, "Maybe and maybe not." He will not make it easy by creating a law. Laws can be obeyed under constraint with no change of heart; prophets want new hearts for God, not just new real estate arrangements. He will empathize with their uncertainty and share his own struggle to discover the way of love. He will not presume to have a simple answer to every lifestyle question.

But he will help them decide. He will say, "Does your house signify or encourage a level of luxury enjoyed in heedless unconcern of the needs of others? Or is it a simple, oft-used retreat for needed rest and prayer and meditation that sends people back to the city with a passion to deny themselves for the evangelization of the unreached and the pursuit of justice?"

He will leave the arrow lodged in their conscience and challenge them to seek a lifestyle in sync with the teaching and life of the Lord Jesus.

WHY HAS GOD GIVEN US SO MUCH?

In Ephesians 4:28, Paul says, "Let the thief no longer steal, but rather let him labor, doing honest work with his own hands, so that he may have something to share with anyone in need." In other words, there are three levels of how to live with things: (1) you can steal to get; (2) or you can work to get; (3) or you can work to get in order to give.

Too many professing Christians live on level two. Almost all the forces of our culture urge them to live on level two. But the Bible pushes us relentlessly to level three. "God is able to make all grace abound to you, so that having all sufficiency in all things at all times, you may abound in every good work" (2 Corinthians 9:8). Why does God bless us with abundance? So we can have enough to live on, and then use the rest for all manner of good works that alleviate spiritual and physical misery. Enough for us; abundance for others.

The issue is not how much a person makes. Big industry and big salaries are a fact of our times, and they are not necessarily evil. The evil is in being deceived into thinking a six-digit salary must be accompanied by a six-digit lifestyle. God has made us to be conduits of His grace. The danger is in thinking the conduit should be lined with gold. It shouldn't. Copper will do.

LIVING ON THE BRINK OF ETERNITY

Our final summary emphasis should be this: In 1 Timothy 6, Paul's purpose is to help us lay hold of eternal life and not lose it. Paul never dabbles in unessentials. He lives on the brink of eternity. That's why he sees things so clearly. He stands there like God's gatekeeper and treats us like reasonable Christian Hedonists: You want life that is life indeed, don't you (v. 19)? You don't want ruin, destruction, and pangs of heart, do you (vv. 9–10)? You want all the gain that godliness can bring, don't you (v. 6)? Then use the currency of Christian Hedonism wisely: Do not desire to be rich, be content with the wartime necessities of life, set your hope fully on God, guard yourself from pride, and let your joy in God overflow in a wealth of liberality to a lost and needy world.

He who loves his wife loves himself.

<small>EPHESIANS 5:28</small>

An excellent wife who can find?
She is far more precious than jewels.

<small>PROVERBS 31:10</small>

MARRIAGE

A Matrix for Christian Hedonism

The reason there is so much misery in marriage is not that husbands and wives seek their own pleasure, but that they do not seek it in the pleasure of their spouses. The biblical mandate to husbands and wives is to seek your own joy in the joy of your spouse. Make marriage a matrix for Christian Hedonism.

TO MAKE A WIFE OF SPLENDOR

There is scarcely a more hedonistic passage in the Bible than the one on marriage in Ephesians 5:25–30:

> Husbands, love your wives, as Christ loved the church and gave himself up for her, that he might sanctify her, having cleansed her by the washing of water with the word, so that he might present the church to himself in splendor, without spot or wrinkle or any such thing, that she might be holy and without blemish. In the same way husbands should love their wives as their own bodies. He who loves his wife loves himself. For no one ever hated his own flesh, but nourishes and cherishes it, just as Christ does the church, because we are members of his body.

Husbands are told to love their wives the way Christ loved the church. How did He love the church? "He gave himself up for her." But why? "That he might sanctify and cleanse her." But why did He want to do that? "That he might present the church to himself in splendor"!

Ah! There it is! "For the joy that was set before him [He] endured the cross" (Hebrews 12:2). What joy? The joy of marriage to His bride, the church. Jesus does not want a dirty and unholy wife. Therefore, He was willing to die to "sanctify and cleanse" His betrothed so He could present to Himself a wife "in splendor."

Pursuing Joy in the Joy of the Beloved

And what is the church's ultimate joy? Is it not to be cleansed and sanctified, and then presented as a bride to the sovereign, all-glorious Christ? So Christ sought His own joy, yes—but He sought it in the joy of the church! That is what love is: the pursuit of our own joy in the joy of the beloved.

In Ephesians 5:29–30, Paul pushes the hedonism of Christ even further: "No one ever hated his own flesh, but nourishes and cherishes it, just as Christ does the church, because we are members of his body." Why does Christ nourish and cherish the church? Because we are members of His own body, and no man ever hates his own body. In other words, the union between Christ and His bride is so close ("one flesh") that any good done to her is a good done to Himself. The blatant assertion of this text is that this fact motivates the Lord to nourish, cherish, sanctify, and cleanse His bride.

By some definitions, this cannot be love. Love, they say, must be free of self-interest—especially Christlike love, especially Calvary love. I have never seen such a view of love made to square with this passage of Scripture. Yet what Christ does for His bride, this text plainly calls love: "Husbands, love your wives, as Christ loved the church...." Why not let the text define love for us, instead of bringing our definition from ethics or philosophy?

According to this text, love is the pursuit of our joy in the holy joy of the beloved. There is no way to exclude self-interest from love, for self-interest is not the same as selfishness. Selfishness seeks its own private happiness at the expense of others. Love seeks its happiness in the happiness of the beloved. It will even suffer and die for the beloved in order that its joy might be full in the life and purity of the beloved.

BUT DID NOT JESUS SAY, "HATE YOUR LIFE"?

When Paul says, "No one ever hated his own flesh, but nourishes and cherishes it," and then uses Christ Himself as an example, is he contradicting John 12:25, where Jesus says, "Whoever loves his life loses it, and whoever hates his life in this world will keep it for eternal life"? No! There is no contradiction. On the contrary, the agreement is remarkable.

The key phrase is "in this world": He who hates his life in this world will keep it for eternal life. This is not an ultimate hating, because by doing it, you keep your life forever. So there is a kind of hating of life that is good and necessary, and this is not what Paul denies when he says no one hates his life. This kind of hating is a means to saving and is therefore a kind of love. That's why Jesus has to limit the hating He commends with the words *in this world.* If you take the future world into view, it can't be called hating anymore. Hating life in this world is what Jesus did when He "gave himself for the church." But He did it for the joy set before Him. He did it that He might present His bride to Himself in splendor. Hating His own life was the deepest love for His own life—and for the church!

Nor is Paul's word here a contradiction of Revelation 12:11: "And they have conquered him by the blood of the Lamb and by the word of their testimony, for *they loved not their lives even unto death.*" They were willing to be killed for Jesus, but by hating their lives in this way, they "conquered" Satan and gained the glory of heaven: "Be faithful unto death, and I will give you the crown of life" (Revelation 2:10). This "not loving life unto death" was indeed a loving of life beyond death.

EVERYONE SEEKS HAPPINESS

No man in this world ever hates his own flesh in the ultimate sense of choosing what he is sure will produce the greater misery. This has been the conclusion of many great knowers of the human heart. Blaise Pascal put it like this:

All men seek happiness. This is without exception. Whatever different means they employ, they all tend to this end. The cause of some going to war, and of others avoiding it, is the same desire in both, attended with different views. The will never takes the least step but to this object. This is the motive of every action of every man, even of those who hang themselves.[1]

Jonathan Edwards tied it to the Word of Christ:

Jesus knew that all mankind were in the pursuit of happiness. He has directed them in the true way to it, and He tells them what they must become in order to be blessed and happy.[2]

Edward Carnell generalizes the point:

The Christian ethic, let us remember, is premised on the self's love for the self. Nothing motivates us unless it appeals to our interests.[3]

Karl Barth, in his typically effusive manner, writes for pages on this truth. Here is an excerpt:

The will for life is the will for joy, delight, happiness.... In every real man the will for life is also the will for joy. In everything he wills, he wills and intends also that this, too, exist for him in some form. He strives for different things with the spoken or unspoken, but very definite, if unconscious, intention of securing for himself this joy.... It is hypocrisy to hide this from oneself. And the hypocrisy would be at the expense of the ethical truth that he should will to enjoy himself, just as he should will to eat, drink, sleep, be healthy, work, stand for what is

1. Blaise Pascal, *Pascal's Pensees,* trans. W. F. Trotter (New York: E. P. Dutton, 1958), 113, thought #425.
2. Jonathan Edwards, *The Works of Jonathan Edwards,* vol. 2 (Edinburgh: Banner of Truth, 1974), 905. The quote is found in a sermon on Matthew 5:8 entitled "Blessed Are the Pure in Heart."
3. E. J. Carnell, *Christian Commitment* (New York: Macmillan, 1957), 96.

right and live in fellowship with God and his neighbor. A person who tries to debar himself from this joy is certainly not an obedient person.[4]

For a husband to be an obedient person, he must love his wife the way Christ loved the church. That is, he must pursue his own joy in the holy joy of his wife.

In the same way husbands should love their wives as their own bodies. He who loves his wife loves himself. (Ephesians 5:28)

This is clearly Paul's paraphrase of Jesus' command, which he took from Leviticus 19:18: "You shall love your neighbor as yourself" (Matthew 22:39). The popular misconception is that this command teaches us to learn to esteem ourselves so we can love others. This is not what the command means.[5] Jesus does not command us to love ourselves. He assumes that we do. That is, He assumes, as Edwards said, that we all pursue our own happiness; then He makes the measure of our innate self-love the measure of our duty to love others. "As you love yourself, so love others."

Paul now applies this to marriage. He sees it illustrated in Christ's relationship to the church. And he sees it illustrated in the fact that husbands and wives become "one flesh" (v. 31). "Husbands should love their wives as their own bodies. He who loves his wife loves himself" (v. 28). In other words, husbands should devote the same energy and time and creativity to making their wives happy that they devote naturally to making themselves happy. The result will be that in doing this, they will make themselves happy. For he who loves his wife loves himself. Since the wife is one flesh with her husband, the same applies to her love for him.

Paul does not build a dam against the river of hedonism; he builds a channel for it. He says, "Husbands and wives, recognize that in marriage you have

4. Karl Barth, *The Doctrine of Creation*, Church Dogmatics, vol. 3, 4, trans. A. T. Makay, et. al. (Edinburgh: T. & T. Clark, 1961), 375.
5. See my article "What Does It Mean to Love Your Neighbor as Yourself?" in *Christianity Today* (12 August 1977): 6–9, also available online at http://desiringgod.org/dg/id227_m.htm.

become one flesh. If you live for your private pleasure at the expense of your spouse, you are living against yourself and destroying your joy. But if you devote yourself with all your heart to the holy joy of your spouse, you will also be living for your joy and making a marriage after the image of Christ and His church."

THE PATTERN FOR CHRISTIAN HEDONISM IN MARRIAGE

Now what does this love between husband and wife look like? Does Paul teach a pattern for married love in this text?

Ephesians 5:31 is a quotation of Genesis 2:24: "Therefore a man shall leave his father and his mother and hold fast to his wife, and they shall become one flesh." Paul adds in verse 32: "This mystery is profound, and I am saying that it refers to Christ and the church." Why does he call Genesis 2:24 a "profound mystery"?

Before we answer, let's go back to the Old Testament context and see more clearly what Genesis 2:24 meant.

THE OLD TESTAMENT CONTEXT

According to Genesis 2, God created Adam first and put him in the garden alone. Then the Lord said, "It is not good that the man should be alone; I will make him a helper fit for him" (18). This is not necessarily an indictment of Adam's fellowship with God or proof that care for the garden was too hard for one person. Rather, the point is that God made man to be a sharer. God created us not to be cul-de-sacs of His bounty, but conduits. No man is complete unless he is conducting grace (like electricity) between God and another person. (No person who is single should conclude that this can happen only in marriage![6])

It must be another person, not an animal. So in Genesis 2:19–20, God paraded the animals before Adam to show him that animals would never do as a "helper fit for him." Animals help plenty, but only a person can be a fellow heir

---

6. See John Piper, *For Single Men and Women (and the Rest of Us)* (Louisville, Ky.: Council of Biblical Manhood & Womanhood, 1992); available online at http://www.cbmw.org/Online-Books/Recovering-Biblical-Manhood-and-Womanhood/for-Single-Men-and-Women-and-the-Rest-of-Us.

of the grace of life (1 Peter 3:7). Only a person can receive and appreciate and enjoy grace. What a man needs is another person with whom he can share the love of God. Animals will never do! There is an infinite difference between sharing the northern lights with your beloved and sharing them with your dog.

Therefore, according to verse 21–22, "The LORD God caused a deep sleep to fall upon the man, and while he slept took one of his ribs and closed up its place with flesh. And the rib that the LORD God had taken from the man he made into a woman and brought her to the man." Having shown the man that no animal would do for his helper, God made another human from man's own flesh and bone to be like him—and yet very unlike him. He did not create another male. He created a female. And Adam recognized in her the perfect counterpart to himself—utterly different from the animals: "This at last is bone of my bones and flesh of my flesh; she shall be called Woman, because she was taken out of Man" (Genesis 2:23).

By creating a person *like* Adam, yet very *unlike* Adam, God provided the possibility of a profound unity that otherwise would have been impossible. A different kind of unity is enjoyed by the joining of diverse counterparts than is enjoyed by joining two things just alike. When we all sing the same melody line, it is called unison, which means "one sound." But when we unite diverse lines of soprano and alto and tenor and bass, we call it harmony; and everyone who has an ear to hear knows that something deeper in us is touched by great harmony than by mere unison. So God made a woman, and not another man. He created heterosexuality, not homosexuality.[7]

Notice the connection between verses 23 and 24, signaled by the word *therefore* in verse 24:

Then the man said, "This at last is bone of my bones and flesh of my flesh; she shall be called Woman, because she was taken out of Man." Therefore a man shall leave his father and his mother and hold fast to his wife, and they shall become one flesh.

7. See http://desiringgod.org/resource-library/topic-index/homosexuality.

In verse 23 the focus is on two things: objectively, the fact that woman is part of man's flesh and bone; and subjectively, the joy Adam has in being presented with the woman. *"At last,* this is bone of my bones and flesh of my flesh"! From these two things the writer draws an inference about marriage in verse 24: "Therefore a man shall leave his father and his mother and hold fast to his wife, and they shall become one flesh."

In other words, in the beginning God took woman out of man as bone of his bone and flesh of his flesh, and then God presented her back to the man to discover in living fellowship what it means to be one flesh. Verse 24 draws out the lesson that marriage is just that: a man leaving father and mother because God has given him another; a man holding fast to this woman alone and no other; and a man discovering the experience of being one flesh with this woman.

THE GREAT MYSTERY OF MARRIAGE

Paul looks at this and calls it a "profound mystery." Why?

He had learned from Jesus that the church is Christ's body (Ephesians 1:23). By faith a person is joined to Jesus Christ. Thus, a person becomes one with all believers so that we "are all one in Christ Jesus" (Galatians 3:28). Believers in Christ are the body of Christ. We are the organism through which He manifests His life and in which His Spirit dwells.

Knowing this about the relationship between Christ and the church, Paul sees a parallel with marriage. He sees that husband and wife become one flesh and that Christ and the church become one body. So in 2 Corinthians 11:2, for example, he says to the church, "I feel a divine jealousy for you, for I betrothed you to one husband to present you as a pure virgin to Christ." He pictures Christ as the husband, the church as the bride, and conversion as an act of betrothal that Paul had helped bring about. The bride's presentation to her husband probably will happen at the Lord's second coming, referred to in Ephesians 5:27 ("that he might present the church to himself in splendor").

It looks as though Paul uses the relationship of human marriage, learned from Genesis 2, to describe and explain the relationship between Christ and the church. But if that were the case, *marriage* would not be a mystery, as Paul calls it in

Ephesians 5:32; it would be the clear and obvious thing that explains the mystery of Christ and the church. So there is more to marriage than meets the eye. What is it?

The mystery is this: God did not create the union of Christ and the church after the pattern of human marriage—just the reverse! He created human marriage on the pattern of Christ's relation to the church.

The mystery of Genesis 2:24 is that the marriage it describes is a parable or symbol of Christ's relation to His people. There was more going on in the creation of woman than meets the eye. God doesn't do things willy-nilly. Everything has a purpose and meaning. When God engaged to create man and woman and to ordain the union of marriage, He didn't roll the dice or draw straws or flip a coin as to how they might be related to each other. He patterned marriage very purposefully after the relationship between His Son and the church, which He had planned from all eternity.[8]

Therefore, marriage is a mystery—it contains and conceals a meaning far greater than what we see on the outside. God created man male and female and ordained marriage so that the eternal covenant relationship between Christ and His church would be imaged forth in the marriage union. As Geoffrey Bromiley has written, "As God made man in his own image, so he made marriage in the image of his own eternal marriage with his people."[9]

The inference Paul draws from this mystery is that the roles of husband and wife in marriage are not arbitrarily assigned, but are rooted in the distinctive roles of Christ and His church. Those of us who are married need to ponder again and again how mysterious and wonderful it is that God grants us in marriage the privilege to image forth stupendous divine realities infinitely bigger and greater than ourselves.

This is the foundation of the pattern of love that Paul describes for marriage. It is not enough to say that each spouse should pursue his or her own joy in the joy of the other. It is also important to say that husbands and wives

---

8. The covenant that binds Christ to the church is called in Hebrews 13:20 an "eternal covenant": "May the God of peace who brought again from the dead our Lord Jesus, the great shepherd of the sheep, by the blood of the eternal covenant...." Therefore the relationship between Christ and the church has eternally been in God's mind, and in the order of His thought, it precedes and governs the creation of marriage.

9. Geoffrey Bromiley, *God and Marriage* (Grand Rapids, Mich.: Eerdmans, 1980), 43.

should consciously copy the relationship God intended for Christ and the church.[10]

THE WIFE TAKES HER SPECIAL CUES
FROM THE CHURCH

Accordingly, wives are to take their cues from the purpose of the church in its relation to Christ: "Wives, submit to your own husbands, as to the Lord. For the husband is the head of the wife even as Christ is the head of the church, his body, and is himself its Savior. Now as the church submits to Christ, so also wives should submit in everything to their husbands" (Ephesians 5:22–24).

To understand the wife's submission, we need to understand the husband's "headship" because her submission is based on his headship. ("Wives be subject… for the husband is the head.") What is the meaning of *head* in Ephesians 5:23?

The Greek word for *head (kephalē)* is used in the Old Testament sometimes to refer to a chief or leader (Judges 10:18; 11:8–9; 2 Samuel 22:44; Psalm 18:43; Isaiah 7:8). But it is not at first obvious why *head* should be used to refer to a leader. Perhaps its position at the top of the body gave the head its association with high rank and power.

For some ancients, the leading faculty of thought was in the heart, not in the head, though according to Charles Singer in the *Oxford Classical Dictionary,* Aristotle's opinion that intelligence is in the heart "was contrary to the views of some of his medical contemporaries, contrary to the popular view, and contrary to the doctrine of [Plato's] Timaeus."[11] The most pertinent Greek witness for the meaning of *head* in Paul's time would be his contemporary, Philo, who said:

> Just as nature conferred the sovereignty of the body on the head when
> she granted it also possession of the citadel as the most suitable for its
> kingly rank, conducted it thither to take command and established it

---

10. These themes are treated at length in John Piper, *This Momentary Marriage: A Parable of Permanence* (Wheaton, Ill: Crossway, 2009).
11. N. G. L. Hammond and H. H. Scullard, eds., *The Oxford Classical Dictionary* (Oxford: Clarendon, 1970), 59.

on high with the whole framework from neck to foot set below it, like the pedestal under the statue, so too she has given the lordship of the senses to the eyes.[12]

This was the popular view in Paul's day, according to Heinrich Schlier, as is evident from Stoic sources besides Philo.[13] Therefore, contemporary critics are wrong when they claim that "for Greek speaking people in New Testament times, who had little opportunity to read the Greek translation of the Old Testament, there were many possible meanings for 'head' but 'supremacy over' or 'being responsible to' were not among them."[14]

"Supremacy" is precisely the quality given to the head by Philo and others. But most important is that Paul's own use of the word *head* in Ephesians 1:22 "unquestionably carries with it the idea of authority."[15]

In Ephesians 1:20–22, Paul says:

[God] worked in Christ when he raised him from the dead and seated him at his right hand in the heavenly places, far above all rule and authority and power and dominion, and above every name that is named…. And he put all things under his feet and gave him as head over all things to the church.

Even if the word *head* could mean "source" as some claim,[16] this would be a foreign idea here where Christ is installed as supreme over all authorities. Nor is

---

12. Philo, *The Special Laws,* III, 184, in Loeb Classical Library, 8:591.
13. *Theological Dictionary of the New Testament,* ed. Gerhard Kittle (Grand Rapids, Mich.: Eerdmans, 1965), 3:674.
14. Alvera and Berkeley Mickelsen, "Does Male Dominance Tarnish Our Translations?" *Christianity Today* 22, no. 23 (5 October 1979): 25.
15. Stephen Bedale, "The Meaning of *kephalē* in the Pauline Epistles," *Journal of Theological Studies* 5 (1954): 215.
16. Among others, Gilbert Bilezekian, *Beyond Sex Roles,* 2nd ed. (Grand Rapids, Mich.: Baker, 1985), 157–62; Catherine Clark Kroeger, "Head," in *Dictionary of Paul and His Letters,* ed. Gerald F. Hawthorne, Ralph P. Martin, and Daniel G. Reid (Downers Grove, Ill.: InterVarsity, 1993), 376–7. But Wayne Grudem has shown that this is an extremely unlikely meaning for the singular use of *head* in Paul's day. See "The Meaning of *Kephalē* ("Head"): A Response to Recent Studies" in *Recovering Biblical Manhood and Womanhood,* 425–68, 534–41, as well as his more recent, "The Meaning of *kephalē* ("Head"): An Evaluation of New Evidence, Real or Alleged," *Journal of the Evangelical Theological Society* 44, no. 1 (March 2001): 25–65.

it at all likely that this idea was in Paul's mind in Ephesians 5:23, where the wife's "subordination" suggests most naturally that her husband is "head" in the sense of leader or authority.

But, let's suppose that "source" were the sense of *head* in this passage. What would that mean in this context? The husband is pictured as the head of the wife, as Christ is pictured as the head of the church, *His body* (Ephesians 5:29–30). You cannot say that *head* is the head of a river or something like that. Paul is very specific what kind of "head" he has in mind. It is the head connected to a neck on top of a "body."

Now if the head means "source," what is the husband the source of? What does the body get from the head? It gets *nourishment* (that's mentioned in verse 29: "No one ever hated his own flesh but *nourishes* it and cherishes it, just as Christ does the church"). And we can understand this, because the mouth is in the head, and nourishment comes through the mouth to the body. But that's not all the body gets from the head. It gets *guidance* because the eyes are in the head. And it gets *alertness* and *protection* because the ears are in the head.

In other words, if the husband as head is one flesh with his wife, his body, and if he is therefore her source of guidance and food and alertness, then the natural conclusion is that the head, the husband, has a primary responsibility for leadership and provision and protection.

So even if you give *head* the meaning "source," the most natural interpretation of these verses is that husbands are called by God to take primary responsibility for Christlike servant leadership and protection and provision in the home. And wives are called to honor and affirm their husbands' leadership and help carry it through according to their gifts.

Therefore, when Paul says, "Wives, submit to your own husbands...for the husband is the head of the wife," he means a wife should recognize and honor her husband's greater responsibility to lead the home. She should be disposed to yield to her husband's authority and should be inclined to follow his leadership.

The reason I say a *disposition* to yield and an *inclination* to follow is that no submission of one human being to another is absolute. The husband does not replace Christ as the woman's supreme authority. She must never follow her husband's leadership into sin. But even when a Christian wife may have to stand with Christ against the sinful will of her husband, she can still have a spirit of submission. She can show by her attitude and behavior that she does not like resisting his will and that she longs for him to forsake sin and lead in righteousness so that her disposition to honor him as head can again produce harmony.

Another reason for stressing the disposition and inclination of submission, rather than any particular acts, is that the specific behaviors growing out of this spirit of submission are so varied from marriage to marriage. They can even appear contradictory from culture to culture.

The Husband Takes His Special Cues from Christ

So in this mysterious parable of marriage, the wife is to take her special cue from God's purpose for the church in its relation to Christ.[17] And to the husbands Paul says, "Take your special cues from Christ": "Husbands, love your wives, as Christ loved the church and gave himself up for her" (v. 25). If the husband is the head of the wife, as verse 23 says, let it be very plain to every husband that this means primarily leading out in the kind of love that is willing to die to give her life.

As Jesus says in Luke 22:26, "Let…the leader [become] as one who serves." The husband who plops himself down in front of the TV and orders his wife around like a slave has abandoned the way of Christ. Jesus bound Himself with a towel and washed the apostles' feet. Woe to the husband who thinks his maleness requires of him a domineering, demanding attitude toward his wife. If you want to be a Christian husband, you become a servant, not a boss.

It is true that verse 21 puts this whole section under the sign of mutual submission: "submitting to one another out of reverence for Christ." But it is utterly unwarranted to infer from this verse that the *way* Christ submits Himself to the church and the way the church submits herself to Christ are the same. The church submits to Christ by a disposition to follow His leadership. Christ

---

17. Again, these themes are treated at length in Piper, *Momentary Marriage.*

submits to the church by a disposition to exercise His leadership in humble service to the church.

When Christ said, "Let the leader become as one who serves," He did not mean let the leader cease to be a leader. Even while He was on His knees washing their feet, no one doubted who the leader was. Nor should any Christian husband shirk his responsibility under God to provide moral vision and spiritual leadership as the humble servant of his wife and family.

I address the men directly for a moment: Do not let the rhetoric of unbiblical feminism cow you into thinking that Christlike leadership from husbands is bad. It is what our homes need more than anything. For all your meekness and all your servanthood and all your submission to your wife's deep desires and needs, you are still the head, the leader.

What I mean is this: *You* should feel the greater responsibility to take the lead in the things of the Spirit; you should lead the family in a life of prayer, in the study of God's Word, and in worship; you should lead in giving the family a vision of its meaning and mission; you should take the lead in shaping the moral fabric of the home and in governing its happy peace. I have never met a woman who chafes under such Christlike leadership. But I know of too many wives who are unhappy because their husbands have abdicated their God-ordained leadership and have no moral vision, no spiritual conception of what a family is for, and therefore no desire to lead anyone anywhere.

A famous cigarette billboard pictures a curly-headed, bronze-faced, muscular macho with a cigarette hanging out the side of his mouth. The sign says, "Where a man belongs." That is a lie. Where a man belongs is at the bedside of his children, leading in devotion and prayer. Where a man belongs is leading his family to the house of God. Where a man belongs is up early and alone with God seeking vision and direction for his family.

FORMS OF SUBMISSION

To the wife it should be said that the form your submission takes will vary according to the quality of your husband's leadership. If the husband is a godly man who has a biblical vision for his family and leads out in the things of the

Spirit, a godly woman will rejoice in this leadership and support him in it. You will no more be squelched by this leadership and support than the disciples were squelched by the leadership of Jesus.

If you think your husband's vision is distorted or his direction is unbiblical, you will not sit in dumb silence, but query him in a spirit of meekness, and you may often save his foot from stumbling. The husband's headship does not mean infallibility or hostility to correction. Nor does a wife's involvement in shaping the direction of the family involve insubordination.

There is no necessary correlation between leadership and intelligence or between submission and the lack of intelligence. A wife will always be superior in some things and a husband in others. But it is a mistake to ignore that God-ordained pattern of husband leadership on the grounds that the woman is a more competent leader. Any man with zeal to obey the Word of God can be a leader, no matter how many superior competencies his wife has.

A small example: Suppose the husband has a hard time reading. When he tries to read the Bible aloud, he gets it all twisted and pronounces the words wrong. His wife, meanwhile, is a gifted leader. Leadership does not require that he do all the reading during family devotions. Leadership may consist in this one announcement: "Hey, kids, come on into the living room. It's time for devotions. Let's pick up where we left off last time. Mama will read for us." Dad may even be an invalid and still be recognized as the leader. It has to do with the husband's spirit of initiative and responsibility and with the wife's open support for this spirit.

But what if a Christian woman is married to a man who provides no vision and gives no moral direction, takes no lead in the things of the Lord? First Peter 3:1 makes plain that submission is still the will of God. ("Wives, be subject to your own husbands, so that even if some do not obey the word, they may be won without a word by the conduct of their wives.") Yet the form of submission in this case will be different.

Under the lordship of Christ, she will not join her husband in sin even if he wants her to, since she is called to submit to Christ, who forbids sinning (Ephesians 5:22). But she will go as far as her conscience allows in supporting her husband and doing with him what he likes to do.

Where she can, she will give a spiritual vision and moral direction to her children, without communicating a cocky spirit of insubordination to her unbelieving husband. Even when, for Christ's sake, she must do what her husband disapproves, she can try to explain in a tranquil and gentle spirit that it is not because she wants to go against him, but because she is bound to Christ. Yet it will do no good to preach at him. At the root of his being, there is guilt that he is not assuming the moral leadership of his house. She must give him room and win him in quietness by her powerful and sacrificial love (1 Peter 3:1–6).

REDEEMING FALLEN HEADSHIP AND FALLEN SUBMISSION

I have argued that there is a pattern of love in marriage ordained by God. The roles of husband and wife are not the same. The husband is to take his special cues from Christ as the head of the church. The wife is to take her special cues from the church as submissive to Christ. In doing this, the sinful and damaging results of the Fall begin to be reversed. The Fall twisted man's loving headship into hostile domination in some men and lazy indifference in others. The Fall twisted woman's intelligent, willing submission into manipulative obsequiousness in some women and brazen insubordination in others.

The redemption we anticipate at the coming of Christ is not the dismantling of the created order of loving headship and willing submission,[18] but a *recovery* of it. This is precisely what we find in Ephesians 5:21–33. Wives, redeem your fallen submission by modeling it after God's intention for the church! Husbands, redeem your fallen headship by modeling it after God's intention for Christ!

The point of all of this has been to give direction to those who are persuaded that married love is the pursuit of our own joy in the holy joy of our spouses. I find in Ephesians 5:21–33 these two things: (1) the display of Christian Hedonism in marriage and (2) the direction its impulses should take.

---

18. Headship and submission did not originate with the Fall, as so many people claim, but in their pure form were part of God's intention from the beginning of creation before the Fall. See Raymond C. Ortlund Jr., "Male-Female Equality and Male Headship: Genesis 1–3," in *Recovering Biblical Manhood and Womanhood,* 95–112.

Wives, seek your joy in the joy of your husband by affirming and honoring his God-ordained role as leader in your relationship. Husbands, seek your joy in the joy of your wife by accepting the responsibility to lead as Christ led the church and gave Himself for her.

Not that my personal testimony could add anything to the weight of the Word of God, yet I would like to bear witness to God's goodness in my life. I discovered Christian Hedonism the same year I got married, in 1968. Since then, Noël and I, in obedience to Jesus Christ, have pursued as passionately as we can the deepest, most lasting joys possible. All too imperfectly, all too half-heartedly at times, we have stalked our own joy in the joy of each other. And we can testify together: For those who marry, this is the path to the heart's desire. For us, marriage has been a matrix for Christian Hedonism. As each pursues joy in the joy of the other and fulfills a God-ordained role, the mystery of marriage as a parable of Christ and the church becomes manifest for His great glory and for our great joy.[19]

19. I have tried elsewhere, with others, to give explanation and justification for the vision of manhood and womanhood in this chapter. See *Recovering Biblical Manhood and Womanhood*. I commend to you the work of The Council on Biblical Manhood and Womanhood (www.cbmw.org), whose mission involves "helping the church deal biblically with gender issues."

Most men are not satisfied with the permanent output of their lives. Nothing can wholly satisfy the life of Christ within his followers except the adoption of Christ's purpose toward the world he came to redeem. Fame, pleasure and riches are but husks and ashes in contrast with the boundless and abiding joy of working with God for the fulfillment of his eternal plans. The men who are putting everything into Christ's undertaking are getting out of life its sweetest and most priceless rewards.

J. CAMPBELL WHITE
SECRETARY OF THE LAYMEN'S MISSIONARY MOVEMENT

Surely there can be no greater joy than that of saving souls.

LOTTIE MOON
"PATRON SAINT OF BAPTIST MISSIONS"

CHAPTER 9

MISSIONS

The Battle Cry of Christian Hedonism

WHAT IS FRONTIER MISSIONS?

Most men don't die of old age, they die of retirement. I read somewhere that half of the men retiring in the state of New York die within two years. Save your life and you'll lose it. Just like other drugs, other psychological addictions, retirement is a virulent disease, not a blessing.[1]

These are the words of the late Ralph Winter, founder of the United States Center for World Mission. His life and strategy have been a constant summons to young and old that the only way to find life is to give it away. He is one of my heroes. He says so many things that Christian Hedonists ought to say (although he wishes I would not use the word hedonist)!

Not only does he call on retired Christians to quit throwing their lives away on the golf course when they could be giving themselves to the global cause of

---

1. Ralph Winter, "The Retirement Booby Trap," *Mission Frontiers* 7 (July 1985): 25. For those who want to take Winter's words to heart, I would recommend visiting the website of Finishers Project: www.finishers.gospelcom.net. The Finishers Project is a service designed to provide adult Christians information and challenge for processing and discovering ministry opportunities in the missions enterprise—short-term, part-term, or as a second career. The vision statement says, "The Finishers Project is a movement to provide information, challenge and pathways for people to join God in His passion for His glory among the nations. Boomers are and will be the healthiest and best educated generation of empty-nesters ever. This generation is skilled and resourced with a multitude of talents. We can either give them to Jesus to lay up as treasure in Heaven or lose them."

Christ, but he also calls students to go hard after the fullest and deepest joy of life. In his little pamphlet "Say Yes to Missions" he says, "Jesus, for the joy that was set before him, endured the cross, despising the shame.... To follow him is your choice. You're warned! But don't forget the joy."

In fact, in all my reading outside the Bible over the past twenty-five years, the greatest source of affirmation for my emerging Christian Hedonism has been from missionary literature, especially biographies. And those who have suffered most seem to state the truth most unashamedly. In this chapter, I will tell you some of my findings.

But first, back to the issue of retirement. Winter asks, "Where in the Bible do they see that? Did Moses retire? Did Paul retire? Peter? John? Do military officers retire in the middle of a war?"[2] Good questions.[3] If we try to answer them in the case of the apostle Paul, we bump right into a definition of *missions,* which is what we need here at the beginning of this chapter.

As Paul writes his letter to the Romans, he has been a missionary for about twenty years. He was between twenty and forty years old (that's the range implied in the Greek word for "young man" in Acts 7:58) when he was converted. We may guess, then, that he is perhaps around fifty as he writes this great letter.

That may sound young to us. But remember two things: In those days, life expectancy was less, and Paul had led an incredibly stressful life—five times whipped with thirty-nine lashes, three times beaten with rods, once stoned, three times shipwrecked, constantly on the move, and constantly in danger (2 Corinthians 11:24–29).

By our contemporary standards, he should perhaps be "letting up" and planning for retirement. But in Romans 15 he says he is planning to go to Spain! In fact, the reason for writing to the Romans was largely to enlist their support for this great new frontier mission. Paul is not about to retire. Vast areas of the empire are unreached, not to mention the regions beyond! So he says:

2. Ibid.
3. For further reflections on retirement, see John Piper, *Rethinking Retirement: Finishing Life for the Glory of Christ* (Wheaton, Ill: Crossway, 2009), originally published in *Stand: A Call for the Endurance of the Saints,* ed. John Piper and Justin Taylor (Wheaton, Ill: Crossway, 2008).

Now, since I no longer have any room for work in these regions, and since I have longed for many years to come to you, I hope to see you in passing as I go to Spain, and to be helped on my journey there by you, once I have enjoyed your company for a while. (Romans 15:23–24)

Paul was probably killed in Rome before he could fulfill his dream of preaching in Spain. But one thing is certain: He was cut down in combat, not in retirement. He was moving on to the frontier instead of settling down to bask in his amazing accomplishments. Right here we learn the meaning of missions.

How could Paul possibly say in Romans 15:23, "I no longer have any room for work in these regions"? There were thousands of unbelievers left to be converted in Judea and Samaria and Syria and Asia and Macedonia and Achaia. That is obvious from Paul's instruction to the churches on how to relate to unbelievers. But Paul has no room for work!

The explanation is given in verses 19–21:

From Jerusalem and all the way around to Illyricum I have fulfilled the ministry of the gospel of Christ; and thus I make it my ambition to preach the gospel, not where Christ has already been named, lest I build on someone else's foundation, but as it is written, "Those who have never been told of him will see, and those who have never heard will understand."

Paul's missionary strategy was to preach where nobody has preached before. This is what we mean by Frontier Missions. Paul had a passion to go where there were no established churches—that meant Spain.

What is amazing in these verses is that Paul can say he has "fulfilled" the gospel from Jerusalem in southern Palestine to Illyricum northwest of Greece! To understand this is to understand the meaning of Frontier Missions. Frontier Missions is very different from domestic evangelism. There were thousands of people yet to be converted from Jerusalem to Illyricum. But the task of Frontier Missions was finished. Paul's job of "planting" was done and would now be followed by someone else's "watering" (1 Corinthians 3:6).

So when I speak of missions in this chapter, I generally refer to the Christian church's ongoing effort to carry on Paul's strategy: preaching the gospel of Jesus Christ and planting His church among groups of people who have not yet been reached.

THE NEED FOR FRONTIER MISSIONS

My assumption is that people without the gospel are without hope, because only the gospel can free them from their sin. Therefore, missions is utterly essential in the life of a loving church, though not all Christians believe this.

Walbert Buhlmann, a Catholic missions secretary in Rome, spoke for many mainline denominational leaders when he said:

> In the past we had the so-called motive of saving souls. We were convinced that if not baptized, people in the masses would go to hell. Now, thanks be to God, we believe that all people and all religions are already living in the grace and love of God and will be saved by God's mercy.[4]

Sister Emmanuelle of Cairo, Egypt, said, "Today we don't talk about conversion any more. We talk about being friends. My job is to prove that God is love and to bring courage to these people."[5]

It is natural to want to believe in a God who saves all men no matter what they believe or do. But it is not biblical.[6] Essential teachings of Scripture must be rejected to believe in such a God. Listen to the words of the Son of God when He called the apostle Paul into missionary service:

> "I have appeared to you for this purpose, to appoint you as a servant and witness to the things in which you have seen me and to those in

---

4. *Time* (27 December 1982): 52.
5. Ibid., 56.
6. For the detailed support of this claim, see John Piper, *Jesus Christ: The Only Way to God—Must You Hear the Gospel to Be Saved?* (Grand Rapids, Mich.: Baker, 2010), originally printed as chapter 4, "The Supremacy of Christ as the Conscious Focus of All Saving Faith," in John Piper, *Let the Nations Be Glad: The Supremacy of God in Missions,* 3rd ed., (Grand Rapids, Mich.: Baker, 2010).

which I will appear to you, delivering you from your people and from the Gentiles—to whom I am sending you to open their eyes, so that they may turn from darkness to light and from the power of Satan to God, that they may receive forgiveness of sins and a place among those who are sanctified by faith in me." (Acts 26:16–18)

This is an empty commission if in fact the eyes of the nations don't need to be opened and they don't need to turn from darkness to light, and don't need to escape the power of Satan to come to God, and don't need the forgiveness of sins that comes only by faith in Christ, who is preached by the Lord's ambassadors. Paul did not give his life as a missionary to Asia and Macedonia and Greece and Rome and Spain to inform people they were already saved. He gave himself that "by all means [he] might save some" (1 Corinthians 9:22).

So when Paul's message about Christ was rejected (for example, at Antioch by the Jews), he said, "Since you thrust [the Word of God] aside and judge yourselves unworthy of eternal life, behold, we are turning to the Gentiles" (Acts 13:46). At stake in missionary outreach to unreached peoples is *eternal life!* Conversion to Christ from any and every other allegiance is precisely the aim: "There is salvation in no one else, for there is no other name under heaven given among men by which we must be saved" (Acts 4:12).

THE JUSTICE OF GOD IN JUDGMENT AND SALVATION

God is not unjust. No one will be condemned for not believing a message he has never heard. Those who have never heard the gospel will be judged by their failure to own up to the light of God's grace and power in nature and in their own conscience. This is the point of Romans 1:20–21:

His invisible attributes, namely, his eternal power and divine nature, have been clearly perceived, ever since the creation of the world, in the things that have been made. So they are without excuse. For although they knew God, they did not honor him as God or give thanks to him.

Apart from the special, saving grace of God, people are dead in sin, darkened in their understanding, alienated from the life of God, and hardened in heart (Ephesians 2:1; 4:18). And the means God has ordained to administer that special saving grace is the preaching of the gospel of Jesus Christ.

I am under obligation both to Greeks and to barbarians, both to the wise and to the foolish. So I am eager to preach the gospel to you also who are in Rome. For I am not ashamed of the gospel, for it is the power of God for salvation to everyone who believes. (Romans 1:14–16)

THE EFFECTS OF UNIVERSALISM ON MISSIONS

The notion that people are saved without hearing the gospel has wreaked havoc on the missions effort of denominations and churches that minimize the biblical teaching of human lostness without Christ. Though the statistics are somewhat dated, between 1953 and 1980, the overseas missionary force of mainline Protestant churches of North America decreased from 9,844 to 2,813, while the missionary force of evangelical Protestants, who take this biblical teaching more seriously, increased by more than 200 percent. The Christian and Missionary Alliance, for example, with its 200,000 members, supports 40 percent more missionaries than the United Methodist Church, with its 9.5 million members. There is amazing missionary power in taking seriously all the Word of God.[7]

Many Christians thought the end of the colonial era after the Second World War was also the end of foreign missions. The gospel had more or less penetrated every country in the world. But what we have become keenly aware

---

7. In 1980 the Division of Overseas Ministries of the National Council of Churches had a membership of thirty-two missions representing just under five thousand missionaries. Income approached $200 million annually. The Interdenominational Foreign Mission Association represented ninety interdenominational mission boards with roughly 10,700 missionaries and an income of $150 million. The Evangelical Foreign Missions Association had a membership of eighty-two mission agencies representing more than ten thousand missionaries and an income of $350 million.

   During the decade of the seventies, the DOM (the more liberal group) lost 3,462 missionaries, while the IFMA and EFMA (the more evangelical groups) gained 3,785. Incomewise, the DOM increased by $28 million or 24 percent while the IFMA/EFMA increased by $285 million or 293 percent.

   Peter Wagner, *On the Crest of the Wave* (Ventura, Calif.: Regal, 1983), 77–8.

of in the last generation is that the command of Jesus to make disciples of "every nation" does not refer to political nations as we know them today. Nor does it mean every individual, as though the great commission could not be completed until every individual were made a disciple.

WHAT ARE "PEOPLE GROUPS"?

We are increasingly aware that the intention of God is for every "people group" to be evangelized—that a thriving church be planted in every group. No one can exactly define what a people group is. But we get a rough idea from passages like Revelation 7:9:

> After this I looked, and behold, a great multitude that no one could number, from every nation, from all tribes and peoples and languages, standing before the throne and before the Lamb.

It is almost impossible to draw precise distinction between "nations," "tribes," "peoples," and "languages." But what is clear is that God's redemptive purpose is not complete just because there are disciples of Jesus in all twenty-first-century "nations," i.e., political states. Within those countries are thousands of tribes and castes and subcultures and languages.

So the remaining task of Frontier Missions no longer is conceived mainly in geographic terms. The question now is "How many unreached people groups are there, and where are they found?"[8]

In his inspiring book published in 1998, Patrick Johnstone says, "We reckon that there are now nearly 13,000 distinct ethno-linguistic peoples in the countries of the world." Of these, he says that about 3,500 "are still pioneer fields for

---

8. For a detailed exploration of the biblical support for thinking of the great commission in terms of reaching people groups, see chapter 4, "The Supremacy of Christ as the Conscious Focus of All Saving Faith," in *Let the Nations Be Glad.* An excellent discussion of the definition of "unreached peoples" and the problem of counting and locating them is given by Ralph Winter in "Unreached Peoples: The Development of the Concept," *International Journal of Frontier Missions* 1 (1984): 129–61. See also Ralph D. Winter and Bruce A. Koch's "Finishing the Task: The Unreached Peoples Challenge" in *Perspectives on the World Christian Movement,* 4th ed., ed. Ralph D. Winter and Stephen C. Hawthorne (Pasadena, Calif.: William Carey, 2009), 531, available online at http://www.uscwm.org/index.php/resources/detail_page/finishing_the_task/.

mission endeavor. The indigenous Church is either non-existent or still too small or culturally marginalized to impact their entire people in this generation without outside help. Of these probably about 1,200–1,500 peoples have either no indigenous church at all or no residential cross-cultural team of missionaries seeking to reach them."[9] In reality, the statistics are now changing so fast that the reader should consult websites like joshuaproject.net and the U.S. Center for World Mission (uscwm.org) for the most recent state of world evangelization. Concealed within these numbers is the heartrending fact that about 2 billion people live in unevangelized people groups. They are found mainly in the Muslim, Hindu, Buddhist, and Animist peoples of the so-called 10/40 Window.[10]

MISSION IS FINISHABLE, BUT NOT EVANGELISM

To keep us sober in our estimates of the remaining task of reaching the unreached people groups of the world, Ralph Winter reminds us of two facts.

First, evangelism can never be finished, but missions can be finished. The reason is this: Missions has the unique task of crossing language and culture barriers to penetrate a people group and establish a church movement; but evangelism is the ongoing task of sharing the gospel among people within the same culture. This fact allows us to talk realistically about "closure"—the completion of the missionary task—even if there may be millions of people yet to be won to Christ in all the people groups of the world where the church has been planted.

The second fact Winter reminds us of is that there are probably more people groups than the ones listed among the 13,000 ethnolinguistic groups mentioned above. He illustrates by pointing out that tribal divisions along the lines of mutually unintelligible dialects may vary, depending on whether the dialect is spoken or written. So, for example, Wycliffe Bible Translators may detect that a translation of the Bible is readable in a dialect covering a wide area,

---

9. Patrick Johnstone, *The Church Is Bigger Than You Think* (Ross-shire, UK: Christian Focus, 1998), 105–7. Up-to-date estimates about the world's unreached and unengaged peoples are available at www.joshuaproject.net. As of the fall of 2010, the Joshua Project was estimating that there are over 16,500 people groups worldwide, and over 6,800 of those are "unreached."

10. The 10/40 Window refers to the rectangular area on a global map measured horizontally from West Africa to East Asia and vertically from the tenth to the fortieth latitude north of the equator.

while Gospel Recordings may determine that seven or more different audio recordings are needed because of the audible distinctions in the larger dialect.

Thus, Winter asks, which level of people group did Jesus have in mind when He said, "This gospel of the kingdom will be proclaimed throughout the whole world as a testimony to all nations, and then the end will come" (Matthew 24:14)? Winter's answer: "We'll find out...the closer we get to the situation. In the meantime we need to live with guesses.... We can only learn more as we go! And at this hour greater human resources are looming into view than have ever been available to the unfinished task!"[11]

The point of these observations is that the job of Frontier Missions is not complete. In fact, the vast majority of missionaries are working in "fields" where the church has been planted for decades. The need for Frontier Missions is great. The Lord's command to disciple the remaining unreached groups is still in force. And my burden in this chapter is to kindle a desire in your heart to be part of the last chapter of the greatest story in the world.

DRAMATIC GROWTH

There are historical as well as theological reasons for the hope that the task of world missions is finishable. The following chart is truly amazing. It shows a picture of the progress over the first two-thousand-year history of the preaching of the gospel.[12]

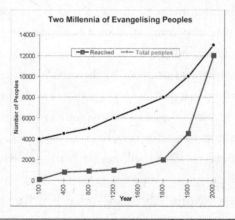

Two Millennia of Evangelising Peoples

---

11. Ralph Winter, "When Jesus Said...," *Missions Frontiers* 17, no. 11–12 (November/December, 1995): 56.
12. Johnstone, *The Church Is Bigger Than You Think,* 105, emphasis added.

Johnstone observes:

It is interesting to see how few of the world's people had been reached by 1800. The number of peoples reached had considerably increased by 1900, but even then more than half the peoples of the world were still completely unreached. The dramatic change has been in the latter part of this century.

Although many people are still unreached, the number is only a fraction of that of 100 years ago. *The goal is attainable in our generation*—if we mobilize in prayer and effort and work together to disciple the remaining least reached peoples.[13]

Even though there is an ongoing and urgent need for more frontier missionaries to penetrate the final unreached peoples with the gospel, it seems that the momentum of closure is accelerating. In addition to the ironclad promise of Jesus in Matthew 24:14 that the gospel will penetrate all the peoples, there is the empirical evidence that this is in fact happening, and at an increasing rate. It is "A Finishable Task."

BECOMING WORLD CHRISTIANS

I would like to believe that many of you who read this chapter are on the brink of setting a new course of commitment to missions: some a new commitment to go to a frontier people, others a new path of education, others a new use of your vocation in a culture less saturated by the church, others a new lifestyle and a new pattern of giving and praying and reading. I want to push you over the brink. I would like to make the cause of missions so attractive that you will no longer be able to resist its magnetism.

Not that I believe everyone will become a missionary, or even should become one. But I pray that every reader of this book might become what David Bryant calls a "World Christian"—that you would reorder your life

---

13. Ibid.

around God's global cause. In his inspiring book *In the Gap*, Bryant defines World Christians as those Christians who say:

> We want to accept personal responsibility for reaching some of earth's unreached, especially from among the billions at the widest end of the Gap who can only be reached through major new efforts by God's people. Among every people-group where there is no vital, evangelizing Christian community there should be, there must be one, there shall be one. Together we want to help make this happen.[14]

THE RICH YOUNG RULER

The biblical basis for a Christian Hedonist's commitment to missions is found in the story of the rich young ruler (Mark 10:17–31):

> As [Jesus] was setting out on his journey, a man ran up and knelt before him and asked him, "Good Teacher, what must I do to inherit eternal life?" And Jesus said to him, "Why do you call me good? No one is good except God alone. You know the commandments: 'Do not murder, Do not commit adultery, Do not steal, Do not bear false witness, Do not defraud, Honor your father and mother.'"
>
> And he said to him, "Teacher, all these I have kept from my youth." And Jesus, looking at him, loved him, and said to him, "You lack one thing: go, sell all that you have and give to the poor, and you will have treasure in heaven; and come, follow me." Disheartened by the saying, he went away sorrowful, for he had great possessions.
>
> And Jesus looked around and said to his disciples, "How difficult it

---

14. The quote is on page 7 of chapter 5 of the online book by David Bryant, *In the Gap*, available at http://www.proclaimhope.org/content/intheGap/ebook. If you want to take a next step in understanding the global purposes of God, I would encourage you to consider taking the course offered around the world entitled "Perspectives on the World Christian Movement." I would also encourage you to get a copy of *Operation World*, edited by Patrick Johnstone and Jason Mandryk, which tells the state of Christianity in all the countries of the world and how to pray for them. I was also greatly helped by Johnstone's *The Church Is Bigger Than You Think*. For my attempt to give a fuller account of mission theology, motivation, and implications, see *Let the Nations Be Glad*.

will be for those who have wealth to enter the kingdom of God!" And the disciples were amazed at his words. But Jesus said to them again, "Children, how difficult it is to enter the kingdom of God! It is easier for a camel to go through the eye of a needle than for a rich person to enter the kingdom of God."

And they were exceedingly astonished, and said to him, "Then who can be saved?" Jesus looked at them and said, "With man it is impossible, but not with God. For all things are possible with God." Peter began to say to him, "See, we have left everything and followed you." Jesus said, "Truly, I say to you, there is no one who has left house or brothers or sisters or mother or father or children or lands, for my sake and for the gospel, who will not receive a hundredfold now in this time, houses and brothers and sisters and mothers and children and lands, with persecutions, and in the age to come eternal life. But many that are first will be last, and the last first."

This story contains at least two great incentives for being totally dedicated to the cause of Frontier Missions.

WITH MAN IT IS IMPOSSIBLE, BUT NOT WITH GOD

First, in Mark 10:25–27 Jesus said to His disciples:

> "It is easier for a camel to go through the eye of a needle than for a rich person to enter the kingdom of God." And they were exceedingly astonished, and said to him, "Then who can be saved?" Jesus looked at them and said, "With man it is impossible, but not with God. For all things are possible with God."

This is one of the most encouraging missionary conversations in the Bible. What missionary has not looked on his work and said, "It's impossible!"? To which Jesus agrees, "Yes, with man it is impossible." No mere human being can liberate another human being from the enslaving power of the love of money.

The rich young ruler went away sorrowful because the bondage to things cannot be broken by man. With man it is impossible! And therefore missionary work, which is simply liberating the human heart from bondage to allegiances other than Christ, is impossible—with men!

If God were not in charge in this affair, doing the humanly impossible, the missionary task would be hopeless. Who but God can raise the spiritually dead and give them an ear for the gospel? "Even when we were dead in our trespasses, [God] made us alive together with Christ" (Ephesians 2:5). The great missionary hope is that when the gospel is preached in the power of the Holy Spirit, God Himself does what man cannot do—He creates the faith that saves.

The call of God does what the call of man can't. It raises the dead. It creates spiritual life. It is like the call of Jesus to Lazarus in the tomb, "Come forth!" (see John 11:43). We can waken someone from sleep with our call, but God's call can summon into being things that are not (Romans 4:17).

God's call is irresistible in the sense that it can overcome all resistance. It is infallibly effective according to God's purpose—so much so that Paul can say, "Those whom [God] called he also justified" (Romans 8:30). In other words, God's call is so effectual that it infallibly creates the faith through which a person is justified. *All* the called are justified. But none is justified without faith (Romans 5:1). So the call of God cannot fail in its intended effect. It irresistibly secures the faith that justifies.

This is what man cannot do. It is impossible. Only God can take out the heart of stone (Ezekiel 36:26). Only God can draw people to the Son (John 6:44, 65). Only God can open the heart so that it gives heed to the gospel (Acts 16:14). Only the Good Shepherd knows His sheep by name. He calls them and they follow (John 10:3–4, 14). The sovereign grace of God, doing the humanly impossible, is the great missionary hope.

What Christian Hedonists Love Best

This sovereign grace is also the spring of life for the Christian Hedonist. For what the Christian Hedonist loves best is the experience of the sovereign grace of God filling him and overflowing for the good of others. Christian Hedonist missionaries love the experience of "not I, but the grace of God that is with me" (1 Corinthians 15:10). They bask in the truth that the fruit of their missionary labor is entirely of God (1 Corinthians 3:7; Romans 11:36). They feel only gladness when the Master says, "Apart from me you can do nothing" (John 15:5). They leap like lambs over the truth that God has taken the impossible weight of new creation off their shoulders and put it on His own.

Without begrudging, they say, "Not that we are sufficient in ourselves to claim anything as coming from us, but our sufficiency is from God" (2 Corinthians 3:5). When they come home on furlough, nothing gives them more joy than to say to churches, "I will not venture to speak of anything except what *Christ* has accomplished through me to bring the Gentiles to obedience" (Romans 15:18). "All things are possible with God!"—in front the words give hope, and behind they give humility. They are the antidote to despair and pride—the perfect missionary medicine.

MISSIONARY INCENTIVES OF SOVEREIGN GRACE

This great confidence of the missionary enterprise is given again by Jesus with different words in John 10:16:

> "I have other sheep that are not of this fold. I must bring them also, and they will listen to my voice. So there will be one flock, one shepherd."

Notice three powerful encouragements in this text for frontier missionaries:

1. *Christ does indeed have other sheep outside the present fold!* They have been "ransomed…from every tribe and language and people and nation" (Revelation 5:9). The children of God are "scattered abroad" (John 11:52). No missionary will ever reach a hidden group and be able to say that God has no people there.

This is precisely how the Lord encouraged Paul when he was downcast in Corinth and confronted with the "impossibility" of planting a church in that rocky soil.

> And the Lord said to Paul one night in a vision, "Do not be afraid, but go on speaking and do not be silent, for I am with you, and no one will

attack you to harm you, *for I have many in this city who are my people.*"
(Acts 18:9–10)

In other words, take heart! It may look impossible, but God has a chosen people (the "other sheep" of John 10:16), and the Good Shepherd knows His own and will call them by name when you faithfully preach the gospel.

JESUS MUST BRING HIS OTHER SHEEP

2. This leads to the second encouragement for missions in John 10:16, namely, the words "I must bring them also." *Christ is under a divine necessity to gather His own sheep. He* must do it. He *must* do it. But of course this does not lead to the hyper-Calvinistic[15] notion that He will do it without using us as a means. William Carey, "father of modern missions," did a great service to the cause of Frontier Missions when he published in 1792 his little book entitled *An Inquiry into the Obligation of Christians to Use Means for the Conversion of the Heathens.*[16]

God will always use means in missions. Jesus makes this plain when He says, "I do not ask for these only, but also for those who will believe in me *through their word*" (John 17:20). Nevertheless, Carey believed, as the Lord taught, that he was helpless and that it is really Christ who calls and saves and works in us what it pleasing in His sight (Hebrews 13:21). After forty years of spectacular accomplishment (for example, he translated the entire Bible into Bengali, Oriya, Marathi, Hindi, Assamese, and Sanskrit, and parts of it into twenty-nine other languages), William Carey died; yet the simple tablet on his grave reads, at his own request:

---

15. Iain Murray writes in *The Forgotten Spurgeon* (Edinburgh: Banner of Truth, 1973), 47:

> Hyper-Calvinism in its attempt to square all truth with God's purpose to save the elect, denies that there is a universal command to repent and believe, and asserts that we have only warrant to invite to Christ those who are *conscious* of a sense of sin and need. In other words, it is those who have been spiritually quickened to seek a Saviour and not those who are in the death of unbelief and indifference, to whom the exhortations of the Gospel must be addressed. In this way a scheme was devised for restricting the Gospel to those who there is reason to suppose are elect.

> This is an excellent book to show how Charles Spurgeon, the Baptist pastor in London in the latter half of the nineteenth century, held together strong (Calvinistic) views of the sovereignty of God with a powerful and fruitful soul-winning ministry. He fought against the hyper-Calvinists on the one side, and the Arminians on the other in a way I consider exemplary.

16. For a biography of Carey, see Timothy George, *Faithful Witness: The Life and Mission of William Carey* (Birmingham, Ala.: New Hope, 1991).

WILLIAM CAREY
BORN AUGUST 17TH, 1761
DIED JUNE, 1834
A WRETCHED, POOR AND HELPLESS WORM,
ON THY KIND ARMS I FALL

The great encouragement from John 10:16 is that the Lord Himself will do what is impossible for "poor and helpless worms" like us. "I have other sheep that are not of this fold. I must bring them also."

THEY WILL HEAR HIS VOICE

3. The third encouragement from this verse is that the sheep He calls will surely come: "I must bring them also, and *they will listen to my voice."* What is impossible with man is possible with God! When Paul was finished preaching in the city of Antioch, Luke described the result like this: "As many as were appointed to eternal life believed" (Acts 13:48). God has a people in every people group. He will call them with Creator power. And they *will* believe!

What power is in these words for overcoming discouragement in the hard places of the frontiers! The story of Peter Cameron Scott is a good illustration of the power of John 10:16.

Born in Glasgow in 1867, Scott became the founder of the Africa Inland Mission. But his beginnings in Africa were anything but auspicious. His first trip to Africa ended in a severe attack of malaria that sent him home. He resolved to return after he recuperated.

This return was especially gratifying to him because this time his brother John joined him. But before long, John was struck down by fever. All alone, Peter buried his brother and in the agony of those days recommitted himself to preach the gospel in Africa. Yet his health gave way again, and he had to return to England.

How would he ever pull out of the desolation and depression of those days? He had pledged himself to God. But where could he find the strength to go back to Africa? With man it was impossible!

He found strength in Westminster Abbey. David Livingstone's tomb is still there. Scott entered quietly, found the tomb, and knelt in front of it to pray. The inscription reads:

OTHER SHEEP I HAVE
WHICH ARE NOT OF THIS FOLD;
THEM ALSO I MUST BRING.

He rose from his knees with a new hope. He returned to Africa. And today the mission he founded is a vibrant, growing force for the gospel in Africa.

If your greatest joy is to experience the infilling grace of God overflowing from you for the good of others, then the best news in all the world is that God will do the impossible through you for the salvation of the hidden peoples. "With man it is impossible, but not with God. For all things are possible with God."

YOU WILL RECEIVE BACK A HUNDREDFOLD

The second great incentive in Mark 10:17–31 for being dedicated to the cause of Frontier Missions is found in verses 28–30:

Peter began to say to [Jesus], "See, we have left everything and followed you." Jesus said, "Truly, I say to you, there is no one who has left house or brothers or sisters or mother or father or children or lands, for my sake and for the gospel, who will not receive a hundredfold now in this time, house and brothers and sisters and mothers and children and lands, with persecutions, and in the age to come eternal life.

This text does not mean you get materially rich by becoming a missionary—at least not in the sense that your own private possessions increase. If you volunteer for mission service with such a notion, the Lord will confront you with these words: "Foxes have holes, and birds of the air have nests; but the Son of Man has nowhere to lay his head" (Luke 9:58).

Instead, the point seems to be that if you are deprived of your earthly family in the service of Christ, it will be made up a hundredfold in your spiritual family, the church. But even this may be too limiting. What about the lonely missionaries who labor for years without being surrounded by hundreds of sisters and brothers and mothers and children in the faith? Is the promise not true for them?

HE MAKES UP FOR EVERY SACRIFICE

Surely it is. Surely what Christ means is that He Himself makes up for every sacrifice. If you give up a mother's nearby affection and concern, you get back one hundred times the affection and concern from the ever-present Christ. If you give up the warm comradeship of a brother, you get back one hundred times the warmth and comradeship of Christ. If you give up the sense of at-homeness you had in your house, you get back one hundred times the comfort and security of knowing that your Lord owns every house and land and stream and tree on earth. To prospective missionaries, Jesus says, "I promise to *work* for and *be* for you so much that you will not be able to speak of having sacrificed anything."

John G. Paton, missionary to the New Hebrides (today's Vanuatu in the South Pacific) gives a beautiful testimony of the nearness and friendship of Christ when he was utterly alone, having lost his wife and child, and now surrounded by hostile natives as he hid in a tree.

> I climbed into the tree and was left there alone in the bush. The hours I spent there live all before me as if it were but of yesterday. I heard the frequent discharging of muskets, and the yells of the Savages. Yet I sat there among the branches, as safe in the arms of Jesus. Never, in all my sorrows, did my Lord draw nearer to me, and speak more soothingly in my soul, than when the moonlight flickered among these chestnut leaves, and the night air played on my throbbing brow, as I told all my heart to Jesus. Alone, yet not alone! If it be to glorify my God, I will not grudge to spend many nights alone in such a tree, to feel again my Savior's spiritual presence, to enjoy His consoling fellowship. If thus thrown back upon your own soul, alone, all alone, in the midnight, in

the bush, in the very embrace of death itself, have you a Friend that will not fail you then?[17]

What was Jesus' attitude to Peter's "sacrificial" spirit? Peter said, "We have left everything and followed you." Is this the spirit of "self-denial" commended by Jesus? No, it is rebuked. Jesus said, "No one ever sacrifices anything for me that I do not pay back a hundredfold—yes, in one sense even in this life, not to mention eternal life in the age to come." Why did Jesus rebuke Peter for thinking in terms of sacrifice? Jesus Himself had demanded "self-denial" (Mark 8:34). The reason seems to be that Peter did not yet think about sacrifice the way a Christian Hedonist is supposed to.

How is that?

The response of Jesus indicates that the way to think about self-denial is to deny yourself only a lesser good for a greater good. You deny yourself one mother in order to get one hundred mothers. In other words, Jesus wants us to think about sacrifice in a way that rules out all self-pity. This is in fact just what the texts on self-denial teach.

"If anyone would come after me, let him deny himself and take up his cross and follow me. For whoever would save his life will lose it, but whoever loses his life for my sake and the gospel's will save it." (Mark 8:34–35)[18]

The argument is inescapably hedonistic. Saint Augustine captured the paradox in these words:

If you love your soul, there is danger of its being destroyed. Therefore you may not love it, since you do not want it to be destroyed. But in not wanting it to be destroyed you love it.[19]

17. John G. Paton, *John G. Paton: Missionary to the New Hebrides, An Autobiography Edited by His Brother* (Edinburgh: Banner of Truth, 1965, orig. 1889, 1891), 200.
18. See also Matthew 10:39 and 16:24–26, Luke 9:24–25 and 17:33, John 12:25, and Revelation 12:11.
19. Saint Augustine, *Migne Patrologia Latina* 39, 1652, Sermon 368.

Jesus knew this. It was the basis of His argument. He does not ask us to be indifferent to whether we are destroyed. On the contrary, He assumes that the very longing for true life (1 Peter 3:10) will move us to deny ourselves all the lesser pleasures and comforts of life. If we were indifferent to the value of God's gift of life, we would dishonor it. The measure of your longing for life is the amount of comfort you are willing to give up to get it. The gift of eternal life in God's presence is glorified if we are willing to "hate our lives in this world" in order to get it (John 12:25). Therein lies the God-centered value of self-denial.

TWO KINDS OF SELF-LOVE

When Peter blurted out that he had sacrificed everything, he had not thought as deeply as David Brainerd and David Livingstone. As a young missionary to the Indians of New England, Brainerd wrestled with the issue of self-love and self-denial. On January 24, 1744, he wrote in his diary:

> In the evening, I was unexpectedly visited by a considerable number of people, with whom I was enabled to converse profitably of divine things. Took pains to describe the difference between a regular and irregular self love; the one consisting with a supreme love to God, but the other not; the former uniting God's glory and the soul's happiness that they became one common interest, but the latter disjoining and separating God's glory and man's happiness, seeking the latter with a neglect of the former. Illustrated this by that genuine love that is founded between the sexes, which is diverse from that which is wrought up towards a person only by rational argument, or the hope of self-interest.[20]

Brainerd knew in his soul that in seeking to live for the glory of God, he was loving himself! He knew there was no ultimate sacrifice going on, though

---

20. Jonathan Edwards, ed., *The Life and Diary of David Brainerd* (Chicago: Moody Press, 1949, original, 1749), 149. By "self-interest" I take Brainerd to mean "worldly, self-interest that does not have the glory of God for its pleasure." He goes on to say that "love is a pleasing passion; it affords pleasure to the mind where it is." But the object of love is never that pleasure. The object is God and the love is pleasurable. This is why it is confusing at times when we speak of seeking pleasure. It sounds as though pleasure has taken the place of God. But this is not the case. As Brainerd says, God's glory and our happiness become one common interest. We seek pleasure in God. Not from God.

he was dying of tuberculosis. Yet he knew that Jesus condemned some form of self-love and commended some form of self-denial. So he endorsed a distinction between a self-love that separates our pursuit of happiness from our pursuit of God's glory, and a self-love that combines these pursuits into "one common interest." In other words, he did not make Peter's mistake of thinking that his suffering for Christ was ultimately sacrificial. With everything he gave, there came new experiences of the glory of God. A hundredfold!

"I NEVER MADE A SACRIFICE"

On December 4, 1857, David Livingstone, the great pioneer missionary to Africa, made a stirring appeal to the students of Cambridge University, showing that he had learned through years of experience what Jesus tried to teach Peter:

> For my own part, I have never ceased to rejoice that God has appointed me to such an office. People talk of the sacrifice I have made in spending so much of my life in Africa. Can that be called a sacrifice which is simply paid back as a small part of a great debt owing to our God, which we can never repay? Is that a sacrifice which brings its own blest reward in healthful activity, the consciousness of doing good, peace of mind, and a bright hope of a glorious destiny hereafter? Away with the word in such a view, and with such a thought! It is emphatically no sacrifice. Say rather it is a privilege. Anxiety, sickness, suffering, or danger, now and then, with a foregoing of the common conveniences and charities of this life, may make us pause, and cause the spirit to waver, and the soul to sink; but let this only be for a moment. All these are nothing when compared with the glory which shall hereafter be revealed in and for us. *I never made a sacrifice.*[21]

One sentence of this quote is, I think, unhelpful and inconsistent: "Can that be called a sacrifice which is simply paid back as a small part of a great debt owing to our God, which we can never repay?" I don't think it is helpful

---

21. Cited in Samuel Zwemer, "The Glory of the Impossible," *Perspectives on the World Christian Movement*, 4th ed., ed. Ralph D. Winter and Stephen C. Hawthorne (Pasadena, Calif.: William Carey, 2009), 333, emphasis added.

to describe our obedience as an attempt (albeit impossible) to pay God back for His grace.[22] It is a contradiction of free grace to think of it that way. Not only is it unhelpful; it is inconsistent with the rest of what Livingstone says. He says his obedience is in fact more receiving—healthful, peaceful, hopeful. It would honor God's grace and value more if we dropped the notion of paying Him back at all. We are not involved in a trade or purchase. We have received a gift. But this reservation aside, the last line is magnificent: "I never made a sacrifice."

This is what Jesus' rebuke to Peter's sacrificial (self-pitying?) spirit was supposed to teach. Our great incentive for throwing our lives into the cause of Frontier Missions is the 10,000 percent return on the investment. Missionaries have borne witness to this from the beginning—since the apostle Paul.

Paul was bold to say that everything was garbage[23] compared to knowing and suffering with Jesus:

> But whatever gain I had, I counted as loss for the sake of Christ. Indeed, I count everything as loss because of the surpassing worth of knowing Christ Jesus my Lord. For his sake I have suffered the loss of all things and count them as rubbish, in order that I may gain Christ...that I may know him and the power of his resurrection, and may share his sufferings. (Philippians 3:7–8, 10)

> This slight momentary affliction is preparing for us an eternal weight of glory beyond all comparison. (2 Corinthians 4:17)

> I consider that the sufferings of this present time are not worth comparing with the glory that is to be revealed to us. (Romans 8:18)

22. See John Piper, *Future Grace* (Sisters, Ore.: Multnomah, 1995), passim.
23. BDAG, the standard Greek lexicon, says that *skubalon*, in various senses, means "excrement, manure, garbage, kitchen scraps." See Walter Bauer, *A Greek-English Lexicon of the New Testament and Other Early Christian Literature,* rev. and ed. Frederick W Danker, 3rd ed. (Chicago/London: University of Chicago Press, 2000).

I do it all for the sake of the gospel, that I may share with them in its blessings. (1 Corinthians 9:23)[24]

HOLY MISSIONARIES ARE MOST HEDONISTIC

It is simply amazing how consistent are the testimonies of missionaries who have suffered for the gospel. Virtually all of them bear witness to the abundant joy and overriding compensations (a hundredfold!).

Colin Grant describes how the Moravian Brethren were sending missionaries out from the mountains of Saxony in central Europe sixty years before William Carey set out for India. Between 1732 and 1742, with utter abandon, they reached the West Indies, Surinam, North America, Greenland, South Africa, China, and Persia—"a record without parallel in the post–New Testament era of world evangelization." In recounting the main characteristics of this movement, Grant puts "glad obedience" at the top of the list: "In the first place, *the missionary obedience of the Moravian Brethren was essentially glad and spontaneous,* 'the response of a healthy organism to the law of its life.'"[25]

Andrew Murray refers to this "law of life" in his missionary classic, *Key to the Missionary Problem.* Nature teaches us that every believer should be a soulwinner: "It is an essential part of the new nature. We see it in every child who loves to tell of his happiness and to bring others to share his joys."[26] Missions is the automatic outflow and overflow of love for Christ. We delight to enlarge our

---

24. On this last text Adolf Schlatter comments powerfully:

> Paul cannot look at his position as a Christian in isolation, separated from his work in the service of Jesus, as though the way he performed his ministry had no significant connection with his salvation. Since it was the Lord who gave him his ministry Paul stays bound to Him only if he carries it out faithfully. And the Gospel would no longer be valid in his own life, if he forsook his ministry. That gives Paul's love its purity. He enters into community with all, that he might win them. But his will remains free from the presumption that says to others that only they are in danger and need salvation. Rather the question of salvation retains for him, as also for them its full seriousness. He takes pains therefore that he save others for his own salvation.

> *Die Korintherbriefe*, vol. 6, *Erlaeuterungen zum Neuen Testament* (Stuttgart: Calwer Verlag, 1974), 118.

25. Colin A. Grant, "Europe's Moravians: A Pioneer Missionary Church" in *Perspectives on the World Christian Movement*, 274. Grant is using Harry Boer's words in the last phrase.
26. Andrew Murray, *Key to the Missionary Problem* (Fort Washington, Penn.: Christian Literature Crusade, 1979, orig. 1905), 127.

joy in Him by extending it to others. As Lottie Moon said, "Surely there can be no deeper joy than that of saving souls."[27]

What Lottie Moon did in promoting the cause of foreign missions among Southern Baptist women in the United States, Amy Carmichael did among the Christian women of all denominations in the United Kingdom. She wrote thirty-five books detailing her fifty-five years in India. Sherwood Eddy, a missionary statesman and author who knew her well, said, "Amy Wilson Carmichael was the most Christlike character I ever met, and…her life was the most fragrant, the most joyfully sacrificial, that I ever knew."[28] "Joyfully sacrificial!" That is what Jesus was after when he rebuked Peter's sacrificial spirit in Mark 10:29–30.

John Hyde, better known as "Praying Hyde," led a life of incredibly intense prayer as a missionary to India at the turn of the century. Some thought him morose. But a story about him reveals the true spirit behind his life of sacrificial prayer.

A worldly lady once thought she would have a little fun at Mr. Hyde's expense. So she asked, "Don't you think, Mr. Hyde, that a lady who dances can go to heaven?" He looked at her with a smile and said quietly, "I do not see how a lady can go to heaven *unless* she dances." Then he dwelt on the joy of sin forgiven.[29]

Samuel Zwemer, famous for his missionary work among the Muslims, gives a stirring witness to the joy of sacrifice. In 1897 he and his wife and two daughters sailed to the Persian Gulf to work among the Muslims of Bahrein. Their evangelism was largely fruitless. The temperatures soared regularly to 107 "in the coolest part of the verandah." In July 1904 both the daughters, ages four and seven, died within eight days of each other. Nevertheless, fifty years later Zwemer looked back on this period and wrote, "The sheer joy of it all comes back. Gladly would I do it all over again."[30]

---

27. Cited in Ruth Tucker, *From Jerusalem to Irian Jaya*, 2nd ed. (Grand Rapids, Mich.: Zondervan, 2004), 297. Charlotte Diggs (Lottie) Moon was born in 1840 in Virginia and sailed for China as a Baptist missionary in 1873. She is known not only for her pioneering work in China, but also for mobilizing the women of the Southern Baptist Church for the missionary cause.
28. Cited in Tucker, ibid., 299. For a wonderful biography of Carmichael, see Elisabeth Elliot, *A Chance to Die: The Life and Legacy of Amy Carmichael* (Grand Rapids, Mich.: Fleming H. Revell, 1987).
29. E. G. Carre, *Praying Hyde* (South Plainfield, N. J.: Bridge, n. d.), 66.
30. Cited in Tucker, *From Jerusalem to Irian Jaya*, 240.

In the end, the reason Jesus rebukes us for a self-pitying spirit of sacrifice is that He aims to be glorified in the great missionary enterprise. And the way He aims to be glorified is by keeping Himself in the role of benefactor and keeping us in the role of beneficiaries. He never intends for the patient and the physician to reverse roles. Even if we are called to be missionaries, we remain invalids in Christ's sanatorium. We are still in need of a good physician. We are still dependent on Him to do the humanly impossible in us and through us. We may sacrifice other things to enter Christ's hospital, but we are there for our spiritual health—not to pay back a debt to the doctor!

INVALIDS MAKE THE BEST MISSIONARIES

Daniel Fuller uses this picture of patient and doctor to show how the effective missionary avoids the presumption of assisting God:

> An analogy for understanding how to live the Christian life without being a legalist is to think of ourselves as being sick and needing a doctor's help in order to get well. Men begin life with a disposition so inclined to evil that Jesus called them "children of hell" (Matthew 23:15).... In Mark 2:17 and elsewhere Jesus likened Himself to a doctor with the task of healing a man's sins; He received the name "Jesus" because it was His mission to "save His people from their sins" (Matthew 1:21). The moment we turn from loving things in this world to bank our hope on God and His promises summed up in Jesus Christ, Jesus takes us, as it were, into His clinic to heal us of our hellish dispositions.... True faith means not only being confident that one's sins are forgiven but also means believing God's promises that we will have a happy future through eternity. Or, to revert to the metaphor of medicine and the clinic, we must entrust our sick selves to Christ as the Great Physician, with confidence that He will work until our hellishness is transformed into godliness.
>
> [One] implication to be drawn from the doctor analogy is that while he will prescribe certain general instructions for all his patients to follow,

he will also make up individual health regimens for the particular needs of each patient. For example, he may direct some to leave their homeland to go to proclaim the Gospel in a foreign land. There is great temptation in such circumstances for people to revert to the legalism of thinking that they are being heroes for God because they are leaving their homeland to endure the rigors of living in a foreign land [this was Peter's problem]. Those who are dedicated to do hard jobs for God must remind themselves that these rigors are simply for their health. As these difficulties help them become more like Christ, they will sing a song of praise to God, and as a result "many will see it and fear and put their trust in the LORD" (Psalm 40:3). People who regard themselves as invalids rather than heroes will make excellent missionaries.[31]

EXPECTING FIRST, THEN ATTEMPTING

William Carey, at first glance, may appear to be an exception to the idea that missionaries should see their ministry as God's treatment for their spiritual disease of sin. On Wednesday, May 31, 1792, he preached his famous sermon from Isaiah 54:2–3 ("Enlarge the place of your tent..."), in which his most famous dictum was pronounced: "Expect great things from God; attempt great things for God." Is this the way an invalid talks about his relationship with his physician-therapist?

Yes! Emphatically, yes! If a therapist says to a partially paralyzed invalid, "Hold on to me and stand up out of your chair," the invalid must first trust the therapist and "expect great help." Mary Drewery's interpretation of Carey's motto surely accords with his intention:

Once he was convinced of his missionary call, Carey put his complete faith in God to guide him and to supply all his needs. "Expect great things from God" had been the first part of his command at the Association Meeting in Nottingham in 1792. Though the expectations were not always met in the form or at the time Carey anticipated,

---

31. Daniel Fuller, *Gospel and Law: Contrast or Continuum?* (Grand Rapids, Mich.: Eerdmans, 1980), 117–9.

nonetheless, he would claim that the help did always come to an ever-increasing extent. Thus he was able to "achieve great things for God." The blessings were not a reward for work done; they were a prerequisite for carrying out the work.[32]

Confirmation of this interpretation from Carey himself is found in the words he requested on his tombstone, as we have seen: "A wretched, poor and helpless worm, On Thy kind arms I fall." This is a perfect description of an invalid and his kind and loving physician-therapist. It was true in life ("Expect great things from God"), and it was true in death ("On Thy kind arms I fall").

THE POWERFUL RESTING OF HUDSON TAYLOR

The same was true of Hudson Taylor, founder of the China Inland Mission. His son compiled a short work in 1932 called *Hudson Taylor's Spiritual Secret*. This secret is that Hudson Taylor learned to be a happy patient in the Savior's clinic of life.

> Frequently those who were wakeful in the little house at the Chinkiang might hear, at two or three in the morning, the soft refrain of Mr. Taylor's favorite hymn ["Jesus, I am resting, resting in the joy of what Thou art..."]. He had learned that for him, only one life was possible— just that blessed life of resting and rejoicing in the Lord under all circumstances, while He dealt with the difficulties, inward and outward, great and small.[33]

It almost goes without saying that every therapy is painful: "Through many tribulations we must enter the kingdom of God" (Acts 14:22). This is what

---

32. Mary Drewery, *William Carey, A Biography* (Grand Rapids, Mich.: Zondervan, 1978), 157.

33. Dr. and Mrs. Howard Taylor, *Hudson Taylor's Spiritual Secret* (Chicago: Moody, n. d., orig. 1932), 209. Consistently, he once answered an admirer's praise with these words: "I often think that God must have been looking for someone small enough and weak enough for Him to use, and that He found me" (201ff.). His son comments that he would have been fully in accord with Andrew Murray, who wrote, "Take time to read His Word as in His presence, that from it you may know what He asks of you and what He promises you. Let the Word create around you, create within you a holy atmosphere, a holy heavenly light, in which your soul will be refreshed and strengthened for the work of daily life" (236).

Jesus meant when He said our hundredfold benefit in mission therapy would be "with persecutions" (Mark 10:30). No naïveté here. For some, the therapy includes even death, for the clinic bridges heaven and earth: "They will lay their hands on you and persecute you…and some of you they will put to death.… But not a hair of your head will perish. By your endurance you will gain your lives" (Luke 21:12, 16, 18–19).

CALLING DEATH SWEET NAMES

This is why martyr missionaries have often called death sweet names. "Though we have but a hard breakfast, yet we shall have a good dinner, we shall very soon be in heaven."[34] The faithful missionary invalid is promised a hundredfold improvement in this life, with persecutions, and in the age to come eternal life.

Missionaries are not heroes who can boast in great sacrifice for God. They are true Christian Hedonists. They know that the battle cry of Christian Hedonism is missions. They have discovered a hundred times more joy and satisfaction in a life devoted to Christ and the gospel than in a life devoted to frivolous comforts and pleasures and worldly advancements. And they have taken to heart the rebuke of Jesus: Beware of a self-pitying spirit of sacrifice! Missions is gain! Hundredfold gain!

SUMMARY AND EXHORTATION

These, then, are two great incentives from Jesus to become a World Christian and to dedicate yourself to the cause of Frontier Missions as we begin the twenty-first century.

1. Every impossibility with men is possible with God (Mark 10:27). The conversion of hardened sinners will be the work of God and will accord with His sovereign plan. We need not fear or fret over our weakness. The battle is the Lord's, and He will give the victory.

2. Christ promises to work for us and to be for us so much that when our missionary life is over, we will not be able to say we've sacrificed anything (Mark

---

34. Jeremiah Burroughs, *The Rare Jewel of Christian Contentment* (Edinburgh: Banner of Truth, 1964, orig. 1648), 83.

10:29–30). When we follow His missionary prescription, we discover that even the painful side effects work to improve our condition. Our spiritual health, our joy, improves a hundredfold. And when we die, we do not die. We gain eternal life.

I do not appeal to you to screw up your courage and sacrifice for Christ. I appeal to you to renounce all you have to obtain life that satisfies your deepest longings. I appeal to you to count all things as rubbish for the surpassing value of standing in service of the King of kings. I appeal to you to take off your store-bought rags and put on the garments of God's ambassadors. I promise you persecutions and privations—but "remember the joy"! "Blessed are those who are persecuted for righteousness' sake, for theirs is the kingdom of heaven" (Matthew 5:10).

On January 8, 1956, five Auca Indians of Ecuador killed Jim Elliot and his four missionary companions as they were trying to bring the gospel to the Auca tribe of sixty people. Five young wives lost husbands and nine children lost their fathers. Elisabeth Elliot wrote that the world called it a nightmare of tragedy. Then she added, "The world did not recognize the truth of the second clause in Jim Elliot's credo:

> He is no fool who gives what he cannot keep
> to gain what he cannot lose."[35]

---

35. Elisabeth Elliot, *Shadow of the Almighty: The Life and Testament of Jim Elliot* (New York: Harper & Brothers, 1958), 19.

*If in this life only we have hoped in Christ, we are
of all people most to be pitied.*

1 CORINTHIANS 15:19

The noble army of the martyrs praise thee.

TE DEUM

*I rejoice in my sufferings for your sake, and in my flesh I am filling up what is
lacking in Christ's afflictions for the sake of his body, that is, the church.*

COLOSSIANS 1:24

CHAPTER 10

SUFFERING

The Sacrifice of Christian Hedonism

SITTING AT THE FEET OF A SUFFERING SAINT

I have never been the same since sitting at the feet of Richard Wurmbrand. It was literally at his feet. He took off his shoes and sat in a chair on the slightly raised platform at Grace Baptist Church in south Minneapolis. (I learned later it had to do with damage to his feet during the torture he had received in a Romanian prison.) Before him—and below him—sat about a dozen pastors. He spoke of suffering. Again and again he said that Jesus "chose" suffering. He chose it. It did not merely happen to him. He chose it: "No one takes [my life] from me, but I lay it down of my own accord" (John 10:18). He asked us if we would choose suffering for the sake of Christ.

Wurmbrand died in 2001. But his impact continues. His devotional book, *Reaching Toward the Heights,* introduces him like this:

Richard Wurmbrand is an evangelical Lutheran pastor of Jewish origin who was born in 1909 in Romania. When the Communists seized his native land in 1945, he became the leader in the underground church. In 1948 he and his wife, Sabina, were arrested, and he served fourteen years in Red Prisons, including three years in solitary confinement in a subterranean cell, never seeing the sun, the stars, or flowers. He saw no

one except his guards and torturers. Christian friends in Norway purchased his freedom for $10,000 in 1964.[1]

HOW BEAUTIFUL IS SACRIFICE?

One of the stories he tells is about a Cistercian abbot who was interviewed on
Italian television. The interviewer was especially interested in the Cistercian tradition of living in silence and solitude. So he asked the abbot, "And what if you
were to realize at the end of your life that atheism is true—that there is no God?
Tell me, what if that were true?"

The Abbot replied, "Holiness, silence, and sacrifice are beautiful in themselves, even without promise of reward. I still will have used my life well."

Few glimpses into the meaning of life have had a greater impact on my contemplations about suffering. The first impact of the abbot's response was a
superficial, romantic surge of glory. But then something stuck. It did not sit
well. Something was wrong. At first I could not figure it out. Then I turned to
the great Christian sufferer, the apostle Paul, and was stunned by the gulf
between him and the abbot.

Paul's answer to the interviewer's question was utterly contrary to the
abbot's answer. The interviewer had asked, "What if your way of life turns out
to be based on a falsehood, and there is no God?" The abbot's answer in essence
was, "It was a good and noble life anyway." Paul gave his answer in 1
Corinthians 15:19: "If in this life only we have hoped in Christ, we are of all
people most to be pitied." This is the exact opposite of the abbot's answer.

Why did Paul not agree with the monk? Why didn't Paul say, "Even if
Christ is not raised from the dead, and even if there is no God, a life of love and
labor and sacrifice and suffering is a good life"? Why didn't he say that "even
without the reward of resurrection, we are not to be pitied"? Why did he say
instead, "If our hope in Christ proves false in the end, we are to be pitied more
than anyone"?

---

1. Richard Wurmbrand, *Reaching Toward the Heights* (Bartlesville, Okla.: Living Sacrifice, 1992), back
cover.

DOES LIFE GO BETTER WITH CHRIST?

This is an utterly crucial question for the Christian church, especially in prosperous, comfortable lands like America and Western Europe. How many times do we hear Christian testimonies to the effect that becoming a Christian has made life easier? I once heard the quarterback of a professional football team say that after he prayed to receive Christ, he felt good about the game again and was proud of their eight-and-eight record because he was able to go out every Sunday and give it his best.

It seems that most Christians in the prosperous West describe the benefits of Christianity in terms that would make it a good life, even if there were no God and no resurrection. Think of all the psychological benefits and relational benefits. And of course these are true and biblical: The fruit of the Holy Spirit is love, joy, and peace. So if we get love, joy, and peace from believing these things, then is it not a good life to live, even if it turns out to be based on a falsehood? Why should we be pitied?

What's wrong with Paul, then? Was he not living the abundant life? Why would he say that if there is no resurrection, we are of all men most to be pitied? It does not seem to be pitiable to live your threescore and ten in a joyful and satisfying delusion, if that delusion makes no difference whatever for the future. If delusion can turn emptiness and meaninglessness into happiness, then why not be deluded?

The answer seems to be that the Christian life for Paul was not the so-called good life of prosperity and ease. Instead, it was a life of freely chosen suffering beyond anything we ordinarily experience. Paul's belief in God and his confidence in resurrection and his hope in eternal fellowship with Christ did not produce a life of comfort and ease that would have been satisfying even without resurrection. No, what his hope produced was a life of chosen suffering. Yes, he knew joy unspeakable. But it was a "rejoicing in hope" (Romans 12:12, NASB). And that hope freed him to embrace sufferings that he never would have chosen apart from the hope of his own resurrection and the resurrection of those for whom he suffered. If there is no resurrection, Paul's sacrificial choices, by his own testimony, were pitiable.

Yes, there was joy and a sense of great significance in his suffering. But the joy was there only because of the joyful hope beyond suffering. This is the point of Romans 5:3–4: "We exult in our afflictions, knowing that affliction produces endurance, and endurance produces proven genuineness, and genuineness produces *hope*" (author's translation). So there is joy in affliction. But the joy comes because of the hope that affliction itself is helping to secure and increase. So if there is no hope, Paul is a fool to embrace this affliction and an even bigger fool to rejoice in it. But there is hope. And so Paul chooses a way of life that would be foolish and pitiable without the hope of joy beyond the grave. He answers Richard Wurmbrand's question, Yes. He chooses suffering.

IS THERE A DIFFERENCE BETWEEN CONFLICT AND CANCER?

Let's take a brief detour for a moment. Someone may ask at this point, "What about suffering I do not choose? Like cancer. Or the death of my child in a car accident? Or a severe depression? Is this chapter about any of that?" My answer is that most of this chapter is about the suffering Christians accept as part of a choice to be openly Christian in risky situations. And all situations are risky, one way or the other.

The most significant difference between sickness and persecution is that persecution is an intentional hostility from someone because we are known to be Christians, but sickness is not. Therefore, in some situations, to choose to be public Christians is to choose a way of life that accepts suffering, if God wills (1 Peter 4:19). But suffering may result from living as a Christian even when there is no intentional hostility from unbelievers. For example, a Christian may go to a disease-ridden village to minister, and then contract the disease. This is suffering as a Christian, but it is not persecution. It is a choice to suffer, if God wills, but not from the hostility of others.

But then, when you stop to think about it, all of life, if it is lived earnestly by faith in the pursuit of God's glory and the salvation of others, is like the Christian who goes to the disease-ridden village. The suffering that comes is part of the price of living where you are in obedience to the call of God. In choosing to follow Christ in the way He directs, we choose all that this path includes under His sovereign providence. Thus, all suffering that comes in the path of obedience is suffering with Christ and for Christ—whether it is cancer or conflict. And it is "chosen"—that is, we willingly take the path of obedience where the suffering befalls us, and we do not murmur against God. We may pray—as Paul did—that the suffering be removed (2 Corinthians 12:8); but if God wills, we embrace it in the end as part of the cost of discipleship in the path of obedience on the way to heaven.

ALL SUFFERING IN A CHRISTIAN CALLING IS WITH CHRIST AND FOR CHRIST

All experiences of suffering in the path of Christian obedience, whether from persecution or sickness or accident, have this in common: They all threaten our faith in the goodness of God and tempt us to leave the path of obedience. Therefore, every triumph of faith and all perseverance in obedience are testimonies to the goodness of God and the preciousness of Christ—whether the enemy is sickness, Satan, sin, or sabotage.

Therefore, all suffering, of every kind, that we endure in the path of our Christian calling is a suffering "with Christ" and "for Christ." *With Him* in the sense that the suffering comes to us as we are walking with Him by faith and in the sense that it is endured in the strength He supplies through His sympathizing high-priestly ministry (Hebrews 4:15). *For Him* in the sense that the suffering tests and proves our allegiance to His goodness and power and in the sense that it reveals His worth as an all-sufficient compensation and prize.

SATAN'S AND GOD'S DESIGN IN THE SAME SUFFERING

Not only that, but the suffering of sickness and the suffering of persecution also have this in common: They are both intended by Satan for the destruction of our faith and governed by God for the purifying of our faith.

Take first the case of persecution. In 1 Thessalonians 3:4–5, Paul describes his concern for the faith of the Thessalonians in the face of persecution:

> When we were with you, we kept telling you beforehand that we were to suffer affliction, just as it has come to pass, and just as you know. For this reason, when I could bear it no longer, I sent to learn about your faith, for fear that somehow the tempter had tempted you and our labor would be in vain.

What is plain here is that the design of the "tempter" in this affliction is to destroy faith.

But Satan is not the only designer in this affair. God rules over Satan and gives him no more leash than can accomplish His ultimate purposes. Those purposes are the opposite of Satan's, even in the very same experience of suffering. For example, the writer of Hebrews 12 shows his readers how not to lose heart in persecution because of God's loving purposes in it:

> Consider [Christ] who endured from sinners such hostility against himself, so that you may not grow weary or fainthearted. In your struggle against sin you have not yet resisted to the point of shedding your blood. And have you forgotten the exhortation that addresses you as sons? "My son, do not regard lightly the discipline of the Lord, nor be weary when reproved by him. For the Lord disciplines the one he loves, and chastises every son whom he receives" [Proverbs 3:11–12]. It is for discipline that you have to endure.... For the moment all discipline seems painful rather than pleasant, but later it yields the peaceful fruit of righteousness to those who have been trained by it. (vv. 3–7, 11)

Here is suffering that is coming from "hostility from sinners." This means that Satan has a hand in it, just as he did in the suffering of Jesus (Luke 22:3). Nevertheless, this very suffering is described as governed by God in such a way that it has the loving and fatherly design of purifying discipline. So Satan has one design for our suffering in persecution, and God has a different design for that very same experience.

But persecution is not unique in this. The same is true of sickness. Both the design of Satan and the design of God are evident in 2 Corinthians 12:7–10:

To keep me from exalting myself, there was given me a thorn in the flesh, a messenger of Satan to torment me—to keep me from exalting myself! Concerning this I implored the Lord three times that it might leave me. And He has said to me, "My grace is sufficient for you, for power is perfected in weakness." Most gladly, therefore, I will rather boast about my weaknesses, so that the power of Christ may dwell in me. Therefore I am well content with weaknesses, with insults, with distresses, with persecutions, with difficulties, for Christ's sake; for when I am weak, then I am strong. (NASB)

Here, Paul's physical suffering—the thorn in the flesh—is called "a messenger of Satan." But the design of this suffering is "to keep [Paul] from exalting [himself]," which never would have been Satan's design. So the point is that Christ sovereignly accomplishes His loving, purifying purpose by overruling Satan's destructive attempts. Satan is always aiming to destroy our faith, but Christ magnifies His own power in our weakness.

ARE SUFFERING FROM PERSECUTION AND SICKNESS DISTINGUISHABLE?

Another reason for not distinguishing sharply between persecution and sickness is that the pain from persecution and the pain from sickness are not always distinguishable. Decades after his torture for Christ in a Romanian prison, Richard Wurmbrand still suffered from the physical effects. Was he being "persecuted" as he endured the pain in his feet thirty years later? Or consider the apostle Paul. Among the sufferings that he listed as a "servant of Christ" was the fact that he was shipwrecked three times and spent a night and a day in the water. He also says his sufferings for Christ included "toil and hardship, through many a sleepless night, in hunger and thirst, often without food, in cold and exposure" (2 Corinthians 11:27).

Suppose he got pneumonia from all this work and exposure. Would that have been "persecution"? Paul did not make a distinction between being beaten by rods or having a boating accident or being cold while traveling between towns. For him any suffering that befell him while serving Christ was part of the "cost" of discipleship. When a missionary's child gets diarrhea, we think of this as part of the price of faithfulness. But for any parent walking in the path of obedience to God's calling, it is the same price. What turns sufferings into sufferings *with* and *for* Christ is not how intentional our enemies are, but how faithful we are. If we are Christ's, then what befalls us is for His glory and for our good, whether it is caused by enzymes or by enemies.

IS GLUTTONY THE ALTERNATIVE TO RESURRECTION?

Now we turn from our brief detour to Paul's amazing statement in 1 Corinthians 15:19 that the life he has chosen is pitiable if there is no resurrection. In other words, Christianity as Paul understands it is not the best way to maximize pleasure if this life is all there is. Paul tells us the best way to maximize our pleasures in this life: "If the dead are not raised, 'Let us eat and drink, for tomorrow we die'" (1 Corinthians 15:32). He does not mean something as naïve as sheer Epicureanism or debauchery. That is not the best way to maximize your pleasures, as anyone knows who has followed the path of alcoholism and gluttony. Drunks and gluttons are to be pitied just like Christians if there is no resurrection.

But what he does mean by the phrase "Let us eat and drink" is that without the hope of resurrection, one should pursue ordinary pleasures and avoid extraordinary suffering. This is the life Paul has rejected as a Christian. Thus, if the dead are not raised, and if there is no God and no heaven, he would not have pummeled his body the way he did. He would not have turned down wages for his tentmaking the way he did. He would not have walked into five whippings of thirty-nine lashes. He would not have endured three beatings with rods. He would not have risked his life in deserts and rivers and cities and seas and at the hands of robbers and angry mobs. He would not have accepted sleepless nights and cold and exposure. He would not have endured so long with backsliding and hypocritical Christians (2 Corinthians 11:23–29). Instead, he would have simply lived the good life of comfort and ease as a respectable Jew with the prerogatives of Roman citizenship.

When Paul says, "If the dead are not raised, let us eat and drink," he does not mean "Let's all become lechers." He means there is a normal, simple, comfortable, ordinary life of human delights that we may enjoy with no troubling thoughts of heaven of hell or sin or holiness or God—*if* there is no resurrection from the dead. And what stunned me about this train of thought is that many of the professing Christians seem to aim at just this—and call it Christianity.

Paul did not see his relation to Christ as the key to maximizing his physical comforts and pleasures *in this life*. No, Paul's relation to Christ was a call to choose suffering—a suffering that was beyond what would make atheism "meaningful" or "beautiful" or "heroic." It was a suffering that would have been utterly foolish and pitiable to choose if there is no resurrection into the joyful presence of Christ.

AN ALMOST UNBELIEVABLE INDICTMENT OF WESTERN CHRISTIANITY

This was the thing I finally saw in pondering Wurmbrand's story about the Cistercian abbot. In Paul's radically different viewpoint I saw an almost unbelievable indictment of Western Christianity. Am I overstating this? Judge for yourself. How many Christians do you know who could say, "The lifestyle I have chosen as a Christian would be utterly foolish and pitiable if there is no resurrection"? How many Christians are there who could say, "The suffering I have freely chosen to embrace for Christ would be a pitiable life if there is no resurrection"? As I see it, these are shocking questions.

CHRISTIANITY: A LIFE OF CHOSEN SUFFERING

"If in this life only we have hoped in Christ, we are of all people most to be pitied" (1 Corinthians 15:19). The Christian life for Paul was a life of chosen sacrifice on earth, that he might gain the joy of fellowship with Christ in the age to come. Here is how he put it:

Whatever gain I had, I counted as loss for the sake of Christ. Indeed, I count everything as loss because of the surpassing worth of knowing Christ Jesus my Lord. For his sake I have suffered the loss of all things and count them as rubbish, in order that I may gain Christ.... I share his sufferings…that by any means possible I may attain the resurrection from the dead. (Philippians 3:7–8, 10–11)

I say it again: The call of Christ is a call to live a life of sacrifice and loss and suffering—a life that would be foolish to live if there were no resurrection from the dead. This is a conscious choice for Paul. Listen to his protest: "If the dead are not raised.... Why am I in danger every hour? I protest, brothers, by my pride in you, which I have in Christ Jesus our Lord, I die every day!" (1 Corinthians 15:29–31). This is what Paul has chosen. He "protests" because he does not *have* to live this way. He chooses it: "In danger every hour!" "Dying every day!" This is why he says he should be pitied if there is no resurrection from the dead. He chose a path that leads to trouble and pain virtually every day of his life. "I die every day."

WHY? WHY DOES HE DO IT?

This is not normal. Human beings flee suffering. We move to safer neighborhoods. We choose milder climates. We buy air conditioners. We take aspirin. We come out of the rain. We avoid dark streets. We purify our water. We do not normally choose a way of life that would put us in "danger every hour." Paul's life is out of sync with ordinary human choices. Virtually no advertising slogans lure us into daily dying.

So what is driving the apostle Paul to "share abundantly in Christ's sufferings" (2 Corinthians 1:5) and to be a "fool for Christ's sake" (1 Corinthians 4:10)? Why would he make choices that expose him to "hunger and thirst...[being] poorly dressed...buffeted...homeless...reviled...persecuted... slandered…like the scum of the world, the refuse of all things" (1 Corinthians 4:11–13)?

"I Will Show Him How Much He Must Suffer"

Perhaps it was simple obedience to Christ's commission expressed in Acts 9:15–16. When Jesus sent Ananias to open Paul's eyes after he was blinded on the road to Damascus, He said, "Go, for [Paul] is a chosen instrument of mine to carry my name before the Gentiles and kings and the children of Israel. For *I will show him how much he must suffer for the sake of my name."* In other words, suffering was simply part of Paul's apostolic calling. To be faithful to his calling, he had to embrace what Christ has given him: much suffering.

"Gave" is the right word. Because when writing to the Philippians, Paul, incredibly, calls suffering a gift, just like faith is a *gift:* "To you it has been *granted* (*echaristhē* = freely given) for Christ's sake, not only to believe in Him, but also to *suffer* for His sake" (Philippians 1:29, NASB). But this would mean that the "gift" given to him as part of his apostleship is not viewed by Paul as limited to apostles. It is "granted" to the Philippian believers, the whole church.

Others have made the same strange discovery that suffering is a gift to be embraced. Aleksandr Solzhenitsyn spoke of his time in prison, with all its pain, as a gift:

> It was granted to me to carry away from my prison years on my bent back, which nearly broke beneath its load, this essential experience: how a human being becomes evil and how good. In the intoxication of youthful successes I had felt myself to be infallible, and I was therefore cruel. In the surfeit of power I was a murderer and an oppressor. In my most evil moments I was convinced that I was doing good, and I was well supplied with systematic arguments. It was only when I lay there on rotting prison straw that I sensed within myself the first stirrings of good. Gradually it was disclosed to me that the line separating good and evil passes not through states, nor between classes, nor between political parties either—but right through every human heart—and through all human hearts.… That is why I turn back to the years of my

imprisonment and say, sometimes to the astonishment of those about me: *"Bless you, prison!"* I…have served enough time there. I nourished my soul there, and I say without hesitation: *"Bless you, prison,* for having been in my life!"[2]

Solzhenitsyn agrees with the apostle Paul that suffering is—or can be—a gift not just for apostles, but for every Christian.

TO SHOW HE WAS SIMPLY A CHRISTIAN

Which raises the question: Did Paul, then, embrace his suffering because it would confirm that he was simply a faithful disciple of Jesus? Jesus had said, "If anyone would come after me, let him deny himself and take up his cross daily and follow me. For whoever would save his life will lose it, but whoever loses his life for my sake will save it" (Luke 9:23–24). So there is no true Christianity without cross-bearing and a *daily* dying—which sounds very much like Paul's "I die every day" (1 Corinthians 15:31). Moreover, Jesus had told His disciples, "A servant is not greater than his master. If they persecuted me, they will also persecute you" (John 15:20). So something would be amiss if Paul did not share in the sufferings of Jesus. Jesus gave His disciples an ominous image of their ministry: "Behold, I am sending you out as lambs in the midst of wolves" (Luke 10:3). And so He promised them, "You will be delivered up even by parents and brothers and relatives and friends, and some of you they will put to death. You will be hated by all for my name's sake" (Luke 21:16–17; cf. Matthew 24:9).

Evidently, Paul did not consider these promises of suffering as limited to the original twelve apostles, because he passed them on to his churches. For example, he strengthened all his converts by telling them, "Through many tribulations we must enter the kingdom of God" (Acts 14:22). And he encouraged the suffering Thessalonian believers by exhorting them not to be "moved by these afflictions. For you yourselves know that we are destined for this" (1 Thessalonians 3:3). And when he wrote to Timothy, he made it a general principle: "Indeed, all

---

2. Aleksandr I. Solzhenitsyn, *The Gulag Archipelago: 1918-1956. An Experiment in Literary Investigation,* vol. 2, trans. Thomas P. Whitney (New York: HarperCollins, 1975; Boulder: Westview, 1997), 615–7.

who desire to live a godly life in Christ Jesus will be persecuted" (2 Timothy 3:12). When he spoke of his sufferings, he did not treat them as unique, but said to the churches, "Be imitators of me" (1 Corinthians 4:16). So it would be understandable if Paul embraced a life of suffering because it would simply confirm that he was a Christian. "If they persecuted me, they will also persecute you."

WEANING CHRISTIANS OFF THE BREAST OF SELF-RELIANCE

Since he believed that suffering was part of faithful Christian living, Paul probed into why this might be so. His own experience of suffering drove him deep into the ways of God's love for His children. For example, he learned that God uses our suffering to wean us from self-reliance and cast us on Himself alone. After suffering in Asia, Paul says:

> We do not want you to be ignorant, brothers, of the affliction we experienced in Asia. For we were so utterly burdened beyond our strength that we despaired even of life itself. Indeed, we felt that we had received the sentence of death. But *that was to make us rely not on ourselves but on God* who raises the dead. (2 Corinthians 1:8–9)

This is God's universal purpose for all Christian suffering: more contentment in God and less satisfaction in self and the world. I have never heard anyone say, "The really deep lessons of life have come through times of ease and comfort." But I have heard strong saints say, "Every significant advance I have ever made in grasping the depths of God's love and growing deep with Him has come through suffering."

Malcolm Muggeridge, the Christian journalist who died in 1990, spoke for almost all serious biblical Christians who have lived long enough to wake up from the dreamworld of painlessness when he said:

> Contrary to what might be expected, I look back on experiences that at the time seemed especially desolating and painful, with particular

satisfaction. Indeed, I can say with complete truthfulness that everything I have learned in my seventy-five years in this world, everything that has truly enhanced and enlightened my existence, has been through affliction and not through happiness, whether pursued or attained. In other words, if it ever were to be possible to eliminate affliction from our earthly existence by means of some drug or other medical mumbo jumbo…the result would not be to make life delectable, but to make it too banal or trivial to be endurable. This of course is what the cross [of Christ] signifies, and it is the cross more than anything else, that has called me inexorably to Christ.[3]

Samuel Rutherford said that when he was cast into the cellars of affliction, he remembered that the great King always kept his wine there.[4] Charles Spurgeon said that "they who dive in the sea of affliction bring up rare pearls."[5]

To Magnify Christ As a Superior Satisfaction

The pearl of greatest price is the glory of Christ. Thus, Paul stresses that in our sufferings the glory of Christ's all-sufficient grace is magnified. If we rely on Him in our calamity and He sustains our "rejoicing in hope," then He is shown to be the all-satisfying God of grace and strength that He is. If we hold fast to Him "when all around our soul gives way," then we show that He is more to be desired than all we have lost. Christ said to the suffering apostle, "My grace is sufficient for you, for *my power is made perfect in weakness.*" Paul responded to this: "Therefore I will boast all the more gladly of my weaknesses, *so that the power of Christ may rest upon me.* For the sake of Christ, then, I am content with weaknesses, insults, hardships, persecutions, and calamities. For when I am weak, then I am strong" (2 Corinthians 12:9–10). So suffering clearly is designed by God not only as a way to wean Christians off of self and onto grace,

---

3. Malcom Muggeridge, *Homemade,* July 1990.
4. *Letters of Samuel Rutherford.*
5. Charles Spurgeon, "The Golden Key of Prayer," in *The Metropolitan Tabernacle Pulpit* (Banner of Truth) (Sermon #619), 12 March 1865.

but also as a way to spotlight that grace and make it shine. That is precisely what faith does; it magnifies Christ's future grace.

The deep things of life in God are discovered in suffering. So it was with Jesus Himself: "Although he was a son, he learned obedience through what he suffered" (Hebrews 5:8). The same book where we read this also tells us that Jesus never sinned (4:15). So "learning obedience" does not mean switching from disobedience to obedience. It means growing deeper and deeper with God in the experience of obedience. It means experiencing depths of yieldedness to God that would not have been otherwise demanded.

THE UNSPEAKABLE WORDS OF CHRISTIAN SUFFERING

As Paul contemplated the path of his Master, he was moved to follow. But just at this point I have been astonished by Paul's words. When he describes the relationship between Christ's sufferings and his own, he speaks what seems unspeakable. He says to the Colossian church, "Now I rejoice in my sufferings for your sake, and in my flesh I am filling up *(antanaplērō)* what is lacking in Christ's afflictions *(husterēmata)* for the sake of his body, that is, the church" (Colossians 1:24). This may be the most powerful motive for Paul's choosing a life of suffering. These words have filled me with longing for the church of Jesus Christ. Oh, that we would embrace the necessary suffering appointed for the advancement of Christ's kingdom in the world!

HOW CAN WE COMPLETE THE SUFFERINGS OF CHRIST?

What does Paul mean that he "fills what is lacking in the afflictions of Christ"? Is this a belittling of the all-sufficient, atoning worth of the death of Jesus? Did not Jesus Himself say as He died, "It is finished" (John 19:30)? Is it not true that "by a single offering [Christ] *has perfected for all time* those who are being sanctified" (Hebrews 10:14)? And that "he entered *once for all* into the holy places...by means of his own blood, thus securing an *eternal* redemption" (Hebrews 9:12)? Paul knew and taught that the afflictions of Christ were a complete and sufficient ground for our justification. We are "justified by his blood" (Romans 5:9). Paul taught that Christ chose suffering and was "obedient to the point of death" (Philippians 2:8). That obedient suffering, as the climax of a perfect life of righteousness (Matthew 3:15), was the all-sufficient ground of our righteousness before God. "As by [Adam's] disobedience the many were made sinners, so by the obedience of [Christ] the many will be made righteous" (Romans 5:19). So Paul does not mean that his sufferings complete the atoning worth of Jesus' afflictions.

There is a better interpretation. Paul's sufferings complete Christ's afflictions *not* by adding anything to their worth, but by extending them to the people they were meant to save. What is lacking in the afflictions of Christ is not that they are deficient in worth, as though they could not sufficiently cover the sins of all who believe. What is lacking is that the infinite value of Christ's afflictions is not known and trusted in the world. These afflictions and what they mean are still hidden to most peoples. And God's intention is that the mystery be revealed to all the nations. So the afflictions of Christ are "lacking" in the sense that they are not seen and known and loved among the nations. They must be carried by the ministers of the gospel. And those ministers of the gospel "complete" what is lacking in the afflictions of Christ by extending them to others.

EPAPHRODITUS IS THE KEY

There is a strong confirmation of this interpretation in the use of similar words in Philippians 2:30. There was a man named Epaphroditus in the church at Philippi. When the church there gathered support for Paul (perhaps money or supplies or books), they decided to send them to Paul in Rome by the hand of Epaphroditus. In his travels with this supply, Epaphroditus almost lost his life. He was sick to the point of death, but God spared him (Philippians 2:27).

So Paul tells the church in Philippi to honor Epaphroditus when he comes back (v. 29), and he explains his reason with words very similar to Colossians 1:24. He says, "He nearly died for the work of Christ, risking his life to *complete* [*antanaplērē*, a similar word to the one in Colossians 1:24] *what was lacking* [*ta husterēmata*, same words as in Colossians 1:24] in your service to me." In the Greek original, the phrase *"complete what is lacking* in your service to me" is almost identical with *"complete what is lacking* in Christ's afflictions."

In what sense, then, was the service of the Philippians to Paul "lacking," and in what sense did Epaphroditus "fill up" what was lacking in their service? A hundred years ago commentator Marvin Vincent explained it like this:

> The gift to Paul was a gift of the church as a body. It was a sacrificial offering of love. What was lacking, and what would have been grateful to Paul and to the church alike, was the church's presentation of this offering in person. This was impossible, and Paul represents Epaphroditus as supplying this lack by his affectionate and zealous ministry.[6]

I think that is exactly what the same words mean in Colossians 1:24. Christ has prepared a love offering for the world by suffering and dying for sinners. It is full and lacking in nothing—except one thing, a personal presentation by Christ Himself to the nations of the world. God's answer to this lack is to call the people of Christ (people like Paul) to make a personal presentation of the afflictions of Christ to the world.

In doing this, we "fill up what is lacking in Christ's afflictions." We finish what they were designed for, namely, a personal presentation to the people who do not know about their infinite worth.

Filling Afflictions with Afflictions

But the most amazing thing about Colossians 1:24 is *how* Paul fills up what is lacking in Christ's afflictions. He says that it is *his own sufferings* that fill up Christ's afflictions. "I rejoice in *my sufferings* for your sake, and *in my flesh* I am filling up what is lacking in Christ's afflictions." This means, then, that Paul exhibits the sufferings of Christ by suffering *himself* for those he is trying to win. In *his* sufferings they see Christ's sufferings. Here is the astounding upshot: *God intends for the afflictions of Christ to be presented to the world through the afflictions of His people.* God really means for the body of Christ, the church, to experience some of the suffering He experienced so that when we proclaim the Cross as the

---

6. Marvin Vincent, *Epistle to the Philippians and to Philemon*, I. C. C. (Edinburgh: T. & T. Clark, 1897), 78.

way to life, people will see the marks of the Cross in us and feel the love of the Cross from us. Our calling is to make the afflictions of Christ real for people by the afflictions we experience in bringing them the message of salvation.

Since Christ is no longer on the earth, He wants His body, the church, to reveal *His* suffering in *its* suffering. Since we are His body, our sufferings are His sufferings. Romanian pastor Josef Tson put it like this: "I am an extension of Jesus Christ. When I was beaten in Romania, He suffered in my body. It is not my suffering: I only had the honor to share His sufferings."[7] Therefore, our sufferings testify to the kind of love Christ has for the world.

"I Bear on My Body the Marks of Jesus"

This is why Paul spoke of his scars as the "marks of Jesus." In his wounds people could see Christ's wounds: "I bear on my body the marks of Jesus" (Galatians 6:17). The point of bearing the marks of Jesus is that Jesus might be seen and His love might work powerfully in those who see.

> [We are] always carrying in the body the death of Jesus, so that the life of Jesus may also be manifested in our bodies. For we who live are always being given over to death for Jesus' sake, so that the life of Jesus also may be manifested in our mortal flesh. So death is at work in us, but life in you. (2 Corinthians 4:10–12)

"The Blood of the Martyrs Is Seed"

The history of the expansion of Christianity has proved that "the blood of the martyrs is seed"[8]—the seed of new life in Christ spreading through the world. For almost three hundred years, Christianity grew in soil that was wet with the blood of the martyrs. In his *History of Christian Missions,* Stephen Neil mentions the sufferings of the early Christians as one of the six main reasons the church grew so rapidly:

7. Josef Tson, "A Theology of Maryrdom," an undated booklet of the Romanian Missionary Society, 1415 Hill Avenue, Wheaton, IL 60187, p. 4.
8. Tertullian, *Apologeticus,* c. 50.

Because of their dangerous situation vis-á-vis the law, Christians were almost bound to meet in secret.... Every Christian knew that sooner or later he might have to testify to his faith at the cost of his life.... When persecution did break out, martyrdom could be attended by the utmost possible publicity. The Roman public was hard and cruel, but it was not altogether without compassion; and there is no doubt that the attitude of the martyrs, and particularly of the young women who suffered along with the men, made a deep impression.... In the earlier records what we find is calm, dignified, decorous behaviour; cool courage in the face of torment, courtesy towards enemies, and a joyful acceptance of suffering as the way appointed by the Lord to lead to his heavenly kingdom. There are a number of well-authenticated cases of conversion of pagans in the very moment of witnessing the condemnation and death of Christians; there must have been far more who received impressions that in the course of time would be turned into a living faith.[9]

"How Can I Blaspheme My King Who Saved Me?"

One example of such a powerful witness through suffering was the martyrdom of Polycarp, bishop of Smyrna who died in A.D. 155. His student Irenaeus said that Polycarp had been a student of the apostle John. We know he was very old when he died because when the proconsul commanded him to recant and curse Christ, he said, "Eighty and six years have I served him and he hath done me no wrong; how then can I blaspheme my king who saved me?"[10]

During one season of persecution, a frenzied crowd in Smyrna cried out for a search to be made for Polycarp. He had moved to a town just outside the city, and three days before his death he had a dream from which he concluded, "I must needs be burned alive." So when the search was finally made, instead of fleeing, he said, "The will of God be done." The ancient account of the martyrdom gives the following record:

9. Stephen Neil, *A History of Christian Missions* (Harmondsworth, Middlesex: Penguin Books, 1964), 43–4.
10. Quoted in "The Martyrdom of Polycarp," in *Documents of the Christian Church,* ed. Henry Bettenson (London: Oxford University Press, 1967), 10.

So, hearing of their arrival, he came down and talked with them, while all that were present marveled at his age and constancy, and that there was so much ado about the arrest of such an old man. Then he ordered that something should be served for them to eat and drink, at that late hour, as much as they wanted. And he besought them that they should grant him an hour that he might pray freely. They gave him leave, and he stood and prayed, being so filled with the grace of God that for two hours he could not hold his peace, while they that heard him were amazed, and the men repented that they had come after so venerable an old man.[11]

When he was finally taken away and condemned to be burned, they tried to nail his hands to the stake, but he pled against it and said, "Let me be as I am. He that granted me to endure the fire will grant me also to remain at the pyre unmoved without being secured with nails."[12] When his body seemed not to be consumed by the fire, an executioner drove a dagger into his body. The ancient account concludes: "All the multitude marveled at the great difference between the unbelievers and the elect."[13] In large measure, this is what explains the triumph of Christianity in the early centuries. They triumphed by their suffering. It did not just accompany their witness; it was the capstone of their witness. "They have conquered [Satan] by the blood of the Lamb and by the word of their testimony, *for they loved not their lives even unto death*" (Revelation 12:11).

NOT TILL THE NUMBER OF MARTYRS IS COMPLETE

It is not a fluke of history that the church expands and is strengthened by suffering and martyrdom. This is the way God means it to be. One of the most powerful evidences that God intends to complete His saving purposes in the world by means of suffering is found in the book of Revelation. The setting is a vision of heaven where the souls of the martyrs cry out, "How long, O Lord?" In other words, when will history be complete and Your purposes of salvation

---

11. Ibid., 9–10.
12. Ibid., 11.
13. Ibid., 12.

and judgment be accomplished? The answer is ominous for all of us who want to be a part of the completion of the Great Commission: "They were…told to rest a little longer, until the number of their fellow servants and their brothers should be complete, who were to be killed as they themselves had been" (Revelation 6:11).

What this means is that God has planned to complete His purposes by appointing a certain number of martyrs. When that number is complete, then the end will come. George Otis, Jr. shocked many at the second Lausanne Congress of World Evangelization in Manila in 1989 when he asked, "Is our failure to thrive in Muslim countries owing to the absence of martyrs? Can a covert church grow in strength? Does a young church need martyr models?" Fittingly, he concludes his book *The Last of the Giants* with a chapter titled "Risky Safety." In it he writes:

Should the Church in politically or socially trying circumstances remain covert to avoid potential eradication by forces hostile to Christianity? Or would more open confrontation with prevailing spiritual ignorance and deprivation—even if it produced Christian martyrs—be more likely to lead to evangelistic breakthroughs? Islamic fundamentalists claim that their spiritual revolution is fueled by the blood of martyrs. Is it conceivable that Christianity's failure to thrive in the Muslim world is due to the notable absence of Christian martyrs? And can the Muslim community take seriously the claims of a Church in hiding?… The question is not whether it is wise at times to keep worship and witness discreet, but rather how long this may continue before we are guilty of "hiding our light under a bushel.… The record shows that from Jerusalem and Damascus to Ephesus and Rome, the apostles were beaten, stoned, conspired against and imprisoned for their witness. Invitations were rare, and never the basis for their missions."[14]

---

14. George Otis, Jr., *The Last of the Giants: Lifting the Veil on Islam and the End Times* (Grand Rapids, Mich.: Chosen, 1991), 261, 263.

Otis would no doubt agree with Gregory the Great (pope from 590 to 604), when he said, "The death of the martyrs blossoms in the lives of the faithful."[15]

THE BLOOD FLOWED FROM OUR WOUNDS LIKE A FOUNTAIN

There are countless examples in our own day of *choosing* to suffer for the purpose of Colossians 1:24—to fill up what is lacking in Christ's afflictions by presenting them to others through suffering.[16] In late 1995, as I was working on the second edition of this book, a missionary letter describing such suffering came to my attention. I quickly e-mailed the missionary in Africa to confirm the facts. He spoke personally with Dansa, the man in question, and got his permission for me to quote this story in Dansa's words from the letter:

> Around 1980 there was a time of severe persecution from the local officials of the communist government in my area of Wolayta. At the time, I was working in a government office, but I was also serving as the leader of the Christian youth association for all the churches in my area. The communist officials repeatedly came to me to ask for my help in teaching the doctrines of the revolution among the youth. Many other Christians were giving in because the pressure was very great, but I could only say no.
>
> At first, their approach was positive: they offered me promotions and pay increases. But then the imprisonments began. The first two were fairly short. The third time lasted an entire year. During this time communist cadres would regularly come to brainwash the nine of us believers (six men and three women—one of whom would later become my wife) who were being held together. But when one of the cadres converted to Christ, we were beaten and forced to haul water from long distances and carry heavy stones to clear farm land.

15. Quoted in Tson, "A Theology of Martyrdom," 1.
16. See the examples in John Piper, *Let the Nations Be Glad: The Supremacy of God in Missions*, 3nd ed., revised and expanded (Grand Rapids, Mich.: Baker, 2010), chapter 3. See almost any of the books by Richard Wurmbrand; for example, *Tortured for Christ* or *If that Were Christ, Would You Give Him Your Blanket?* or *Victorious Faith*. Other sources include *Called to Suffer, Called to Triumph* by Herbert Schlossberg and *God Reigns in China* by Leslie Lyall.

The worst time came during a two-week period in which the prison official would wake us early while it was still dark when no one would see and force us to walk on our bare knees over a distance up to 1 1/2 kilometers on the gravel road of the town. It would take us about three hours. After the first day, the blood flowed from our wounds like a fountain, but we felt nothing.

On another occasion one particularly brutal prison official forced us to lie on our backs under the blazing sun for six straight hours. I don't know why I said it, but when we finished I told him, "You caused the sun's rays to strike us, but God will strike you." A short time later, the official contracted severe diabetes and died.

When the communist government fell several years later, the head official invited us to preach in the jail. At that time, twelve prisoners being held for murder received Christ. We have continued to minister in the prison, and there are now 170 believers. Most of the prison officials have also believed.

Only God can sort out all the influences that led to this remarkable time of harvest among the prison inmates and officials. But surely it would be naïve to think that the suffering of Dansa was not part of the compelling presentation of the reality of Christ in the lives of those who believed.

"Thank You, Natasha, Wherever You Are"

One of the most moving and incredible accounts of suffering filling up what is lacking in Christ's afflictions is found in Sergei Kourdakov's autobiography, *The Persecutor*. Kourdakov was commissioned by the Russian secret police to raid prayer gatherings and persecute believers with extraordinary brutality. But the afflictions of one believer changed his life:

I saw Victor Matveyev reach and grab for a young girl [Natasha Zhdanova] who was trying to escape to another room. She was a beautiful young girl. *What a waste to be a Believer.* Victor caught her, picked her above his head, and held her high in the air for a second. She was pleading, "Don't, please don't. Dear God, help us!" Victor threw her so hard she hit the wall at the same height she was thrown, then dropped to the floor, semiconscious, moaning. Victor turned and laughed and exclaimed, "I'll bet the idea of God went flying out of her head."

On a later raid, Sergei was shocked to see Natasha again.

I quickly surveyed the room and saw a sight I couldn't believe! There she was, the same girl! It couldn't be. But it was. Only three nights before, she had been at the other meeting and had been viciously thrown across the room. It was the first time I really got a good look at her. She was more beautiful than I had first remembered—a very beautiful girl with long, flowing, blond hair, large blue eyes, and smooth skin, one of the most naturally beautiful girls I have ever seen....

I picked her up and flung her on a table facedown. Two of us stripped her clothes off. One of my men held her down and I began to beat her again and again. My hands began to sting under the blows. Her skin started to blister. I continued to beat her, until pieces of bloody flesh came off on my hand. She moaned but fought desperately not to cry. To suppress her cries, she bit her lower lip until it was bitten through and blood ran down her chin.

At last she gave in and began sobbing. When I was so exhausted I couldn't raise my arm for even one more blow, and her backside was a mass of raw flesh, I pushed her off the table, and she collapsed on the floor.

To Sergei's shock, he later encountered her at yet *another* prayer meeting. But this time something was different:

There *she* was again—Natasha Zhdanova!

Several of the guys saw her too. Alex Gulyaev moved toward Natasha, hatred filling his face, his club raised above his head.

Then something I never expected to see suddenly happened. Without warning, Victor jumped between Natasha and Alex, facing Alex head-on.

"Get out of my way," Alex shouted angrily.

Victor's feet didn't move. He raised his club and said menacingly, "Alex, I'm telling you, don't touch her! No one touches her!"

I listened in amazement. Incredibly, one of my most brutal men was protecting one of the Believers! "Get back!" he shouted to Alex. "Get back or I'll let you have it." He shielded Natasha, who was cowering on the floor.

Angered, Alex shouted, "You want her for yourself, don't you?"

"No," Victor shouted back. "She has something we don't have! Nobody touches her! Nobody!"

…For one of the first times in my life, I was deeply moved… Natasha *did* have something! She had been beaten horribly. She had been warned and threatened. She had gone through unbelievable suffering, but here she was again. Even Victor had been moved and recognized it. She had something we didn't have. I wanted to run after her and ask, "What is it?" I wanted to talk to her, but she was gone. This heroic Christian girl who had suffered so much at our hands somehow touched and troubled me very much.

The Lord later opened Sergei's heart to the glorious good news of Jesus Christ. As he later reflected on Natasha, whom he never saw again, he wrote:

And, finally, to Natasha, whom I beat terribly and who was willing to be beaten a third time for her faith, I want to say, Natasha, largely because of you, my life is now changed and I am a fellow Believer in Christ with you. I have a new life before me. God has forgiven me; I hope you can also.

Thank you, Natasha, wherever you are.

I will never, never forget you.[17]

DEMOTED FOR CHRIST AND FOR SALVATION

Josef Tson has thought deeply about the issue of suffering for Christ as a way to show Christ to the world. He was the pastor of the Second Baptist Church of Oradea, Romania, until 1981, when he was exiled by the government. In his book, *Suffering, Martyrdom and Rewards in Heaven,* he writes in the conclusion: "Suffering and martyrdom have to be seen as part of God's plan; they are His instruments by which He achieves His purposes in history and by which He will accomplish His final purpose with man." I have heard Tson interpret Colossians 1:24 by saying that Christ's suffering is for *propitiation;* our suffering is for *propagation.* He points out that not only Colossians 1:24, but also 2 Timothy 2:10, makes suffering the means of evangelism: "I endure everything for the sake of the elect, that they also may obtain the salvation that is in Christ Jesus." According to Tson, Paul is saying:

> If I had remained a pastor in Antioch, in that affluent and peaceful city, in that wonderful church with so many prophets and such great blessings, nobody in Asia Minor or Europe would have been saved. In order for them to be saved, I have had to accept being beaten with rods, scourged, stoned, treated as the scum of the earth, becoming a walking death. But when I walk like this, wounded and bleeding, people see the love of God, people hear the message of the cross, and they are saved. If we stay in the safety of our affluent churches and we do not accept the cross, others may not be saved. How many are not saved because we don't accept the cross?[18]

He illustrates how the very suffering of Christians is what often provides the means of fruitful evangelism:

---

17. Sergei Kourdakov, *The Persecutor* (Carmel, N.Y.: Fleming H. Revell, 1973), 192, 194, 195, 199, 200, 251.
18. Tson, "A Theology of Martyrdom," 2.

I had a man in an important position whom I baptized come to me and ask, "Now what shall I do? They will convene three or four thousand people to expose me and mock me. They will give me five minutes to defend myself. How should I do it?"

"Brother," I told him, "defending yourself is the only thing you shouldn't do. This is your unique chance to tell them who you were before, and what Jesus made of you; who Jesus is, and what he is for you now."

His face shone and he said, "Brother Josef, I know what I am going to do." And he did it well—so well that afterwards he was severely demoted. He lost almost half of his salary. But he kept coming to me after that saying, "Brother Joseph, you know I cannot walk in that factory now without someone coming up to me. Wherever I go, somebody pulls me in a corner, looks around to see that nobody sees him talking to me, and then whispers, 'Give me the address of your church,' or 'Tell me more about Jesus,' or 'Do you have a Bible for me?'"

Every kind of suffering can become a ministry for other people's salvation.[19]

CHOOSING TO SUFFER FOR THE SAKE OF NATIONS

I conclude, then, that when Paul said, "If in this life only we have hoped in Christ, we are of all men most to be pitied," he meant that Christianity means choosing and embracing a life of suffering for Christ that would be pitiable if Christ proved false. Christianity is not a life that one would embrace as abundant and satisfying without the hope of fellowship with Christ in the resurrection. And what we have seen is that this embracing of suffering is not just an accompaniment of our witness to Christ; it is the visible expression of it. Our sufferings make Christ's sufferings known so that people can see the kind of love Christ offers. We complete Christ's afflictions by providing what they do not have, namely, a personal, vivid presentation to those who do not see Christ suffer in person.

---

19. Ibid., 3.

The startling implication of this is that the saving purposes of Christ among the nations and in our neighborhoods will not be accomplished unless Christians choose to suffer. At the extreme end of this suffering, the number of martyrs is not yet complete (Revelation 6:11). Without them, the final frontiers of world evangelization will not be crossed. Less extreme is the simple costliness in time and convenience and money and effort to replace excessive and addictive leisure with acts of servant love: "Let your light shine before others, so that they may see your good works and give glory to your Father who is in heaven" (Matthew 5:16).

BUT IS THIS CHRISTIAN HEDONISM?

I have titled this chapter "Suffering: The Sacrifice of Christian Hedonism," even though in the previous chapter I quoted David Livingstone as saying that the sufferings of his missionary service were not a "sacrifice." This is not a contradiction to or disagreement with Livingstone. Words are like that. Context is almost everything. When he says suffering is not a sacrifice, he means the blessings outweigh the losses. When I say that suffering is a sacrifice, I mean that there are losses—great losses. When you realize that I agree with Livingstone, it simply implies that I see the blessings as massive.

But I am going to retain the use of the word *sacrifice*. The pain is too great, the losses too real, to pretend that we can talk only in terms of no sacrifice. We must simply keep our definitions clear.

My answer is: Yes, this is Christian Hedonism. The entire New Testament treats suffering in a Christian Hedonist context.

Was Paul pursuing deep and lasting joy when he chose suffering—so much suffering that his life would have been utterly foolish and pitiable if there were no resurrection from the dead? The question virtually answers itself. If it is the resurrection alone that makes Paul's painful life choices *not* pitiable, but praiseworthy (and possible!), then it is precisely his hope and quest for that resurrection that sustains and empowers his suffering. This is in fact exactly what he says: He counts all ordinary human privileges as loss "that I may know [Christ] and the power of his resurrection, and may share his sufferings, becoming like him in his death, *that by any means possible I may attain the resurrection from the dead"* (Philippians 3:10–11). His aim is to so live—and suffer—that he is assured of resurrection from the dead.

Giving All to Gain Christ

Why? Because resurrection meant full, bodily, eternal fellowship with Christ. That was the center of Paul's hope: "I count [all things] as rubbish, in order that I may gain Christ" (Philippians 3:8). Gaining Christ was Paul's great passion and goal in all he did: "To live is Christ and to die is gain" (Philippians 1:21). Gain! Gain! This is the goal of his life and suffering. Paul desired "to depart and be with Christ, for that is *far better"* (Philippians 1:23). "Far better" is not an altruistic motive. It is a Christian Hedonist motive. Paul wanted what would bring the deepest and most lasting satisfaction to his life, namely, being with Christ in glory.

But not alone with Christ in glory!

No one who knows and loves Christ can be content to come to Him alone. The apex of His glory if this: "You were slain, and by your blood you ransomed people for God from every tribe and language and people and nation" (Revelation 5:9). If this is the summit of Christ's glorious mercy, then those who count it their infinite gain cannot live for private pleasures. The pleasures at Christ's right hand are public pleasures, shared pleasures, communal pleasures. When Paul said that he counted everything as loss in order to gain Christ, his losses were all for the sake of bringing others with him to Christ: "If I am to be poured out as a drink offering upon the sacrificial offering of *your faith,* I am glad and rejoice with you all (Philippians 2:17). The pouring out of his life in sufferings was, to be sure, "that he might gain Christ," but it was also that he might gain the *faith* of the nations that magnifies the mercy of Christ.

My Joy, My Crown of Exultation!

This is why Paul describes the people he had won to faith as *his joy:* "My brothers, whom I love and long for, my joy and crown, stand firm thus in the Lord, my beloved" (Philippians 4:1). "What is our hope or *joy* or crown of boasting before our Lord Jesus at his coming? Is it not you? For you are our glory and joy" (1 Thessalonians 2:19–20). The church was his joy because, in their joy in Christ, his joy in Christ was greater. More of Christ's mercy was magnified in multiplied converts to the Cross. So when Paul chose suffering in the cause of world evangelization and said that his aim was to "gain Christ," he meant that his own personal enjoyment of fellowship with Christ would be eternally greater because of the great assembly of the redeemed enjoying Christ with him.

Even though I am not as far along as Paul was in his passionate love for the church, I thank God that there have been key points in my life when God has rescued me from the pit of cynicism. I recall the days when I was finishing college and starting seminary. The mood in the late sixties was inhospitable to the local church. I can remember walking the streets of Pasadena on Sunday mornings in the fall of 1968, wondering if there was any future for the church—like a fish doubting the worth of water or a bird wondering about the reason for wind and air. It was a precious work of grace that God rescued me from that folly and gave me a home with the people of God at Lake Avenue Church for three years and let me see in the heart of Ray Ortlund, my pastor, a man who exuded the spirit of Paul when he looked out on his flock and said, "My joy, my crown of exultation."

Ten years later there was another moment of crisis as I stood at my writing table late at night in October of 1979. The issue was: Would I remain a professor at Bethel College teaching biblical studies, or would I resign and look for a pastorate? One of the things God was doing in those days was giving me a deeper love for the church—the gathered, growing, ministering body of people that meet week in and week out and move into the likeness of Christ. Teaching had its joys. It is a great calling. But that night another passion triumphed, and over the next months, God led me to Bethlehem Baptist Church.

It has been over thirty years. If I allow myself, the tears come fairly easily when I think about what these people mean to me. They know, I hope, that my great passion is to "gain Christ." And unless I am mistaken, they also know that I live for the "furtherance and joy" of their faith (Philippians 1:25, KJV). It is the aim of my writing and preaching to show that these two aims are one. I gain more of Christ in one converted sinner and growing saint than in a hundred ordinary chores. To say that Christ is my joy and Bethlehem is my joy is not double-talk.

If Joy in Suffering Is Admirable, Pursue It

It should not surprise us, even though it is utterly unnatural, that Paul should say in Colossians 1:24, "I *rejoice* in my sufferings for your sake, and in my flesh I am filling up what is lacking in Christ's afflictions." In other words, when I fill up Christ's afflictions by making a personal presentation of them to you in my own afflictions and pain, I rejoice. I rejoice.

Christian Hedonism simply says that this is a good and admirable thing that Paul is doing and that we should go and do likewise. To treat this magnificent spiritual event of joy in suffering as something small or incidental or not to be pursued is close to blasphemy. I say this carefully. When the Holy Spirit Himself does such a great thing, and thus magnifies the all-sufficiency of Christ in suffering, it is close to blasphemy to say, "It is permissible to experience suffering for others, but not to pursue the joy." The Christ-exalting miracle is not just the suffering, but the joy in the suffering. And we are meant to pursue it. In 1 Thessalonians 1:6–7 Paul says, "You…received the word in much affliction, with the *joy of the Holy Spirit,* so that you *became an example* to all the believers in Macedonia and in Achaia." Notice two crucial things: First, joy in tribulation is the work of the Holy Spirit; second, it is an example for others to follow. Beware of those who belittle the miracles of the Spirit of God by saying that they are good gifts, but not good goals.

Rejoice in Persecution—Your Reward Is Great!

Christian Hedonism says that there are different ways to rejoice in suffering as a Christian. All of them are to be pursued as an expression of the all-sufficient, all-satisfying grace of God. One way is expressed by Jesus in Mathew 5:11–12: "Blessed are you when others revile you and persecute you and utter all kinds of evil against you falsely on my account. *Rejoice and be glad, for your reward is great in heaven"* (cf. Luke 6:22–23). One way of rejoicing in suffering comes from fixing our minds firmly on the greatness of the reward that will come to us in the resurrection. The effect of this kind of focus is to make our present pain seem small in comparison to what is coming: "I consider that the sufferings of this present time are not worth comparing with the glory that is to be revealed to us" (Romans 8:18; cf. 2 Corinthians 4:16–18). In making the suffering tolerable, rejoicing over our reward will also make love possible, as we saw in chapter 4. "Love your enemies, and do good, and lend, expecting nothing in return, and *your reward will be great"* (Luke 6:35). Be generous with the poor "and you will be blessed, because they cannot repay you. *You will be repaid at the resurrection of the just"* (Luke 14:14)

REJOICE IN AFFLICTION—IT DEEPENS ASSURANCE!

Another way of rejoicing in suffering comes from the effects of suffering on our assurance of hope. Joy in affliction is rooted in the hope of resurrection, but our experience of suffering also deepens the root of that hope. For example, Paul says, "We exult in our afflictions, knowing that affliction produces endurance, and endurance produces proven genuineness, and genuineness produces hope" (Romans 5:3–4, author's translation). Here, Paul's joy is not merely rooted in his great reward, but in the effect of suffering to solidify his hope in that reward. Afflictions produce endurance, and endurance produces a sense that our faith is real and genuine, and that strengthens our hope that we will indeed gain Christ.

Richard Wurmbrand describes how one may survive the moments of excruciating pain of torture for Christ:

You have been so much tortured, nothing counts any more. If nothing counts any more, my survival doesn't count either. If nothing counts any more, the fact that I should not have pain also does not count. Draw this last conclusion at the stage at which you have arrived and you will see that you will overcome this moment of crisis. If you have overcome this one moment of crisis, it gives you an intense inner joy. You feel that Christ has been with you in that decisive moment.[20]

The "intense joy" comes from the sense that you have endured with the help of Christ. You have been proven in the fire and have come through as genuine. You did not recant. Christ is real in your life. He is for you the all-satisfying God He claims to be. This is what the apostles seemed to experience when, according to Acts 5:41, after being beaten, "they left the presence of the council, *rejoicing that they were counted worthy to suffer dishonor for the name.*" The joy came from the thought that their faith was regarded by God as real and ready to be proved in the fire of affliction.

REJOICE IN SUFFERING WITH CHRIST— IT LEADS TO GLORY!

Another way of rejoicing in suffering is kindled by the truth that our joy itself is a proven pathway to glory. Joy in suffering comes not only (1) from focusing on our reward and (2) from the solidifying effect of suffering on our sense of genuineness, but also (3) from the promise that joy in suffering will secure eternal joy in the future. The apostle Peter expresses it like this: "Rejoice insofar as you share Christ's sufferings, *that* you may also rejoice and be glad when his glory is revealed" (1 Peter 4:13). Joy now in suffering is the appointed pathway to the final rejoicing at the revelation of Christ. Peter is calling us to pursue joy now in suffering (he commands it!) so that we will be found among those who rejoice exceedingly at the coming of Christ.

REJOICE IN SUFFERING FOR OTHERS—THEY SEE CHRIST!

The fourth way of rejoicing in suffering we have seen already. It comes from realizing that through our suffering others are seeing the worth of Christ and standing firm because of our faith in the fire. Paul says to the Thessalonians,

---

20. Richard Wurmbrand, "Preparing for the Underground Church," *Epiphany Journal* 5, no. 4 (Summer 1985): 50.

"Now we live, if you are standing fast in the Lord. For what thanksgiving can we return to God for you, for *all the joy that we feel for your sake before our God?*" (1 Thessalonians 3:8–9). This is the joy of Colossians 1:24, "I rejoice in my sufferings for your sake." When we suffer to show others the love of Christ and the worth of Christ, it is because every new convert that stands firm in faith is a new, unique prism for refracting the all-satisfying glory of Christ. The joy we feel in them is not a different joy than we feel in Christ. The glory of Christ is our "great gain." For this we will suffer the loss of anything and everything. And everyone who sees in our suffering the superior worth of Christ, and believes, is another image and evidence of the great worth—and therefore another reason to rejoice.

THE HAPPIEST PEOPLE IN THE WORLD

The Calvary road with Jesus is not a joyless road. It is a painful one, but it is a profoundly happy one. When we choose the fleeting pleasures of comfort and security over the sacrifices and sufferings of missions and evangelism and ministry and love, we choose against joy. We reject the spring whose waters never fail (Isaiah 58:11). The happiest people in the world are the people who experience the mystery of "Christ in them, the hope of glory" (Colossians 1:27), satisfying their deep longings and freeing them to extend the afflictions of Christ through their own sufferings to the world.

God is calling us to live for the sake of Christ and to do that through suffering. Christ chose suffering; it didn't just happen to Him. He chose it as the way to create and perfect the church. Now He calls us to choose suffering. That is, He calls us to take up our cross and follow Him on the Calvary road and deny ourselves and make sacrifices for the sake of ministering to the church and presenting His sufferings to the world.

Brother Andrew, who heads a ministry called Open Doors and who is most famous for his 1967 book, *God's Smuggler,* describes Christ's call in the mid-1990s like this:

There's not one door in the world closed where you want to witness for Jesus.... Show me a closed door and I will tell you how you can get in.

I won't however, promise you a way to get out....

Jesus didn't say, "Go if the doors are open," because they weren't. He didn't say, "Go if you have an invitation or a red carpet treatment." He said, "Go," because people need his Word....

We need a new approach to missions—an aggressive, experimental, evangelical, no-holds-barred approach...a pioneering spirit...

I'm afraid we'll have to go through a deep valley of need and threatening situations, blood baths; but we'll get there.

God will take away what hinders us if we mean business. If we say, "Lord, at any cost..."—and people should never pray that unless they truly want God to take them at their word—he will answer. Which is scary. But we have to go through the process. This is how it has worked in the Bible for the last two thousand years.

So we face potentially hard times, and we have to go through that.... We play church and we play Christianity. And we aren't even aware we are lukewarm.... We should have to pay a price for our faith. Read 2 Timothy 3:12: "Indeed, all who want to live a godly life in Christ Jesus will be persecuted." The church has been much purified in countries where there was a lot of pressure.... All I can say is to be ready.[21]

NOT TO PROVE OUR POWER, BUT HIS PRECIOUSNESS

The answer to this call is a radical step of Christian Hedonism. We do not choose suffering simply because we are told to, but because the One who tells us to describes it as the path to everlasting joy. He beckons us into the obedience of suffering not to demonstrate the strength of our devotion to duty or to reveal the vigor of our moral resolve or to prove the heights of our tolerance for pain, but rather to manifest, in childlike faith, the infinite preciousness of His all-satisfying promises. Moses *[chose]* rather to be mistreated with the people of God than to enjoy the fleeting pleasures of sin...for he was looking to the

---

21. Brother Andrew, "God's Smuggler Confesses," an interview with Michael Maudlin, in *Christianity Today* (11 December 1995): 46.

reward" (Hebrews 11:25–26). Therefore, his obedience glorified the God of grace, not the resolve to suffer.

THE ESSENCE OF CHRISTIAN HEDONISM

This is the essence of Christian Hedonism. In the pursuit of joy through suffering, we magnify the all-satisfying worth of the Source of our joy. God Himself shines as the brightness at the end of our tunnel of pain. If we do not communicate that He is the goal and the ground of our joy in suffering, then the very meaning of our suffering will be lost. The meaning is this: God is gain. God is gain. God is gain.

The chief end of man is to glorify God. And it is truer in suffering than anywhere else that God *is most glorified in us when we are most satisfied in Him.* My prayer, therefore, is that the Holy Spirit would pour out on His people around the world a passion for the supremacy of God in all things. And I pray that He would make it plain that the pursuit of joy in God, whatever the pain, is a powerful testimony to God's supreme and all-satisfying worth. And so may it come to pass as we "fill up what is lacking in Christ's afflictions" that all the peoples of the world will see the love of Christ and magnify His grace in the gladness of faith.

WHY I HAVE WRITTEN THIS BOOK

Seven Reasons

REASON ONE: IT'S MY PLEASURE!

I wrote as I did, so that when I came I might not suffer pain from those who should have made me rejoice, for I felt sure of all of you, that my joy would be the joy of you all. (2 Corinthians 2:3)

We are writing these things so that our joy may be complete. (1 John 1:4)

When you are a starving man among starving people and you discover a banquet in the wilderness, you become a debtor to all. And the payment of that debt is delightful in proportion to the magnificence of the banquet.

I have felt like the lepers of Samaria. The Syrians surrounded the capital of Israel. Inside the besieged city, the fourth part of a kab of dove's dung sold for five shekels, and women boiled their children for food. But outside the city, unknown to the people within, the Lord had sent the Syrians fleeing. And there in the wilderness was laid a banquet of salvation.

The lepers realized they had nothing to lose. So they ventured into the enemy camp and found that the enemy had gone but left all their provisions behind. At first they began to hoard the treasures for themselves. But then the first rays of Christian Hedonism began to dawn on them:

They said to one another, "We are not doing right. This day is a day of good news. If we are silent and wait until the morning light, punishment will overtake us. Now therefore come; let us go and tell the king's household." (2 Kings 7:9)

This was the text from which Daniel Fuller preached at my ordination service in 1975. It was prophetic. For I have been a leper stumbling again and again onto the banquet of God in the wilderness of this world. And I have discovered that the banquet tastes far sweeter when I eat it with the widows of Samaria than when I hoard it in the desert.

I am radically committed to the pursuit of full and lasting joy. And so my ear has not been deaf to the wisdom of words like these from Karl Barth:

It must be said that we can have joy, and therefore will it, only as we give it to others.... There may be cases where a man can be really merry in isolation. But these are exceptional and dangerous.... It certainly gives us ground to suspect the nature of his joy as real joy if he does not desire—"Rejoice with me"—that at least one or some or many others, as representatives of the rest, should share this joy.... We may succeed in willing joy exclusively for ourselves, but we have to realize that in this case, unless a miracle happens (and miracles are difficult to imagine for such a purpose), this joy will not be true, radiant and sincere.[1]

The motive for writing this book is the desire to double my joy in God's banquet of grace by sharing it with as many as I can. I write this to you that my joy might be full.

REASON TWO: GOD IS BREATHTAKING

One thing have I asked of the LORD, that will I seek after: that I may dwell in the house of the LORD all the days of my life, to gaze upon the beauty of the LORD and to inquire in his temple. (Psalm 27:4)

---

1. Karl Barth, *Church Dogmatics*, III, 4 (Edinburgh: T. & T. Clark, 1961): 379–80.

I saw the Lord sitting upon a throne, high and lifted up; and the train of his robe filled the temple. Above him stood the seraphim. Each had six wings: with two he covered his face, and with two he covered his feet, and with two he flew. And one called to another and said: "Holy, holy, holy is the LORD of hosts; the whole earth is full of this glory." (Isaiah 6:1–3)

If you are a guide on a sightseeing trip and you know the people are longing to enjoy beauty and you come upon some breathtaking ravine, then you should show it to them and urge them to enjoy it. Well, the human race does in fact crave the experience of awe and wonder. And there is no reality more breathtaking than God.

The Preacher said,

[God] has made everything beautiful in its time. Also, he has put eternity into man's heart, yet so that he cannot find out what God has done from the beginning to the end. (Ecclesiastes 3:11)

Eternity is in the heart of man, filling him with longing. But we know not what we long for until we see the breathtaking God. This is the cause of universal restlessness.

Thou madest us for Thyself,
and our heart is restless,
until it rest in Thee.
Saint Augustine[2]

When God at first made man,
Having a glass of blessings standing by,
Let us (said he) pour on him all we can:

---

2. Saint Augustine, *Confessions,* in *Documents of the Christian Church,* ed. Henry Bettenson (London: Oxford University Press, 1967), book 1, chapter 1.

Let the world's riches, which dispersed lie,
Contract into a span.

So strength first made a way;
Then beauty flowed, then wisdom, honour, pleasure:
When almost all was out, God made a stay,
Perceiving that alone of all his treasure,
Rest in the bottom lay.

For if I should (said he)
Bestow this jewel also on my creature,
He would adore my gifts instead of me,
And rest in Nature, not the God of Nature:
So both should losers be.

Yet let him keep the rest,
But keep them with repining restlessness;
Let him be rich and weary, that at least,
If goodness lead him not, yet weariness
May toss him to my breast.
George Herbert, "The Pulley" [3]

The world has an inconsolable longing. It tries to satisfy the longing with scenic vacations, accomplishments of creativity, stunning cinematic productions, sexual exploits, sports extravaganzas, hallucinogenic drugs, ascetic rigors, managerial excellence, et cetera. But the longing remains. What does this mean?

If I find in myself a desire which no experience in this world can satisfy, the most probable explanation is that I was made for another world.[4]

---

3. George Herbert, *The Complete English Poems* (Harmondworth, Middlesex: Penguin Books, 1991), 150.
4. C. S. Lewis, *A Mind Awake: An Anthology of C. S. Lewis,* ed. Clyde Kilby (New York: Harcourt, Brace & World, 1968), 22.

It was when I was happiest that I longed most.... The sweetest thing in all my life has been the longing...to find the place where all the beauty came from.[5]

The tragedy of the world is that the echo is mistaken for the Original Shout. When our back is to the breathtaking beauty of God, we cast a shadow on the earth and fall in love with it. But it does not satisfy.

The books or the music in which we thought the beauty was located will betray us if we trust to them; it was not in them, it only came through them, and what came through them was longing. These things—the beauty, the memory of our own past—are good images of what we really desire; but if they are mistaken for the thing itself they turn into dumb idols, breaking the hearts of their worshipers. For they are not the thing itself; they are only the scent of a flower we have not found, the echo of a tune we have not heard, news from a country we have never yet visited.[6]

I have written this book because the breathtaking Beauty has visited us: "The Word became flesh and dwelt among us, and we have seen his glory [His beauty!], glory as of the only Son from the Father, full of grace and truth" (John 1:14). How can we not cry, "Look!"

Reason Three: The Word of God Commands Us to Pursue Our Joy

Delight yourself in the LORD. (Psalm 37:4)

Rejoice in the Lord always; again I will say, Rejoice. (Philippians 4:4)

And the Word of God threatens terrible things if we will not be happy:

---

5. Ibid., 25.
6. Ibid., 22–3.

Because you did not serve the LORD your God with joyfulness and gladness of heart, because of the abundance of all things, therefore you shall serve your enemies whom the LORD will send against you. (Deuteronomy 28:47–48)

But there are numerous objections to Christian Hedonism at this point.

Objection One

Someone may object, "No, you should not pursue your joy. You should pursue God." This is a helpful objection. It forces us to make several needed clarifications.

The objector is absolutely right that if we focus our attention on our own subjective experience of joy, we will most certainly be frustrated, and God will not be honored. When you go to an art museum, you had better attend to the paintings, and not your pulse. Otherwise, there will be no delight in the beauty of the art.

But beware of jumping to the conclusion that we should no longer say, "Come and take delight in these paintings." Do not jump to the conclusion that the command to pursue joy is misleading, while the command to look at the paintings is not.

What would you say is wrong with the person who comes to the art museum looking for a particular painting because he knows he can make a big profit if he buys and resells it? He goes from room to room, looking carefully at each painting. He is not the least preoccupied with his subjective, aesthetic experience. What is wrong here?

He is mercenary. His reason for looking is not the reason the painting was created. You see, it is not enough to say our pursuit should simply be the paintings. For there are ways to pursue the paintings that are bad.

One common way of guarding against this mercenary spirit is to say we should pursue art for art's sake. But what does this mean? It means, I think, pursuing art in a way that honors art, not money. But how do you honor art? I would answer: You honor art mainly by experiencing an appropriate emotion when you look at it.

We know we will miss this emotion if we are self-conscious while beholding the painting. We also know we will miss it if we are money-conscious or fame-conscious or power-conscious when we look at the painting. It seems to me, therefore, that a helpful way to admonish visitors to the art museum is to say, "Delight yourself in the paintings!"

The word *delight* guards them from thinking they should pursue money or fame or power with the paintings. And the phrase "in the paintings" guards them from thinking the emotion that honors the paintings could be experienced any other way than by focusing on the paintings themselves.

So it is with God. We are commanded by the Word of God: "Delight yourself in the LORD." This means: Pursue joy in God. The word *joy*, or *delight*, protects us from a mercenary pursuit of God. And the phrase "in God" protects us from thinking joy somehow stands alone as an experience separate from our experience of God Himself.

Objection Two

The most common objection against the command to pursue joy is that Jesus commanded just the opposite when He called for our self-denial: "Whoever would save his life will lose it, but whoever loses his life for my sake and the gospel's will save it" (Mark 8:35). We have dealt with this already (p. 241), but it may be helpful to draw in one other text to illustrate that *biblical* self-denial means "Deny yourselves lesser joys so you don't lose the big ones." Which is the same as saying: *Really* pursue joy! Don't settle for anything less than full and lasting joy.

Consider Hebrews 12:15–17 as an example of how one person failed to practice self-denial, to his own destruction:

> See to it that no one fails to obtain the grace of God; that no "root of bitterness" springs up and causes trouble, and by it many become defiled; that no one is sexually immoral or unholy like Esau, who sold his birthright for a single meal. For you know that afterward, when he desired to inherit the blessing, he was rejected, for he found no chance to repent, though he sought it with tears.

Esau lost his life because he preferred the pleasure of a single meal above the blessings of his birthright in the chosen family. This is a picture of all people who refuse to deny themselves the "fleeting pleasures of sin" (Hebrews 11:25). But note well! The main evil is not in choosing a meal, but in despising his birthright. Self-denial is never a virtue in itself. It has value precisely in proportion to the superiority of the reality embraced above the one denied. Self-denial that is not based on a desire for some superior goal will become the ground of boasting.

Objection Three

The third objection to the command to seek our joy can be stated like this:

> You have argued that the pursuit of pleasure is a necessary part of all worship and virtue. You have said that if we try to abandon this pursuit, we cannot honor God or love people. But can you make this square with Romans 9:3 and Exodus 32:32? It seems that Paul and Moses do indeed abandon the pursuit of their own pleasure when they express a willingness to be damned for the salvation of Israel.

These are startling verses!

In Romans 9:3, Paul expresses his heartaches over the cursed condition of most of his Jewish kinsmen. He says, "I could wish that I myself were accursed and cut off from Christ for the sake of my brothers, my kinsmen according to the flesh."

In Exodus 32 the people of Israel have committed idolatry. The wrath of God burns against them. Moses takes the place of a mediator to protect the people. He prays, "Alas, this people have sinned a great sin. They have made for themselves gods of gold. But now, if you will forgive their sin—but if not, blot me out of your book that you have written" (vv. 31–32).

First, we must realize that these two instances do not present us with the same problem. Moses' prayer does not necessarily include a reference to eternal damnation like Paul's does. We must not assume that the "book" he refers to here carries the same eternal significance that the "book of life" does, say, in Philippians 4:3 and Revelation 13:8; 17:8; 20:15; and 21:27.

George Bush (the Old Testament scholar, not the former president of the United States!) argues that in Exodus 32:32 being blotted out of the book is tantamount to being taken out of life while others survive:

> There is no intimation in these words of any secret book of the divine decrees, or of anything involving the question of Moses' final salvation or perdition. He simply expressed the wish rather to die than witness the destruction of his people. The phraseology is an allusion, probably, to the custom of having the names of a community enrolled in a register, and whenever one died, of erasing his name from the number.[7]

A person's willingness to die is not necessarily at odds with Christian Hedonism. Hebrews 11:26 says that Moses "considered the reproach of Christ greater wealth than the treasures of Egypt, for he was looking to the reward." There is no reason to think Moses stopped looking to the all-compensating reward when he struggled with the sin of Israel.

But this, of course, does not remove the main problem, which is Romans 9:3. Paul had written, "I could wish that I myself were accursed and cut off from Christ for the sake of my brothers." This appears to be a willingness to abandon the pursuit of happiness. Did Paul then cease to be a Christian Hedonist in expressing this kind of love for the lost?

Notice that he says, "I *could wish* that I myself were accursed." The reason for translating the verb as "I could wish" is that the Greek imperfect tense is used to soften the expression and show that it cannot be carried through. Henry Alford says, "The sense of the imperfect in such expression is the proper and strict one...the act is unfinished, an obstacle intervening."[8] Buist Fanning says that this "desiderative imperfect" is used "to contemplate the desire, but fail to bring oneself actually to the point of wishing."[9]

---

7. George Bush, *Notes on Exodus,* vol. 2 (Minneapolis: James & Klock, 1976, orig. 1852), 225.
8. Henry Alford, *The Greek New Testament,* vol. 2 (Chicago: Moody, 1958, orig. 1852), 225.
9. B. M. Fanning, *Verbal Aspect in New Testament Greek* (Oxford: Clarendon, 1999), 251, cited in Daniel B. Wallace, *Greek Grammar Beyond the Basics: An Exegetical Syntax of the New Testament* (Grand Rapids, Mich.: Zondervan, 1996), 552 n. 27. Wallace translates it, "I could almost wish myself accursed."

The obstacle is the immediately preceding promise of Romans 8:38–39: "For I am sure that neither death nor life, nor angels nor rulers, nor things present nor things to come, nor powers, nor height nor depth, nor anything else in all creation, will be able to separate us from the love of God in Christ Jesus our Lord." Paul knows it is impossible to take the place of his kinsmen in hell.

But he says he is potentially willing to! This is the problem for Christian Hedonism. We simply must take this seriously. Paul ponders the hypothetical possibility of a world in which such a thing might be possible. Suppose there were a world in which an unconverted sinner and a man of faith could stand before the bar of God to receive judgment. And suppose that if the saint were willing, God would reverse their roles. If the saint were willing, God would withdraw His saving grace from the saint so he becomes fit for hell in unbelief and rebellion, and He would give converting grace to the unbeliever so that he trusts Christ and becomes fit for heaven.

In such a world, what would love require? It would require total self-sacrifice. And the principle of Christian Hedonism would cease to apply. But mark well! This hypothetical world does not exist! God did not create a world in which a person could be eternally damned for an act of love.

In the real world God made, we are never asked to make such a choice: Are you willing to become damnable for the salvation of others? Instead, we are constantly told that doing good to others will bring us great reward *and* that we should pursue that reward.

Paradoxically, Paul's willingness to reach for a hypothetical case of ultimate sacrifice is a deep and dramatic way of saying with as much force as he knows how, "This, even this, is how much I delight in the prospect of Israel's salvation!" But immediately we see the impossibility of carrying through the wish: If their salvation were such a great delight to him, would hell really be hell? Could we really speak of hell as the place where Paul could achieve his deepest and noblest desire of love? This is the sort of incongruity you run into in hypothetical worlds that do not exist.

Happiness would be impossible in any case in such a world. For if God were to give a saint the option of becoming damnable to save another, such a saint could never live with himself if he said no. And he would suffer forever in hell if he said yes. He loses both ways.

But Christian Hedonism is not a philosophy for hypothetical worlds. It is based on the real world God has established and regulated in Holy Scripture. In this real world we are never urged or required to become evil that good may abound. We are always required to become good. This means becoming the kind of people who delight in the good, not just doing it dutifully. The Word of God commands us to pursue our joy.

REASON FOUR: AFFECTIONS ARE ESSENTIAL TO THE CHRISTIAN LIFE, NOT OPTIONAL

It is astonishing to me that so many people try to define true Christianity in terms of decisions, and not affections. Not that decisions are unessential. The problem is that they require so little transformation to achieve. They are evidence of no true work of grace in the heart. People can make "decisions" about the truth of God while their hearts are far from Him.

We have moved far away from the Christianity of Jonathan Edwards. Edwards pointed to 1 Peter 1:8 and argued that "true religion, in great part, consists in the affections."

> Though you have not seen him, you love him. Though you do not now see him, you believe in him and rejoice with joy that is inexpressible and filled with glory. (1 Peter 1:8)

He points out that "true religion" has two kinds of operation in the souls of the saints, according to this test: love to Christ ("though you have not seen him, you love him") and joy in Christ ("you rejoice with joy inexpressible and filled with glory"). Both of these operations in the soul are affections, not merely decisions. Edwards's conception of true Christianity was that the new birth really brought into being a new nature that had new affections.[10]

---

10. Jonathan Edwards, *Treatise Concerning Religious Affections,* in *The Works of Jonathan Edwards,* vol. 1 (Edinburgh: Banner of Truth, 1974), 236.

I find this supported throughout Scripture. We are commanded to feel, not just to think or decide. We are commanded to experience dozens of emotions, not just to perform acts of willpower.

For example, we are commanded not to covet (Exodus 20:17), and it is obvious that every commandment not to have a certain feeling is also a commandment to feel a certain way. The opposite of covetousness is contentment with what we have, and in Hebrews 13:5 this is exactly what we are commanded to experience ("Be content with what you have").

We are commanded to bear no grudge, but to forgive from the heart (Leviticus 19:17–18). Note: The law does not say, "Make a mere decision to drop the matter." Rather, it says, "Experience an event in the heart" (see Matthew 18:35). Similarly, the intensity of the heart is commanded in 1 Peter 1:22 ("Love one another *earnestly* from a pure heart") and in Romans 12:10 ("Love one another with brotherly *affection*").

Among other examples of emotions that the Scriptures command are these:

joy	(Psalm 100:2; Philippians 4:4; 1 Thessalonians 5:16; Romans 12:8, 12, 15)
hope	(Psalm 42:5; 1 Peter 1:13)
fear	(Luke 12:5; Romans 11:20; 1 Peter 1:17)
peace	(Colossians 3:15)
zeal	(Romans 12:11)
grief	(Romans 12:15; James 4:9)
desire	(1 Peter 2:2)
tenderheartedness	(Ephesians 4:32)
brokenness and contrition	(Psalm 51:17)
gratitude	(Ephesians 5:20; Colossians 3:17)
lowliness	(Philippians 2:3)

I do not believe it is possible to say that Scriptures like these all refer to optional icing on the cake of decision. They are commanded by the Lord who said, "Why do you call me 'Lord, Lord,' and not do what I tell you?" (Luke 6:46).

It is true that our hearts are often sluggish. We do not feel the depth or intensity of affections appropriate for God or His cause. It is true that at those times we must, insofar as it lies within us, exert our wills and make decisions that we hope will rekindle our joy. Though joyless love is not our aim ("God loves a cheerful giver!"), nevertheless it is better to do a joyless duty than not to do it, provided there is a spirit of repentance for the deadness of our hearts.

I am often asked what a Christian should do if the cheerfulness of obedience is not there. It is a good question. My answer is not to simply get on with your duty because feelings are irrelevant! My answer has three steps. First, confess the sin of joylessness. Acknowledge the culpable coldness of your heart. Don't say that it doesn't matter how you feel. Second, pray earnestly that God would restore the joy of obedience. Third, go ahead and do the outward dimension of your duty in the hope that the doing will rekindle the delight.[11]

This is very different from saying, "Do your duty because feelings don't count." These steps are predicated on the assumption that there is such a thing as hypocrisy. They are based on the belief that our goal is the reunion of pleasure and duty and that a justification of their separation is a justification of sin. John Murray puts it like this:

> There is no conflict between gratification of desire and the enhancement of man's pleasure, on the one hand, and fulfillment of God's command on the other.... The tension that often exists within us between a sense of duty and wholehearted spontaneity is a tension that arises from sin and a disobedient will. No such tension would have invaded the heart of unfallen man. And the operations of saving grace redirected to the end of removing the tension so that there may be, as there was with man at the beginning, the perfect complementation of duty and pleasure, of commandment and love.[12]

This is the goal of saving grace and the goal of this book.

---

11. For more practical counsel on fighting for joy, see John Piper, *When I Don't Desire God: How to Fight for Joy* (Wheaton, Ill.: Crossway, 2004).
12. John Murray, *Principles of Conduct* (Grand Rapids, Mich.: Eerdmans, 1957), 38–9.

REASON FIVE: CHRISTIAN HEDONISM COMBATS PRIDE AND SELF-PITY

God does everything He does to exalt His mercy and abase man's pride:

> So that in the coming ages he might show the immeasurable riches of his grace…so that no one may boast. (Ephesians 2:7, 9)

> In love He predestined us to adoption as sons through Jesus Christ…to the praise of the glory of His grace. (Ephesians 1:4–6, NASB)

> God chose what is low and despised in the world…so that no human being might boast in the presence of God. (1 Corinthians 1:28–29)

Christian Hedonism combats pride by putting man in the category of an empty vessel beneath the fountain of God. It guards us from the presumption of trying to be God's benefactors. Philanthropists can boast. Welfare recipients can't. The primary experience of the Christian Hedonist is *need*. When a little, helpless child is swept off his feet by the undercurrent on the beach and his father catches him just in time, the child does not boast; he hugs.

The nature and depth of human pride are illuminated by comparing boasting with self-pity. Both are manifestations of pride. Boasting is the response of pride to success. Self-pity is the response of pride to suffering. Boasting says, "I deserve admiration because I have achieved so much." Self-pity says, "I deserve admiration because I have sacrificed so much." Boasting is the voice of pride in the heart of the strong. Self-pity is the voice of pride in the heart of the weak. Boasting sounds self-sufficient. Self-pity sounds self-sacrificing.

The reason self-pity does not look like pride is that it appears to be needy. But the need arises from a wounded ego, and the desire of the self-pitying is not really for others to see them as helpless, but as heroes. The need self-pity feels does not come from a sense of unworthiness, but from a sense of unrecognized worthiness. It is the response of unapplauded pride.

Christian Hedonism severs the root of self-pity. People don't feel self-pity when suffering is accepted for the sake of joy.

"Blessed are you when others revile you and persecute you and utter all kinds of evil against you falsely on my account. *Rejoice and be glad, for your reward is great in heaven,* for so they persecuted the prophets who were before you." (Matthew 5:11–12)

This is the ax laid to the root of self-pity. When we have to suffer on account of Christ, we do not summon up our own resources like heroes. Rather, we become like little children who trust the strength of their father and who want the joy of his reward. As we saw in the last chapter, the greatest sufferers for Christ have always deflected praise and pity by testifying to their Christian Hedonism.

"I never made a sacrifice," said Hudson Taylor in later years, looking back over a life in which that element was certainly not lacking. But what he said was true, for the compensations were so real and lasting that he came to see that giving up is inevitably receiving, when one is dealing heart to heart with God.... The sacrifice was great, but the reward far greater.

"Unspeakable joy [he tells us] all day long and every day, was my happy experience. God, even my God, was a living bright reality, and all I had to do was joyful service."[13]

"Giving up is inevitably receiving." This is the motto of Christian Hedonism and the demise of self-pity. You can see the principle at work among the godly again and again. For example, I knew a seminary professor who also served as an usher in the balcony of a big church. Once when he was to have part in a service, the pastor extolled him for his willingness to serve in this unglamorous role

---

13. Dr. and Mrs. Howard Taylor, *Hudson Taylor's Spiritual Secret* (Chicago: Moody, n. d., original 1932), 30.

even though he had a doctorate in theology. The professor humbly deflected the praise by quoting Psalm 84:10:

> For a day in your courts is better than a thousand elsewhere. I would rather be a doorkeeper in the house of my God than dwell in the tents of wickedness.

In other words, don't think I am heroically overcoming great obstacles of disinclination to keep the doors of the sanctuary. The Word of God says it will bring great blessing!

Most people can recognize that doing something for the joy of it is a humbling experience. When a man takes friends out for dinner and picks up the check, his friends may begin to say how good it was of him to pay for them. But he simply lifts his hand in a gesture that says, "Stop." And he says, "It's my pleasure." In other words, if I do a good deed for the joy of it, the impulse of pride is broken.

The breaking of that impulse is the will of God, and that is one of the reasons I have written this book.

Reason Six: Christian Hedonism Promotes Genuine Love for People

No one has ever felt unloved because he was told that the attainment of his joy would make another person happy. I have never been accused of selfishness when justifying a kindness on the basis that it delights me. On the contrary, loving acts are genuine to the degree that they are not done begrudgingly. And the good alternative to begrudgingly is not neutrally or dutifully, but gladly. The authentic heart of love "loves kindness" (Micah 6:8); it doesn't just do kindness. Christian Hedonism forces this truth into consideration.

> By this we know that we love the children of God, when we love God and obey his commandments. For this is the love of God, that we keep his commandments. And his commandments are not burdensome. For everyone who has been born of God overcomes the world. (1 John 5:2–4)

Read these sentences in reverse order and notice the logic. First, being born of God gives a power that conquers the world. This is given as the ground or basis ("For") for the statement that the commandments of God are not burdensome. So being born of God gives a power that conquers our worldly aversion to the will of God. Now His commandments are not "burdensome," but are the desire and delight of our heart. This is the love of God: not just that we do His commandments, but also that they are not burdensome.

Then in verse 2 the evidence of the genuineness of our love for the children of God is said to be the love of God. What does this teach us about our love for the children of God? Since love for God is doing His will gladly rather than with a sense of burden, and since love for God is the measure of the genuineness of our love for the children of God, therefore our love for the children of God must also be done gladly rather than begrudgingly. Christian Hedonism stands squarely in the service of love, for it presses us on to glad obedience.

Jesus was big on giving to the needy. How did He motivate giving? He said, "Sell your possessions, and give to the needy. Provide yourselves with moneybags that do not grow old, with a treasure in the heavens that does not fail" (Luke 12:33). In other words, stop craving two-bit possessions on earth when you can have endless treasures in heaven by giving alms! (Remember Hudson Taylor: "Giving up is inevitably receiving.")

Or, a bit differently, but basically the same, He said, "When you give to the needy, do not let your left hand know what your right hand is doing, so that your giving may be in secret. And your Father who sees in secret will reward you" (Matthew 6:3–4). In other words, stop being motivated by the praises of men, and let the thought of God's reward move you to love.

Yes, it is real love when our giving is motivated by the heavenly treasure. It is not exploitation, because the loving almsgiver aims for His alms to rescue the beggar for that same reward. A Christian Hedonist is always aware that his own enjoyment of the Father's reward will be even greater when shared with the ones He has drawn into the heavenly fellowship.

My point is this: If Jesus thought it wise to motivate acts of love with promises of reward (Matthew 6:4) and treasures in heaven (Luke 12:33), it accords with His teaching to say that Christian Hedonism promotes genuine love for people.

Consider another illustration. Hebrews 13:17 gives the following counsel to every local church:

> Obey your leaders and submit to them, for they are keeping watch over your souls, as those who will have to give an account. Let them do this with joy and not with groaning, for that would be of no advantage to you.

Now, if it is not profitable for pastors to do their oversight sadly instead of joyfully, then a pastor who does not seek to do his work with joy does not care for his flock. Not to pursue our joy in ministry is not to pursue the profit of our people. This is why Paul admonished those who do acts of mercy to do them "with cheerfulness" (Romans 12:8), and why God loves a "cheerful giver" (2 Corinthians 9:7). Begrudging service does not qualify as genuine love.

The pursuit of joy through mercy is what makes love real. And that is one of the reasons I have written this book.

REASON SEVEN: CHRISTIAN HEDONISM GLORIFIES GOD

We have come back to where we began. And this is as it should be: "For from him and through him and to him are all things" (Romans 11:36).

Does Christian Hedonism put man's pleasure above God's glory? No. It puts man's pleasure in God's glory. Our quest is not merely joy. It is joy *in* God. And there is no way for a creature to consciously manifest the infinite worth and beauty of God without delighting in Him. It is better to say that we pursue our joy *in* God than to simply say that we pursue God. For one can pursue God in ways that do not honor Him:

> "What to me is the multitude of your sacrifices?" says the LORD; "I have had enough of burnt offerings of rams and the fat of well-fed beasts." (Isaiah 1:11)

Our solemn assemblies may be a stench in God's nose (Amos 5:21–24). It is possible to pursue God without glorifying God. If we want our quest to honor God, we must pursue Him for the joy in fellowship with Him.

Consider the Sabbath as an illustration of this. The Lord rebukes His people for seeking "their own" pleasure on His holy day. But what does He mean? He means they are delighting in their business and not in the beauty of their God. He does not rebuke their hedonism. He rebukes the weakness of it. They have settled for secular interests and thus honor them above the Lord.

> If you turn back your foot from the Sabbath,
>   from doing your pleasure on my holy day,
>   and *call the Sabbath a delight*
>   *and the holy day of the Lord honorable;*
>   if you honor it, not going your own ways,
>   or seeking your own pleasure, or talking idly;
>   then you shall *take delight in the* LORD,
>   and I will make you ride on the heights of the earth;
>   I will feed you with the heritage of Jacob your father,
>   for the mouth of the LORD has spoken. (Isaiah 58:13–14)

Notice that calling the Sabbath a *delight* is parallel to calling the holy day of the Lord *honorable.* This simply means you honor what you delight in. Or you glorify what you enjoy.

The enjoyment and the glorification of God are one. His eternal purpose and our eternal pleasure unite. To magnify His name and multiply your joy is the reason I have written this book, for:

The chief end of man is to glorify God
by
enjoying Him forever.

WHY CALL IT CHRISTIAN HEDONISM?

I am aware that calling this philosophy of life "Christian Hedonism" runs the risk of ignoring Bishop Ryle's counsel against "the use of uncouth and new-fangled terms and phrases in teaching sanctification."[1] Nevertheless, I stand by the term for at least six reasons.

1. My old *Webster's Collegiate Dictionary* of 1961, which has been within arm's reach since I was in the tenth grade, defines *hedonism* as "a living for pleasure." Forty years later, the authoritative *American Heritage Dictionary of the English Language, Fourth Edition* has as its first definition: "pursuit of or devotion to pleasure." That is precisely what I mean by it. If the chief end of man is to enjoy God forever, human life *should* be a "living for pleasure."

In previous editions of this book I cited at this point the article on hedonism in *The Encyclopedia of Philosophy, which defined hedonism as* "a theory according to which a person is motivated to produce one state of affairs in preference to another if, and only if, he thinks it will be more pleasant, or less unpleasant for himself."[2] This has proved to be confusing, because while such a

---

1. J. C. Ryle, *Holiness* (Grand Rapids, Mich.: Baker, 1979, orig. 1883), xxix.
2. See under "Hedonism," in *The Encyclopedia of Philosophy*, ed. Paul Edwards (New York: Macmillan, 1972 reprint; first published 1967), 3:433.

theory of motivation may be true,[3] it is not part of what I mean by Christian Hedonism. My definition of Christian Hedonism on p. 28 does not include this conviction. What matters to me is not that all people *are* motivated by the pursuit of pleasure, but that all people *should be* motivated by the pursuit of full and everlasting pleasure in God. That is what this book is about. And the main reason is that God is most glorified in us when we are most satisfied in him.

2. Other people, smarter and older than I am, have felt themselves similarly driven to use the term *hedonism* in reference to the Christian way of life.

For example, C. S. Lewis counsels his friend "Malcolm" to be aware of committing idolatry in his enjoyment of nature. To be sure, he must enjoy the "sunlight in a wood." But these spontaneous pleasures are "patches of Godlight" and one must let one's mind "run back up the sunbeam to the sun." Then Lewis comments:

> You notice that I am drawing no distinction between the sensuous and aesthetic pleasures. But why should I? The line is almost impossible to draw and what use would it be if one succeeded in drawing it? If this is *Hedonism,* it is also a somewhat arduous discipline.[4]

We will find that it is indeed an arduous discipline!

In *The Simple Life,* Vernard Eller delights himself in some of the great parables of Søren Kierkegaard. One of his favorites is the parable of the lighted carriage and starlit night. We could also call it the crisis of Christian Hedonism. It goes like this:

> When the prosperous man on a dark but starlit night drives comfortably in his carriage and has the lanterns lighted, aye, then his is safe, he fears no difficulty, he carries his light with him, and it is not dark close

---

3. Mark Talbot, in a serious critique of "Christian Hedonism" argues that it is not true. "When All Hope Has Died: Meditations on Profound Christian Suffering" in: Sam Storms and Justin Taylor, editors, *For the Fame of God's Name: Essays in Honor of John Piper* (Wheaton: Crossway Books, 2010), pp. 70-101.
4. C. S. Lewis, *Letters to Malcolm: Chiefly on Prayer* (New York: Harcourt Brace Jovanovich, 1963), 90.

around him. But precisely because he has the lanterns lighted, and has a strong light close to him, precisely for this reason, he cannot see the stars. For his lights obscure the stars, which the poor peasant, driving without lights, can see gloriously in the dark but starry night. So those deceived ones live in the temporal existence: either, occupied with the necessities of life, they are too busy to avail themselves of the view, or in their prosperity and good days they have, as it were, lanterns lighted, and close about them everything is so satisfactory, so pleasant, so comfortable—but the view is lacking, the prospect, the view of the stars.[5]

Eller comments, "Clearly, 'the view of the stars' here intends one's awareness and enjoyment of God."[6] The rich and busy who surround themselves with the carriage lights of temporal comfort, or the busy who cover themselves with troublesome care, cut themselves off from what Kierkegaard calls "the absolute joy":

What indescribable joy!—joy over God the Almighty.... For this is the absolute joy, to adore the almighty power with which God the Almighty bears all thy care and sorrow as easily as nothing.[7]

Eller applies all this to the so-called "simple life" and says,

The motive of Christian simplicity is not the enjoyment of simplicity itself; that and any other earthly benefit that comes along are part of 'all the rest' [Matthew 6:33]. But the sole motive of Christian simplicity is the enjoyment of God himself (and if that be *hedonism*, let's make the most of it!)—it is "the view of the stars."[8]

This is indeed hedonism! And I have done my best to make the most of it in this book.

---

5. V. Eller, *The Simple Life* (Grand Rapids, Mich.: Eerdmans, 1973), 12.
6. Ibid.
7. Ibid., 109.
8. Ibid., 121–2.

Precisely! Christian Hedonism does not make a god out of pleasure. It says you have already made a god out of whatever you take most pleasure in.

3. The third reason I use the term Christian Hedonism is that it has an arresting and jolting effect. My heart has been arrested and my life has been deeply jolted by the teaching of Christian Hedonism. It is not an easy or comfortable philosophy. It is extremely threatening to nominal Christians. That is why when I wrote a condensed version of this book, I gave it the title *The Dangerous Duty of Delight* (Multnomah, 2011).

It is based on the devastating truth of Christ when He said, "Because you are lukewarm, and neither cold nor hot, I will spit you out of my mouth" (Revelation 3:16). This is utterly shocking. Should we not then find words to shock ourselves into realizing that eternity is at stake when we disobey the commandment, "Delight yourself in the LORD" (Psalm 37:4)?

Most of us are virtually impervious to the radical implications of familiar language. What language shall we borrow to awaken joyless believers to the words of Deuteronomy 28:47–48?

> Because you did not serve the LORD your God *with joyfulness and gladness of heart*…therefore you shall serve your enemies whom the LORD will send against you…. And he will put a yoke of iron upon your neck until he has destroyed you.

How shall we open their ears to the shout of Jeremy Taylor: "God threatens terrible things, if we will not be happy!"?[9]

I have found over the years that there is a correlation between people's willingness to get over the offensiveness of the term *Christian Hedonism* and their willingness to yield to the offensive biblical truth behind it. The chief effect of the term is not that it creates a stumbling block to the truth, but that it wakens people to the fact that the truth itself is a stumbling block—and often a very different one than they expected.

---

9. Quoted in C. S. Lewis, *George MacDonald: An Anthology* (London: Geoffrey Bles, 1946), 19.

4. To the objection that the term *hedonism* carries connotations too worldly to be redeemed, I answer with the precedent of Scripture. If Jesus can describe His coming as the coming of a "thief" (Matthew 24:43–44), if He can extol a "dishonest manager" as a model of shrewdness (Luke 16:8), and if the inspired psalmist can say that the Lord awoke from sleep "like a strong man shouting because of wine" (Psalm 78:65), then it is a small thing for me to say the passion to glorify God by enjoying Him forever is indeed Christian Hedonism.

5. Remarkably, the apostle Paul describes his own experience of weakness and suffering with a Greek word that is at the root of the English word *hedonism.* He quotes Christ as saying, "My grace is sufficient for you, for my power is made perfect in weakness." Then he responds, "Therefore I will boast all the more *gladly* (h[dista, *hedonista*) of my weaknesses, so that the power of Christ may rest upon me" (2 Corinthians 12:9). And a few verses later he says, "I will most *gladly* (h[dista, *hedonista*) spend and be spent for your souls" (2 Corinthians 12:15). This word *"hedonista"* has no special spiritual connotations that would make it fitting for Paul's use here. He simply chooses an ordinary pleasure word from this culture and shocks us with his use of it in relation to weakness and love.

6. Finally, by attaching the adjective *Christian* to the word *hedonism,* I signal loud and clear that this is no ordinary hedonism. For me, the word *Christian* carries this implication: Every claim to truth that flies under the banner of Christian Hedonism must be solidly rooted in the Christian Scriptures, the Bible. And the Bible teaches that man's chief end is to glorify God *BY* enjoying Him forever.

GROUP STUDY GUIDE

by Desiring God

(with an Explanation of the Resource
and an Introduction for Leaders)

I f God is most glorified in us when we are most satisfied in Him, then we must make it our aim to be as happy as we possibly can be in God. In other words: to be a Christian is to be a hedonist.

For nearly three decades John Piper has labored to show the biblical foundation for a vision of God and the Christian life, which he calls Christian Hedonism, and to call people to pursue it with all their might. One of his earliest formulations of this vision came in a sermon series in the early eighties, which later was turned into the book *Desiring God: Meditations of a Christian Hedonist.*

Our hope is that churches will use the book and its study resources to foster group study of Scripture and encourage group reflection on a God-centered vision of life, and that through this discussion God would ignite a passion in churches and individuals to seek after the deepest pleasure available, that which is found in seeing and savoring Jesus. This could happen in a number of ways, whether these resources are used at leadership retreats or gatherings, or in small group studies, or in personal study, or in some other fresh, creative, and Christ-exalting way that the Spirit of God may lead.

We want you to see from Scripture that God is uppermost in His affections. We want you to know that a Christian is one who savors God's glory in Jesus Christ above all competing treasures. We long for you to pursue worship as an end in itself. And we pray that you discover (perhaps for the first time) that love is the overflow of joy in God that gladly meets the needs of others; that Scripture and prayer sustain our pursuit of ultimate and lasting joy in God; that money and marriage and all material reality are means to our exaltation of and exultation in God; and that costly, risk-taking missions of love are also efforts to double our joy in God. May God bless individuals, churches, and communities such that they learn more and more that the chief end of man is to glorify God by enjoying him forever.

EXPLANATION OF THE STUDY GUIDE

In an effort to encourage discussion and deeper engagement with *Desiring God*, we have developed a ten-week study of the book. Each week consists of reading a chapter of the book, meditation upon concepts and Scriptures, and answering/discussing correlating study questions found in the study guide. The study guide is divided into the various sections explained below.

Note: We feel that these study resources would work best in a group setting. Not only do we believe in the biblical principle that iron sharpens iron, we also long to see church communities strengthened together in the foundations of the gospel. Nevertheless, we hope that these study resources can also be of benefit for individual study and reflection. We would strongly encourage any individuals who choose to use these resources for their own study to find other believers with whom to discuss the themes and Scriptures encountered in the material.

Reading and Reflection

Each week the reader will work through a chapter of *Desiring God* (typically around twenty to thirty pages; week 6 covers two chapters). Ten core study questions are provided in the study guide to stimulate the learner to interact with *Desiring God* and with Scripture. The focus of these questions ranges from comprehension of the reading, to personal examination, to group discussion. It may be most convenient to break these questions down into five daily portions of two questions each (with a sixth day devoted to "Going Deeper"; see below).

These questions are intended to help the reader locate the key concepts within the text of *Desiring God* itself and to challenge the reader to dig further into Scripture. For this reason, we have included the page number(s), usually in parentheses, where the ideas these questions cover can be found in *Desiring God*. The questions are listed in order of appearance within *Desiring God*. Readers should feel free to answer these questions as they read, but if it is preferred, these questions could be answered after reading the chapter(s). If used in this way, the questions would serve as a good way to review the reading.

We recommend obtaining a separate notepad to write out answers as well as other thoughts, reflections, and resolutions that may develop during reading and study. Group participants are expected to bring both the study guide (with their answers) and *Desiring God* (if owned) to the group meetings.

The questions with an asterisk (*) are those we feel would be particularly germane to group discussion. Group participants should familiarize themselves with these questions prior to the group meeting (see "For Leaders" below for more details). Participants should also be mindful during their personal study of any other questions that would stir meaningful discussion, noting them in the guide and bringing them up in the group discussion. Such questions may be felt to be particularly suited to the group's context, or they may be questions with which the participant is particularly wrestling and struggling to answer.

Throughout the study guide the learner will repeatedly be challenged to utilize their biblical knowledge by thinking of or locating relevant Scriptures. These may either add support to the concepts discussed or seem to conflict with them, and should be discussed with the group. Learners should, therefore, always have a Bible when working through the reading and study guide (a concordance would also be quite helpful). Regardless of how deep one considers their biblical understanding, everyone should bring what they know to bear on their study and discussion and strive to discover more of Scripture in the process.

Going Deeper

A short section appears at the conclusion of every week containing two or three questions aimed at internalization of the truths being studied. The questions here will often be pointed toward personal examination and application. In this section learners are also presented with opportunities to further study especially difficult concepts arising in the reading. Optional further readings are noted in an effort to aid the learner's meditation on such concepts. These optional readings include the Epilogue and Appendix as well as a few articles which can be found on the Desiring God Web site (www.desiringGod.org).

Praying the Psalms

We believe that times of group prayer are essential in the fight for joy in God. Furthermore, we have found the psalms to be filled with the language and experience of Christian Hedonism. Therefore, to foster a spirit of group prayer and as a way of reinforcing the truths encountered during each week, we have selected a psalm for the group (or individual) to pray through in conclusion to each time of discussion. This way of concluding each time of discussion ultimately stems from the convictions that Scripture is "kindling for Christian Hedonism" and prayer is the "power of Christian Hedonism" and that they always work in conjunction.

We want you to experience the mingling of Scripture and prayer by praying together praises to God and supplications for yourselves and your communities, being guided by what the psalmists prayed under divine inspiration. We trust that using a different psalm each week will be a fitting and fruitful way to conclude your time of study, discussion, and mutual encouragement. For direction on how to "pray a psalm," see "For Leaders" below.

For Leaders

As the group facilitator, you are expected to familiarize yourself with the layout of the study guide and have an idea of how to structure group discussions from the outset of the study. Read thoroughly the "Explanation of the Study Guide" above as well as the rest of this section before the first meeting. Also, skim each week's study with an eye to key themes being introduced or further developed in each week's reading and study.

Before class each week you will want to review the chapter and each of the corresponding study questions. We strongly recommend that you read all the optional readings found in the "Going Deeper" sections of the study guide. (Note: it would also be helpful to direct the group each week to where the additional readings for the coming week may be found, whether in *Desiring God* or on our Web site.)

At every stage of preparation, immerse yourself in prayer for your own soul and for your group. Only by the Spirit's power and guidance will the concepts covered, the biblical texts discussed, and the resolutions made prove to be of lasting value in each other's lives.

Finally, you should develop a basic blueprint of the group meetings. A suggested blueprint for a one-hour meeting is below, which includes advice for how to conduct each portion of the meeting. This blueprint can and should be adapted to your particular group's needs and context. Plan to set aside at least two hours for preparation each week.

Introduction (10 minutes)

Open each class with prayer to set the tone of the meeting as one of humble expectation for the Spirit's movement in minds and hearts, and to direct everyone to God as the supreme treasure of our pursuit. One way to introduce the group discussion would be to have the group explain the meaning of the subtitle of the chapter read during the week. For example, you might open the discussion of chapter 1 with the question, "Why is the happiness of God considered the foundation of Christian Hedonism?" Such discussion will inevitably recall the main points encountered in the chapter and key definitions. It may also be appropriate (in weeks 2–10) to review the previous week's reading and discussion and to ask how the current week's reading and study build upon that.

Note: It may be appropriate to use the introductory time differently in the first meeting. Specifically, you will want to use this time to introduce the book and the study guide. Be sure to inform the group of the approximate number of pages to read each week (typically twenty to thirty) and how the study questions relate to the reading. Encourage the group to use the study questions as launching points for their own study of Scripture. It may also be helpful to talk about strategies for reading and working through the study guide during the week. For example, they may find it works best to read only a few pages and answer two study questions a day, using the sixth day for answering the "Going Deeper" questions and for further reflection. Most importantly for the first meeting, you will want to introduce the members of the group to one another and think of creative ways to help the class become comfortable with one another and in the group environment.

Discussion (40 minutes)

Throughout the study guide, the questions with an asterisk (*) are those we feel would be fruitful and engaging in group discussion. Group participants are especially encouraged to familiarize themselves with these questions before the group meeting. These highlighted questions are only suggestions. In your own study, you should note any other questions that are particularly suited to your group's context and would stir meaningful discussion during the group meeting. Furthermore, we encourage you to develop your own questions for discussion. Questions tailor-made for a group's context, situation, level of understanding, etc., are often the most helpful and have the deepest impact. Our hope is that the study guide will be a resource that gets you started and that launches other creative and worthwhile efforts to deepen knowledge, faith, and love.

You may facilitate group discussion by introducing questions (from the study guide or from your own preparation) and encouraging members to respond.

How did they answer the questions in the study guide? What new concepts did they encounter? What new understandings of Scripture were they introduced to and which Scriptures did they study and meditate upon? What new insights on the Christian life and mission did they discover and how might those insights impact our lives today? What, if anything, did they disagree with and why? What confused them? It is okay if there is initial silence after a question is raised.

As the discussion advances and as the weeks go by, the participants of the group will become more comfortable with sharing their answers and expressing their thoughts. Try to curb the temptation to always break silence with "the answer," and throughout the study beware of dominating the discussion. Also, seek to affirm each individual's input as much as possible to encourage them to continue contributing to the discussions. When you need to address false ideas, do so with love and gentleness.

Do not be afraid to linger on a particular question or topic if the Spirit seems to be moving in a special way during discussion; however, as the leader you must also be sensitive to whether the discussion needs to move forward. Also, you should try to include all members in the discussion, being mindful of those who may have something to contribute to the discussion but remain silent. Pray for such Spirit-led sensitivity to the needs and flow of your time together both before and during the meeting.

It might be beneficial to use the final five or ten minutes of the discussion time to address any practical effects the themes considered have on our daily lives. In particular, review the questions in the "Going Deeper" section of the study guide. Ask what resolutions were made by the members of the group and what practical strategies were thought up to implement the biblical truths encountered.

Prayer (10 minutes)

We also want to encourage extended times of group prayer during your meetings. We suggest using at least the final ten minutes of the time for prayer. You may choose to pray as a large group or to break into smaller groups. You could break into small groups that change from week to week or maintain the same smaller prayer groups throughout the study. Whatever you may choose, we hope that prayer for one another will be an integral part of your time together, both during the group meetings and throughout the week as you progress through this study.

To encourage a commitment to group prayer, and to help the group learn by practice and experience the crucial role the Word plays in prayer, we have suggested a psalm to pray through together at the end of the discussion (see "Praying the Psalms" in the study guide). Some individuals in the group may not be familiar with the concept of "praying the psalms" and may be unsure of how to do it. Encourage them that it is taking the words of the psalmists (divinely inspired) and using them to inform the spirit, manner, goals, and content of our prayers. To give you an idea of how the psalms can inspire and inform our own prayers, we will conclude this introduction to this study of *Desiring God* with a prayer for you and your group derived from Psalm 84.

Lord of Hosts, Your dwelling places are altogether lovely.
May it be that as people read and study and discuss Your Word
together that they might long and yearn to be in Your courts
where they might see and savor You.
Cause the hearts, and even the bodies, of Your people to be filled
with rejoicing in You, the living God.
Even the birds of the air rest in Your presence and find comfort and
security and joy in Your altars, O Lord of Hosts, our King and
our God.
So too are all who dwell in Your house; their joy is as unceasing as
their praise.

May the peoples and the churches and the groups who join together
in this study be blessed, finding their strength in You.
May there be in their hearts a highway leading straight to Your throne.
Cause them to be immeasurably strengthened and to appear before You
without fear and with great happiness.

Hear our prayer, Father God, and listen to our supplication, God
of Israel.

You are a shield; shed Your light and Your gracious blessing on the
faces of churches and groups and individuals who join together
in this study, so that they might see You.

For a day in your courts, in Your presence, is better than a thousand
anywhere else.

Transform hearts to see this and believe it; give all of us affections such
that we would rather stand at the doorway of Your house than live
a life of comfort and material prosperity and prestige in houses
established on wickedness.

You are a sun filled with warmth and life and a shield to protect us
from every attack.

Grant Your people grace and glory.

You withhold nothing good from those who walk in your ways, so
cause Your people to walk in Your ways, and lavish them with
good.

O Lord of hosts, how blessed are those who trust in You! Bless Your
people, we pray. Amen.

How I Became a Christian Hedonist

Reading and Reflection

*1. The first answer in the Westminster Shorter Catechism states: "The chief end of man is to glorify God and enjoy Him forever." According to the author, how does the clause about glorifying God relate to the clause about enjoying God forever (pp. 17–18)?

2. What initial discovery did Blaise Pascal help the author to make on his way to becoming a Christian Hedonist (p. 19)?

*3. What insight did C. S. Lewis add to Pascal's (p. 19–20)? This was shocking to the author; is it for you? Why or why not?

4. What was the third insight that the author says "seems so patently obvious" in retrospect (p. 21)?

*5. What is the relationship between praise and joy that the author discovered with the help of C. S. Lewis and Jonathan Edwards (pp. 21–22)? How does this help clarify the meaning of *hypocrisy* (p. 23)?

*6. What does it mean that God "is the end of our search [for pleasure], not the means to some further end" (p. 24)? What other ends besides God Himself might we tend to view Him as a means to acquiring?

*7. According to the author, why doesn't Christian Hedonism "make a god out of pleasure" (p. 24)?

8. In your own words explain what is meant by a "general theory of moral justification" (p. 24)? How does the author respond to the criticism that Christian Hedonism is such a theory (pp. 24–25)?

9. How does the author describe the relationship between love and happiness? Why does the author consider the phrase "Let's all be good because it will make us happy" over-simplistic? What essential, radically

life-changing, defining point about virtue is missed in such an oversimplification? (pp. 25–26)

10. Rewrite each of the five convictions that Christian Hedonism is built on
     in your own words (p. 28).

Going Deeper

- Select five to ten psalms to read and meditate upon. Write down
  any "language of Hedonism" that you encounter. How do the
  psalmists view the goodness and grace and character and worth
  of God?

- In these psalms, what does God command with respect to your
  heart and emotions? How do these demands over your
  heart/emotions land on you individually, personally? Are they
  freeing? frightening? imprisoning? why?

- Read the Epilogue, "Why I Have Written This Book: Seven
  Reasons" (pp. 289–307), to orient yourself to the author's motivations and purposes in writing this book. Write down any
  uncertainties, questions, or objections you might have concerning the author's conception of the Christian life. Refer to these
  throughout the study.

Praying the Psalms

Psalm 100

CHAPTER 1

THE HAPPINESS OF GOD:
FOUNDATION FOR CHRISTIAN HEDONISM

Reading and Reflection

*1. Why does the author think it might sound strange to say, "The chief end of *God* is to glorify God and enjoy Himself forever" (p. 31)? What are some reasons we might be more accustomed to think about our duty rather than God's design? Are these all good reasons, or they all bad reasons, or are they mixed? Evaluate them.

*2. Why does the author say that God's happiness is the foundation for Christian Hedonism (pp. 32–33)?

3. According to the author, what does it mean to say that God is sovereign (p. 32)? Why is God's sovereignty the foundation for God's happiness (p. 33)? In light of this, what must the author do before he can explain why the happiness of God is the foundation for Christian Hedonism?

4. How much of what occurs in the universe is owing ultimately to God's sovereign purpose? What is the clearest example in history that even the morally wicked decisions and actions of human beings are part of God's sovereign design? (pp. 33–36)

*5. Describe what the author means by looking at a wicked event "through a narrow lens or through a wide-angle lens" (p. 39–40). What is the difference between God's "will of command" and His "will of decree," and what light does this shed on our understanding of God's sovereign purposes even over evil (see footnote 5 on p. 39)?

6. What is the important transition in the author's argument that happens on page 41; what question will he now try to answer? What is the answer he suggests (pp. 41–42)?

*7.   Why would God be unrighteous if He Himself were not uppermost in His affections (pp. 42–43)? How does Jesus Christ relate to God's supreme delight in Himself (p. 43)?

8.   What does the author mean when he says that God's works are the "spillover" of His joy in Himself (p. 45)? To what does the author liken this expansive quality of God's joy? How should we understand the relationship of God's activity in Creation and Redemption to what God delights in most of all?

9.   On pages 44–45 a crucial transition occurs in the author's argument. What question arises from the truth that God is uppermost in His affections, which the author will spend the remainder of the chapter trying to answer? Restate the question in your own words.

*10.   What is meant by a "second-hander"? Why should we not consider God to be a second-hander? What biblical texts show that the similarity between God's purpose to display His own glory and the vanity of second-handers is only superficial? What other biblical texts can you think of besides the ones mentioned by the author? (pp. 46–47)

Going Deeper

- On page 47 the author makes a very important statement: "Because God is unique as an all-glorious, totally self-sufficient Being, He must be for Himself if He is to be for us." Restate each part of this sentence in your own words in a way that both makes sense to you and genuinely reflects the author's intended meaning. What must God give to us if He is to love us infinitely? How does His demand to praise Him relate to His granting us this supremely valuable gift? (pp. 48–49)

- Many people are not convinced that God's ultimate goal in all that He does is to uphold and to display His glory and that God is uppermost in God's affections. It simply sounds contradictory to one understanding of love that is prevalent. Can you think of examples in biblical history where God tells us He was acting for the sake of His name? Describe in your own words how God's pursuit of His own glory is the foundation of His love for us and the foundation of our hope for grace.

Praying the Psalms

Psalm 135

CHAPTER 2

CONVERSION:
THE CREATION OF A CHRISTIAN HEDONIST

Reading and Reflection

1. What is the twofold aim of this chapter (p. 54)?

*2. Why does the author want to introduce terminology like "Christian Hedonism" and "becoming a Christian Hedonist" and "treasuring Jesus above all other things" (p. 54–55)?

*3. In your own words, define *conversion*. What two human acts are involved in conversion (pp. 63–64)? Why does the author say that these two acts "are really two sides of the same coin" (p. 64)?

*4. Why should we view conversion as a gift of God? What are some biblical texts that lead us to this conclusion? (pp. 64–70)

5. Write down all the reasons you think the raising of Lazarus is a good picture of God's work of regeneration (pp. 66–67).

*6.   What does the author mean when he says that conversion is a condition for salvation? Why is this not "a way of earning salvation"? How does a lack of clarity in the definition of *salvation* lead to confusion over this matter? (pp. 67–70)

7.   Describe the relationship between joy and faith. How is joy the fruit of faith? How is joy the root of faith? How is joy part of the essence of what faith is? (pp. 70–74)

8.   What things, besides love for the light, might motivate a person to "come to the light"? Why would any such motives be dishonoring to the light? (p. 72)

*9.   According to the author, what is "saving faith" (cf. pp. 72–73)? Explain why this definition leads the author to say that conversion is the creation of a Christian Hedonist.

*10.   What is the ultimate good that Christ died to secure for those who trust wholly in him (pp. 72–73)? Examine your own heart. Is this ultimate good the supreme treasure of your heart? Why or why not? According to Scripture, what are some ways in which we can evaluate our own hearts?

Going Deeper

- On page 73 the author asks, "Would you want to go to heaven if God were not there, only His gifts?" Answer this question and explain why you answer the way you do. What gifts tend to compete for your supreme affections? Pray for deeper delight in God Himself as the supreme delight of your heart.

- Read the second paragraph on p. 65 and footnote 12. What is the difference between a "physical inability" and a "moral inability"? For help, read "A Response to J. I. Packer on the So-Called Antinomy Between the Sovereignty of God and Human Responsibility" (it can be found by performing a title search on the Desiring God Web site: www.desiringGod.org). What Scriptures can you think of that tell us of our moral inability?

- Many people stumble over the term "Christian Hedonism." However, as was seen in this chapter, the author thinks that the term is both harmonious with biblical teaching and extremely helpful in our contemporary culture. Do you have any reservations about or objections to the term "Christian Hedonism"? If so, what are they? Write down any remaining questions or concerns you have and discuss them with the group.

Praying the Psalms

Psalm 130

CHAPTER 3

WORSHIP:
THE FEAST OF CHRISTIAN HEDONISM

Reading and Reflection

*1. Why are the how and whom of worship more important than the where? What two words in John 4:23 correspond to "how" and "whom"? Explain the correspondence. What happens when one or the other is missing from one's effort at worship? (pp. 81–82)

*2. In the author's analogy of "fuel, furnace, and heat" on p. 82, what is the fuel, what is the furnace, and what is the heat of worship? What part does the Holy Spirit play?

3. Even though worship involves some kind of outward act, why should

we consider worship to be "a way of gladly reflecting back to God the radiance of His worth" (p. 84)? What possible misunderstanding could the word *gladly* cause? What possible worse misunderstanding could be caused by not using the word *gladly*? (pp. 84–85)

*4. What makes an act of worship vain? What are some motivations besides genuine affection for God that might lead a person to perform an act of worship? (pp. 85–86)

*5. Explain what is meant by the phrase "Worship is an end in itself." How does this phrase relate to "spontaneous affections"? If worship is an end in itself, does it ever lead to anything else? If so, how is this possible, and what might it lead to? (pp. 90–92)

6. In the author's illustration of buying roses for his wife on their anniversary (pp. 93–94), why would saying, "It's my duty," be dishonoring to his wife? In what ways would saying, "It's my joy," be honoring to her? What, then, is the real duty of worship? How is it a "duty"?

*7. Respond to the following objection: "In making the joy of worship an end in itself, we make God a means to our end rather than our being a means to His end. Christian Hedonism, therefore, is man-centered." (Cf. pp. 94–96.)

8. In your own words, list the three stages of worship (pp. 96–97). How might knowing about these three stages be an encouragement for us?

9. How does the notion that the pursuit of joy is submoral or immoral destroy the possibility of true worship (pp. 98–102)? Read the quote from Carl Zylstra in footnote 14 on page 100. Why does the author say, "When the question is put like this, it cannot be answered truthfully"?

10. What must genuine affection for God be rooted in and shaped by and why (pp. 102–104)? This chapter discusses the reality "that true worship always combines heart and head, emotion and thought, affection and reflection, doxology and theology" (p. 102). The majority of the chapter focuses on the first halves of these pairs (i.e., heart, emotion, affection, doxology). Why do you think this is so?

Going Deeper

- Reflect upon the statement, "Where feelings for God are dead, worship is dead" (p. 88). Choose two of the affections the author talks about on pages 86–87 and contemplate what it is about God that should cause these affections or feelings to arise in our hearts. Examine your own self to see whether these qualities of God cause such emotions to swell in your heart. Now do the same thing for two other "inward feelings that reflect the worth of God's glory," which are not mentioned by the author.

- Reflect upon pages 104–108. What implications does this chapter have on forms of worship?

- Read footnote 6 on page 93. Explain what E. J. Carnell means by "moral fulfillment." How is worship a fruit, not a work? Now read Matt 25:31–40. In what ways do Carnell's insights relate to this passage? Have the sheep addressed by Jesus committed good and loving deeds for others? Why are they surprised at Jesus' words? Why should we consider a heart that truly loves both God and others to be a miracle? What implications does this have on our understanding of prayer?

Praying the Psalms

Psalm 63

CHAPTER 4

LOVE:
THE LABOR OF CHRISTIAN HEDONISM

Reading and Reflection

1. The author makes an important shift in chapter 4 from vertical Christian Hedonism to what (pp. 112–113)? In your own words, describe what this means. How will this chapter differ from chapters 1–3? What similarities will this chapter share with chapters 1–3?

2. What is the essential argument of this chapter (p. 112, cf. 115)?

*3. What two clues in the immediate context of 1 Corinthians 13:5 show us that it is not wrong to intentionally pursue our own gain in our love of others? List any other biblical texts that you can think of which support this. What, according to Edwards, is the "gain" we are to be motivated by? What kind of "gain" would it be wrong to be motivated by? (pp. 112–116)

*4. What is good about the common motto: "Love is not what you feel, but what you do"? Why is this an insufficient and possibly misleading way of describing love? Why can't love be equated merely with action? How is it possible to give away all your possessions to the poor and yet not be truly loving? (pp. 116–117)

*5. What four observations from 2 Corinthians 8:1–4, 8 does the author make in coming to an understanding of genuine love? What is the author's definition of biblical love? (pp. 118–120) What is the connection between vertical Christian Hedonism, that is, joy in God, and love for other people on the horizontal plane?

6. According to 2 Corinthians 2:2 what gives Paul great joy? According to 2:3 what does Paul expect to be the joy of the Corinthians? What do

these observations tell us about love? How does this perspective of what love is relate to the perspective found in 2 Corinthians 8 (pp. 121–124)?

*7.   What is the great obstacle to both true worship of God and genuine love for neighbor (pp. 128–129)? How do we overcome this obstacle? Why is this good news?

*8.   Explain what the author means by "dissatisfied contentment" (pp. 124–125). How is the weeping of compassion related to joy? Why does the author say the joy of love is costly (pp. 129–136)? How can grief and anguish and tears coexist in a loving heart that overflows with joy?

9.   Why might some think loving acts that are motivated by reward are not truly loving but are simply mercenary efforts? Based on your reading of this chapter, why is the Christian Hedonist view of love not mercenary (see pp. 125–128)? Explain the relationship between joy in the actual deed of love and joy in the promised reward (pp. 137–139). How does this relationship guard love from becoming a mercenary affair?

10.   Describe the "psychological process that moves us from joy in God to the actual deed of love" (p. 139, cf. pp. 139–141). How does the "doubling" of our joy relate to true love for our neighbor?

Going Deeper

- Interact with the author's assertion that without the pursuit of pleasure it is impossible to truly love others or please God. Why does he assert this? Do you agree or disagree? Why?

- Explain the difference between happiness as a "goal" or a "motive" on the one hand and merely a "consequence" or "unexpected surprise" on the other. Based upon your reading of this chapter, respond to the objections raised by the philosophy professor which are quoted on page 112. Cite other biblical texts not mentioned in the chapter in your response.

Praying the Psalms

Psalm 15

CHAPTERS 5 AND 6

SCRIPTURE:
KINDLING FOR CHRISTIAN HEDONISM
PRAYER:
THE POWER OF CHRISTIAN HEDONISM

Reading and Reflection

1. What is meant by the title of this chapter when it calls Scripture "Kindling for Christian Hedonism"? What is the goal of this chapter, and what three steps are necessary to reach this end? (pp. 143–144)

*2. Choose three of the blessings of the Word of God, discussed on pages 145–152, which are most meaningful to you. How does the Word of God produce these benefits? How do these benefits "kindle" our joy? Think of two other benefits of the Word not mentioned by the author. How does the Word of God produce these and how do they kindle our joy?

*3. Why does the author use the image of "wielding" God's Word? What does he mean when he says that we must *wear* the Word if we are to wield it? What steps should we take to *wear* the Word (consider George Müller's testimony on pages 154–157 for practical outworking)? (Cf. pp. 144, 151, 154.)

*4. How does a proper understanding of prayer help show that the pursuit of our joy and the pursuit of God's glory are one and the same pursuit (pp. 159–161)?

5. How does prayer glorify God? What does a poor prayer life indicate about one's understanding of who God is? Why? (pp. 160–162)

*6. What does "self-centered" mean? Should prayer be considered self-centered? Why or why not? According to James 4:3–5 how might we turn God into a cuckold with our prayers? (pp. 163–165)

7. What keeps our prayers from being a sinfully self-centered and adulterous instrument of idolatry? Is it possible to desire and enjoy creation without being an idolater? Why or why not? (pp. 165–168)

*8. Why must we "*beware of serving God*" (p. 168)? In what way are we not to serve God? How does the meaning of prayer demand the avoidance of serving God in this way? How do these answers point to the uniqueness of God among all the other so-called gods of the world? (pp. 168–172)

9. Why is prayer equated with "waiting for God," and why is it "the antidote for the disease of self-confidence" (pp. 170–171)? In light of this, in what way shall we serve God? How does our effort and our obedience relate to this kind of service? (pp. 172–174)

10. What two reasons can be drawn from the context of John 16:24 for why a deep prayer life leads to fullness of joy? (pp. 174–179)

Going Deeper

- What does the author believe is one of the main reasons many in the church do not have a deep and vibrant prayer life (pp. 182–183)? Resolve to take some practical steps this week in response to the author's closing exhortation on page 183. Write out your resolutions.

- In this study guide, chapters 5 and 6 are the only chapters that are combined into a single lesson. Why do you think these two chapters are combined? What is the relationship of Scripture and prayer? Why ought we always to think of these two things as going hand in hand in the fight for joy?

Praying the Psalms

Psalm 19

CHAPTER 7

MONEY:
THE CURRENCY OF CHRISTIAN HEDONISM

Reading and Reflection

*1. How does the teaching on money in 1 Timothy 6 confirm the central argument of Desiring God (pp. 185–186)?

2. Why is it significant that Paul does not respond to people "selling" godliness for monetary gain by saying, "Don't live for gain"? How does he respond instead? (pp. 186–187)

*3. What is the point of the section entitled: "Getting Raises Is Not the Same as Getting Rich"? Why is this important to realize? What is and isn't Paul warning against in 1 Timothy 6? (pp. 187–188)

4. What three reasons does Paul give in 1 Timothy 6:7–10 for why we should not aspire to be rich? (pp. 188–191)

*5. What kind of "treasure" should we pursue, and how should we pursue it (pp. 192–195)?

6. On page 195 the author mentions that there are over forty places in Luke where "there are promises of reward and threats of punishment connected with the commands of Jesus." Find five of these instances and examine them. Do they commend the type of treasure-pursuing that the author commends? Why or why not?

*7. How do we know that what Paul talks about at the end of 1 Timothy 6:19 is eternal life? How can the author assert that eternal life is at stake in the use of our money while maintaining that we cannot earn eternal life in any way? In light of this, what three directions does Paul give in 1 Timothy 6 to those who are rich? (pp. 196–197, 201)

8. What is a health-wealth-and-prosperity gospel? What is the true half of

such teaching? What is the false half of it? How is 1 Timothy 6:17 different from it? (pp. 197–99)

*9.   What does the author mean by "wartime lifestyle"? What is the war? Why does he not simply commend a "simple lifestyle"? (pp. 199–203)

10.   On pages 201–202 the author gives advice to pastors concerning how to commend a wartime lifestyle to congregations and says, "He will not make it easy by creating a law" (p. 202). What does the author mean by this, that is, "making a law"? Why would this make it "easy"? Why is this not living by faith, that is, treasuring all that God is for us in Jesus?

Going Deeper

- Consider the three levels of how we live with things that are mentioned Ephesians 4:28 (p. 202). Ask yourself to which level you belong. Why has God prospered you? Try to think of specific reasons or areas to where you are being led to channel your abundance.

- One of the weightiest exhortations of this chapter is to live a "wartime lifestyle." Reread pages 199–201. What strategies have you set in place to maximize the effectiveness of your gifts and resources for the good of those in need and for the spread of the gospel? What strategies could you add to these?

Praying the Psalms

Psalm 4

CHAPTER 8

MARRIAGE:
A MATRIX FOR CHRISTIAN HEDONISM

Reading and Reflection

1. Why does the author say of Ephesians 5:25–30, "There is scarcely a more hedonistic passage in the Bible" (p. 205)? List all the "hedonistic" elements in this passage that you can find.

2. What is the difference between self-interest and selfishness? Why can't self-interest be excluded from love? (pp. 206–207)

3. What kind of "hating of life" does Jesus command in John 12:25? How does this "hating of life" not contradict Paul's assertion that "no one ever hated his own flesh"? What is the relationship between the self-love that Paul assumes and the love of husbands for wives and vice versa? (pp. 207–210)

4. Why might we assume that *marriage* isn't the mystery to be explained, but Christ's relationship to the church is the mystery which Paul uses marriage to explain and describe? Why is marriage considered by Paul a mystery to be uncovered and explained? (pp. 210–213)

*5. Why does the author take time to explain the Old Testament context of Genesis 2:24 and the reason marriage is a great mystery? See in particular pages 210 and 213. What is the foundation for the pattern of love in marriage that is described in the rest of the chapter?

*6. What is the most fundamental reason the author gives for believing that a wife "should be disposed to yield to her husband's authority and should be inclined to follow his leadership" (p. 216)? How does he support this (pp. 214–217)? Why does he say it should be a *disposition* and an *inclination*?

*7.   What kind of leadership are husbands to take in marriage, if it is modeled on Christ's leadership? According to the author, what does the responsibility of leadership given to husbands entail, and what doesn't it entail? (pp. 217–218)

*8.   Why is it important that the forms of submission (and headship) necessarily vary, according to pages 218–219? What other reasons can you think of for why this is important to realize (cf. pp. 201–202)?

9.   What did the Fall do to the roles of headship and submission in marriage (p. 220)?

*10.   How does marriage "display Christian Hedonism"?

Going Deeper

- Read an online article entitled "What Does It Mean to Love Your Neighbor as Yourself?" (available at http://www.desiring god.org/dg/id227_m.htm). What is one of the most common contemporary misuses of Luke 10:27? Why does the author believe this use of the second greatest commandment to be mistaken? How does the author suggest we must love our neighbor as ourselves? How might this type of love manifest itself in your own marriage, friendships, and other relationships?

- Read the definitions of masculinity and femininity given in chapter 2, "A Vision of Biblical Complementarity: Manhood and Womanhood Defined According to the Bible," in *Recovering Biblical Manhood and Womanhood* (available in the Online Books section of the Desiring God Web site [pp. 28–43 in the online version]). Write down all the things that the author states masculinity and femininity, respectively, are not. How might knowing that marriage is a matrix for Christian Hedonism guard us from these misunderstandings of what manhood and womanhood are?

Praying the Psalms

Psalm 45

CHAPTER 9

MISSIONS:
THE BATTLE CRY OF CHRISTIAN HEDONISM

Reading and Reflection

1.   Outside of Scripture, where has the author found the greatest confirmation for his vision of Christian Hedonism (p. 224)?

*2.   What does the term "frontier missions" mean (pp. 223–226)? Try to use your own words, and give scriptural illustrations and support.

*3.   Why is missions essential for the church, without which its love will be fundamentally lacking? What is at stake in bringing the gospel to those who have not heard it? How do we know this (i.e., what biblical texts help us to see that this, indeed, is at stake)? (pp. 226–227)

*4.   What is a "people group" (pp. 229–230)? What biblical text does the author cite to help in coming to this definition? What other texts can you think of which show this understanding of "people group" to be true?

5.   What is the first incentive found in Mark 10:25–27 for devoting ourselves to frontier missions (pp. 234–239)? List other biblical texts that support this truth. Why is this particularly good news for the Christian Hedonist (see p. 239)?

6.   What three incentives for missions are found in John 10:16 (pp. 236–239)?

7.   What is the second great incentive found in Mark 10:25–27 for devoting ourselves to frontier missions (pp. 239–242)?

*8.   Respond to the objection that a Christian Hedonist approach to missions ignores or denies the biblical call to self-denial.

9.   What is the fundamental reason that Jesus "rebukes us for a self-pitying spirit of sacrifice" (p. 246)?

*10.   Why do "invalids make the best missionaries" (pp. 247–250)?

Going Deeper

- One error that the church has had to combat in its mission to fulfill the Great Commission is universalism. Read the quotes on page 226 to get an idea of how it might sound today. What does universalism mean? Why is universalism unbiblical? For help, see chapter 4, "The Supremacy of Christ as the Conscious Focus of All Saving Faith," in John Piper, *Let the Nations Be Glad: The Supremacy of God in Missions* (Grand Rapids: Baker, 2010), and listen to the audio excerpt entitled, "What happens to those who have never heard the gospel?" (available at http://www.desiringgod.org/ResourceLibrary/TopicIndex/4_Mi ssions/1751_What_happens_to_those_who_have_never_heard _the_ gospel/).
- On pages 229–230 the author cites statistics on unreached people groups but acknowledges that these statistics quickly get outdated. Find current stats on unreached people groups from Web sites like joshuaproject.net and uscwm.org, and record them. Using these statistics, describe the need for frontier missions. What areas are particularly in need? What areas might be strategic to reach? Are current efforts being made to reach those areas? If so, what are they?
- What is meant by the term "World Christian" (pp. 232–233)? What are some practical steps you can begin taking right now to become more of a World Christian?

Praying the Psalms

Psalm 67

CHAPTER 10

SUFFERING:
THE SACRIFICE OF CHRISTIAN HEDONISM

Reading and Reflection

1. What does Paul mean in 1 Corinthians 15:19 when he says, "If in this life only we have hoped in Christ, we are of all people most to be pitied"? Why does he say this? (pp. 254–256)

*2. What are the similarities between persecution for Christ's name and sickness? What are the differences? (pp. 256–260)

*3. How can Christians view all suffering as suffering for Christ and with Christ? What does it mean that the suffering of Christians is *for* Christ? What does it mean that it is *with* Christ? What makes suffering this way for Christians? (pp. 256–260)

*4. Why does the author call Christianity a life of *chosen* suffering? For what reasons might Paul have chosen a life of suffering? (pp. 261–267)

5. How does the author interpret Colossians 1:24, "Now I rejoice in my sufferings for your sake, and in my flesh I am filling up what is lacking in Christ's afflictions for the sake of his body, that is, the church" (pp. 267–270)? Do you agree with his understanding of this verse and his understanding of the function of suffering in the Christian life? Why or why not? Cite other Scriptures in support.

*6. What does the author mean when he says, "embracing of suffering is not just an accompaniment of our witness to Christ; it is the visible expression of it" (p. 279)? How do the stories of suffering and persecution on pages 274–279 illustrate this reality?

7. Why is it not a contradiction to call suffering the sacrifice of Christian Hedonism and yet, like David Livingston, to say, "I never made a

sacrifice"? Why are the sufferings of Christians to be understood as sacrifices? Why are they to be considered as no sacrifices? (pp. 280–281)

8. Why does Paul's pursuit of joy lead him to a life of chosen suffering? Why is Paul's pursuit of his own deepest joy in Christ in perfect harmony with his deep and pure love for others? That is, how can seeking our own joy and seeking the joy of others be one? (pp. 281–283)

9. In what ways can we rejoice in suffering as Christians (pp. 283–286)? List any other ways of and reasons for rejoicing in suffering as Christians along with supporting biblical texts.

*10. Why should we not view joy in suffering merely as a good gift from God but also a good goal to pursue? Why might some not believe this to be so? What is the fundamental goal and ground of our joy in suffering? (pp. 283–288)

Going Deeper

- One of the most difficult attributes of God for us to understand and to submit to is His absolute sovereignty over all things, including evil and our suffering. What questions concerning God's control over evil in the world still remain in your mind and heart? Discuss these with the group.

- Reflect upon some significant trials and times of suffering in your own life, whether explicit persecution for the name of Jesus or suffering from sickness or loss. What have you learned of God in those times? of His goodness, love, sovereignty, mercy, and wisdom? In what ways can you discern that God has used and is using those times for His good and wise and loving purposes in your life and the lives of those around you? In what ways have those times caused you to doubt God's goodness and love and sovereign wisdom? Perhaps they still are causing you to doubt God. Share these concerns with other trusted believers, and seek to strengthen each other's faith in God as our only hope and joy in all circumstances.

Praying the Psalms

Psalm 43

Proverbs

Ecclesiastes

Isaiah

desiringGod

.If you would like to further explore the vision of God and life presented in this book, we at Desiring God would love to serve you. We have hundreds of resources to help you grow in your passion for Jesus Christ and help you spread that passion to others. At our Web site, desiringGod.org, you'll find almost everything John Piper has written and preached, including more than thirty books. We've made over twenty-five years of his sermons available free online for you to read, listen to, download, and in some cases watch.

In addition, you can access hundreds of articles, find out where John Piper is speaking, learn about our conferences, discover our God-centered children's curricula, and browse our online store. John Piper receives no royalties from the books he writes and no compensation from Desiring God. The funds are all reinvested into our gospel-spreading efforts. Desiring God also has a whatever-you-can-afford policy, designed for individuals with limited discretionary funds. If you'd like more information about this policy, please contact us at the address or phone number below. We exist to help you treasure Jesus Christ and His gospel above all things because He is most glorified in you when you are most satisfied in Him. Let us know how we can serve you!

Desiring God
Post Office Box 2901, Minneapolis, Minnesota 55402
888.346.4700   mail@desiringGod.org

OTHER BOOKS BY THE AUTHOR

⌘

The Pleasures of God
The Dangerous Duty of Delight
Finally Alive
Future Grace
A Hunger for God
Seeing and Savoring Jesus Christ
What's the Difference?
Don't Waste Your Life
When I Don't Desire God
Fifty Reasons Why Jesus Came to Die
God Is the Gospel
What Jesus Demands from the World
When the Darkness Will Not Lift
Spectacular Sins
This Momentary Marriage
A Sweet and Bitter Providence
With Calvin in the Theater of God (with David Mathis)
Think: The Life of the Mind and the Love of God